Rethinking Business Management

Rethinking
Business Management

EXAMINING THE FOUNDATIONS OF
BUSINESS EDUCATION

Edited by Samuel Gregg
and James R. Stoner, Jr.

A project of the Social Trends Institute, Barcelona and New York,

in collaboration with

the Witherspoon Institute, Princeton, New Jersey

PUBLISHED BY THE WITHERSPOON INSTITUTE
2008

Published in the United States by the Witherspoon Institute
16 Stockton Street, Princeton, New Jersey 08540

Library of Congress Control Number: 2008923224

ISBN: 9780981491103

Printed in the United States of America

CONTENTS

ACKNOWLEDGMENTS

THE EFFORTS—indeed, the virtues—of many others besides the authors and ourselves have made possible the production of this volume. Duncan Sahner of the Witherspoon Institute helped organize the conference for which most of the papers were written, and coordinated the flow of documents through the complex process of editing and revision with exemplary efficiency. John Doherty helped him throughout, with thorough attention to the notes. David Mills executed the heroic task of reducing lengthy essays to more readable length, and otherwise proved a master copyeditor. At the Social Trends Institute, Katherine Semler and John Rose gave crucial assistance. At Witherspoon, Alicia Brzycki coordinated the production of the book from its final manuscript, deftly supervising everything from design of the cover to reading the proofs. Arleen Borg proofread, and Megan Muncy assembled the index. Kevin Jackson of Fordham Business School and John Powers of Scepter Publishers, Inc., of New York City, provided valuable professional advice.

Over all these activities presided Luis Tellez of the Witherspoon Institute, whose steady judgment and quiet confidence helped assemble the scholars who participated in the conference and the team who turned its proceedings into this book. And the guiding vision of Carlos Cavallé, Dean Emeritus of the IESE Business School of the University of Navarre and Chairman of the Social Trends Institute, was not only efficient cause of book and conference, but also an enlivening presence at every stage.

To all of these, to the Social Trends Institute of Barcelona and New York and the Witherspoon Institute of Princeton, New Jersey, who provided funding for the conference and the book's production, and to Will and Debbie Garwood and the Clayton Fund of Houston, Texas, who helped support the initial conference, we are very grateful.

S.G. & J.R.S.

FOREWORD

Rethinking Business Management is dedicated to the past and present deans, faculty, staff, alumni, and students of IESE Business School on the occasion of its 50th anniversary. This book has as its origins an initiative that began back in 2005. With IESE's 50th birthday on the horizon, it seemed an appropriate moment to embark on a long-term process of reassessing the state of business management education in light of new developments. The initiative came from the Social Trends Institute (STI), a nonpartisan, international research center based in New York City. STI drew up and submitted a proposal on the matter to its organizational partner and friend, the Witherspoon Institute, whose leaders, Stephen Whelan and Luis Tellez, accepted.

Let me explain the reasons behind this initiative. So much is happening in our modern world that has a bearing on business management. Certain aspects of business are changing much faster than ever before, while business management has a tough time keeping up, let alone leading the way. Still, amidst all of this change, some values, principles, and practices remain the same, or at least should remain the same, no matter what innovations come along tomorrow or the day after. We could refer to them as business management principles, or even business management foundations. They are unshakeable because they correspond to universal human nature, to the very essence of human beings.

Because this is the case, business management must never lose sight of the fact that it is, first and foremost, a human enterprise, composed of and for people. Subscribing to this philosophy, IESE printed in its debut brochure fifty years ago that business organizations are worth what their people are worth. In short, *business management is about people*, a simple truth made complicated by changes in people's environments.

Consider just a few examples of realities that a business manager of, say, only fifteen years ago did not face but which fill the pages of today's financial newspapers: the accelerating pace of globalization, new global capital influxes, the spate of corporate scandals, the incredible rise of Chinese and Indian markets, a current fifteen-year run of world economic prosperity (a feat never before accomplished), and the subprime financial crisis. Undoubtedly, these and countless other recent events have had an impact on people's values and expectations in business, and it should be the duty of educators to observe and analyze the ways in which this has occurred, whether for better or worse. And finally, taking all of this into account, scholars and educators should develop a model of business management suitable for current times, yet loyal to the timeless code of moral conduct as accepted by Aristotle, Judeo-Christians, and many of the world's other major religious traditions. So while the business manager of fifteen years ago inhabited a different world from that of the business manager of today, the two can still share a common sense of purpose and of "right and wrong," elements that place them within the same larger story of business management.

It is therefore pertinent to ask whether modern business education has successfully tied together the discoveries of the present with the wisdom of the past, the ephemeral with the permanent. In many cases, unfortunately, the answer is no. Confusion concerning identity and purpose, and a tension between the short lifespan of popular theories and a desire for more stable concepts (as is true in many sciences), characterizes much of modern business education.

Clearly, rewinding the clock is not a viable solution, but neither can business schools afford to go forward without a metanarrative of identity and purpose and become, by default, mercenary in their approach. *Rethinking Business Management* could be described as an attempt to help illuminate just such a narrative in business management: one that both recognizes the new paradigms in business *and* retains a sense of purpose articulated within a moral framework, reaching above and beyond mere profit and loss. It must be a narrative that sees an ever-present ethical dimension in each and every business decision. Recent experiences continue to remind educators that the answers to the questions "What is business for?" and "What is the business school for?" require an ethical vocabulary, such as we hope can be found in this book.

I would like to thank the contributors to this book. Their reflections and discussions play an important role in our long-term project of revisiting the foundations of business management. In this effort, we are always inspired by the conviction that business management should recognize the immutable aspects of human nature, those present across all eras and cultures. Despite pronouncements about the so-called "economic man," human beings' behavior and aspirations should not be understood in purely economic terms. Business management has the potential to be so much grander by helping to satisfy the human penchant for values and goodness that cannot be expressed in numbers or explained by utilitarian logic. The future belongs to those who are "rethinking business management" accordingly.

Carlos Cavallé
President
Social Trends Institute

Rethinking Business Management

Introduction

SAMUEL GREGG
AND JAMES R. STONER, JR.

To say that business management is in the midst of an ethical crisis or that the schools of business are leading it there would certainly overstate our current situation, but there is a palpable sense among observers that renewed attention is due to the place of ethics and ethics education in the modern global economy. Perhaps this is the result of major scandals in the United States and in Europe. Perhaps it follows from intellectual developments in fields such as philosophical anthropology and psychology that call into question the assumptions about the human person on which modern economics has been based. Perhaps it is simply that, after a generation of experience with the revived prestige of free market economics, the collapse of communism, and the subsequent expansion of free trade and the development of an unprecedented global market, it is simply time to pause and take stock of the state of business in world affairs.

At any rate, on the occasion of the fiftieth anniversary of a major school of business—IESE Business School, at the University of Navarre, in Barcelona, founded in 1958—it seems appropriate to reflect upon business management and how to teach it. Business schools and business education are very much a phenomenon of the second half of the twentieth century. While professional schools for those involved in trade and commerce date back to the Middle Ages, the contemporary business school with its emphasis on producing managers who can literally be employed in any private- (and increasingly public-) sector company or organization is something that first emerged in force after the Second World War. The modern business school continues to shape the management and dynamism of twenty-first century capitalism in a globalized environment, and the number of people studying in such schools continues to rise. In many instances, it is a businessperson's only post-undergraduate point of contact with universities, or at least his only contact with graduate education.

This book contains a collection of essays that reflect upon the state of business schools at the beginning of the twenty-first century. For the most part, they are based upon papers delivered at a public conference titled "Rethinking Business Management," held under the aegis of the Witherspoon Institute and under the direction of Professor Harold James at Princeton University in May 2007. The conference sought to examine experiences of business school education in light of social and ethical responsibilities. The thesis presented for discussion at the conference was that effective management is grounded both on good business science *and* on robust ethical and anthropological conceptions of human flourishing.

A number of considerations helped to frame the conference, many of which manifest themselves in the essays that appear in this volume. A single approach, it was suggested, seems to dominate management education in most of the world's business schools. While this approach invariably speaks about "values" as a driving force behind business decisions, this raises a number of uneasy questions. Which values are identified as central to business? Why are these given priority and not others? The current moral-cultural atmosphere of "neutral morality"—better understood as moral relativism—that marks so much of the educational environment of many Western European and North American universities makes it difficult for a considerable number of people to identify objective moral principles that ought to guide business decision-making. This is complicated by the fact that many business schools educate managers to focus almost exclusively on profits and to base their professional careers largely on monetary achievements.[1] While some business schools have established new departments of social sciences to get beyond an exclusive focus on profit, these seem to impart mostly *pragmatic* values. To be pragmatic, as many of the authors of the following essays insist, is not necessarily the path to virtue and moral flourishing.

In this light, it is little wonder that there is also a growing concern for exploring the anthropological, ethical, and sociological foundations of management in the context of business. Some attention is now being paid to the importance of grounding these foundations upon an accurate philosophical anthropology of the human person, especially the notions that (a) humans are at the same time body and spirit, making a substantial unity, and (b) humans are social and develop within society, of which business is an integral part. There is also growing appreciation of the fact that ethics is not simply prohibitive, but also—at least in its classical form—speaks about the possibility of human fulfillment. This has led some to suggest that the typical business school approach of treating ethics as a compartmentalized subject such as "business ethics" ought to be replaced by a holistic approach to the moral life that should permeate all areas of life in business.

There is also considerable discussion of the nature and goals of business in the wider community. Business is, of course, an essentially social exercise in serving society through the production and distribution of goods and services, thereby creating jobs, creating and accumulating wealth, and contributing to human progress. Some argue that businesses contribute to the common good when they carry out their mission in a sustainable and conscientious relationship with those who are immediately touched by the activity, such as shareholders, employees, clients, and consumers. Others, however, suggest that the social responsibility of business goes beyond these confines, and ought to consider the interests of those whom some describe as stakeholders. Yet others hold that "stakeholderism" is simply an agenda for foisting politically correct objectives onto the operations of business. These questions do and should occupy the attention of business schools, their professors, and their students.

Readers of these essays will observe that the authors generally agree that a free enterprise economy is a basically sound system for organizing economic life, or at least the best available system under contemporary conditions and in light of the fact of human fallibility. The modern return of the free market is accepted—and in some instances celebrated—by the authors, which distinguishes these papers from many other similar collections. It is a mistake to think that all people working in business or teaching in business schools are invariably in favor of free markets. Many are not.

Likewise, although some of these essays raise questions about the issue of the size of business, and a number indicate a preference for smaller-scale enterprises, the authors seem generally to accept that the modern market has global reach. This means that the issues confronting business schools and the executives and managers whom they train cannot be addressed by isolating oneself or one's culture from the larger world. The global economy is here to stay, and business schools need to take this into account when thinking through reform of their curricula and teaching methods.

Lastly, while these essays affirm that the development of a global economy has not been matched by anything like a corresponding growth in adequate moral formation, few suggest that this situation can be resolved by legislation. Many of the markets in question are often already highly regulated—and in some instances, positively over-regulated—and it seems generally to have been agreed that mandating an extra set of additional "ethics rules" would not only increase the costs of compliance, but would fail to address the substantive ethical questions facing business executives, managers, and the schools in which many of them are trained. Instead, the authors appear focused on developing an understanding of the moral life as *more* than a set of rules. It is in fact, they suggest, a matter of developing virtuous human character and ensuring that the prohibitions of morality protect and promote certain virtues rather than simply existing for the sake of making business life more predictable. After all, ethics is in a sense necessarily prior to legislated rules, for one's attitude toward the obligation of rules and toward the incentives they entail is already a question of ethics. A number of essays suggest that the reform of ethics education in business schools should not focus so much on the development of new techniques, but rather address more closely questions of moral formation. In this sense, some of the authors show a distinct preference for the type of reflection about the meaning of morality associated with figures such as Aristotle and Thomas Aquinas, rather than more contemporary scholars such as John Rawls.

We have clustered the essays in three groups. The first group is concerned with the historical and theoretical foundations of business in relation to the human person and to social life as a whole. Historian Harold James addresses the origins of modern business and business education, finding them as a counterpart to the rise of the state and its ability to guarantee by law an extended marketplace that does not rely alone on personal relationships of kinship or friendship; the challenge to business today is to recognize that the establishment of legal personhood in the corporation does not dispense with the need for moral persons in its ranks. Roger Scruton develops a similar theme, applying to modern business Aristotle's distinction between the ends that are sought by means of action and the happiness that comes from acting well; in a healthy corporation, profit comes, like happiness or friendship, not because it is a calculated goal, but as a consequence of doing one's business well, and justice emerges not from a government's seizing and redistributing profits, but from a society permeated by attention to justice as a virtue, as a characteristic of action throughout. A modern Aristotelian and Thomistic analysis of action theory is employed by IESE Professor Antonio Argandoña to develop a dynamic decision theory that illuminates the modern corporation and its management; this approach, he argues, can correct the short-term bias of neo-classical economics by drawing attention to the need for unity and to the role of virtues in the sustained activity of organizations. Philosopher David Novak examines the contribution that natural-law thinking can make toward understanding the predicament of life in the modern economy; instead of accepting that self-interest is the only guiding principle of social life, natural law points to universal rights and duties that are in fact widely known and widely shared. McCormick Professor of Jurisprudence at Princeton, Robert P. George, concludes our study of foundations with reflections originally delivered as a talk at the IESE Global Alumni Reunion on the dynamic character of the modern world economy and the pillars on which any decent and dynamic society rests. These include not only respect for the human person, the rule of law, and institutions of research and learning, but also for families and businesses; George draws attention to how good firms and sound business practices strengthen personhood, law, education, and family, and are in turn sustained by these.

The second group of essays concerns questions of ethics in the management of various social institutions, public as well as private; as a group they are meant to be suggestive, certainly not exhaustive, and they vary markedly in attitude and approach. Anthony Daniels writes from experience as a physician in the British health care system about the incentives, often perverse, that result from modern attempts at bureaucratic management; he casts an eye back to an earlier ethic of public service, a tradition of administration from within the learned professions (e.g., of hospitals by doctors), and an era of institutional pride. Historian Wilfred M. McClay, writing about the American university, takes a seemingly opposite tack, praising the work of Columbia-educated George Keller in bringing the principles of modern management to a recalcitrant setting; according to McClay, Keller at once helped to lay the groundwork for the remarkable success of modern institutions of higher learning and, thanks to his humanist's eye, fostered an appreciation of the diversity of academic institutions and their role in contemporary civil society and our complex economy. Robin Fretwell Wilson, Professor of Law at Washington and Lee, investigates the challenge posed to the formation of family life by the career trajectory of the modern professional, especially the difficulties in store for professional women who also want to be mothers; she recommends ways that management can address this issue, beginning particularly in graduate school, when students are at an age when they might be expected to begin families. Philosophy Professor Sean Kelsey and business executive and consultant Thomas R. Krause suggest that the successful revolution in managing workplace safety over the past generation gives reason for optimism if the same outlook can be applied to workplace ethics, a project that begins, they argue, with a clear understanding of the cooperative character of economic life.

In the final group of essays, several professors at major business schools reflect on the study of ethics in the modern business curriculum and propose different ways to think about ethics and to impart a habit of ethical reflection among their students. University of Virginia Professor of Business Administration, R. Edward Freeman, and his colleague, business executive David Newkirk, argue that reform of business education requires rethinking the character of business itself, understanding the corporation in relation to its stakeholders, not only its shareholders, and adopting, instead of the "separation fallacy" that isolates business activity from other spheres of human activity, an "integration thesis" that connects business seamlessly to ethics and the full range of human affairs. Kevin T. Jackson, who teaches business at Fordham University, refines stakeholder theory by proposing its connection to the traditional attention paid by business managers to shareholders through the concept of "reputational capital." Both essays develop their theoretical perspective before thinking through how business courses could be altered in its light. In separate but congruent essays, Edwin M. Hartman of New York University and James O'Toole of the University of Southern California argue that the key to the reform of business education lies in the study of Aristotle. Both elaborate how Aristotle's account of the human being weaves together economic goods and ethical goodness in a pattern that makes analytical sense and offers practical counsel even for today. Hartman sees in Aristotle a way of addressing the questions that business students ask themselves as they plan their careers: as character depends on virtue and as virtues are formed by habits and choices, according to Aristotle, so students effectively choose the kind of people they will be by where they choose to work, and companies in turn establish their character by the people they employ and the activities they promote. O'Toole looks at the relation between work and leisure, an Aristotelian theme, in the context of individual job choice and company policy. He suggests that Aristotle's account of justice as involving both inequality and equality can prove helpful in considering the distribution of goods within organizations, even, or especially, on the matter of executive compensation. His conclusion, attributed to Aristotle, that "a strong ethical foundation was a requirement for an open society" captures, we think, the spirit of the essays in this volume as a whole.

Note

1. Ian Mitroff, "An Open Letter to the Deans and Faculties of American Business Schools," *Journal of Business Ethics* 54 (October 2004): 185–89.

PART ONE

Foundations

Chapter One

THE ETHICS OF BUSINESS LIFE:

SOME HISTORICAL REFLECTIONS

HAROLD JAMES

THERE EXISTS a long tradition of demonstrating the importance of ethics in the conduct of a business life that is both efficient and just. This tradition did not supply simply utilitarian reasons for behaving ethically, but it did emphasize that ethical behavior brings many benefits, and that an unethical society is dissatisfied and destructive.

Its most elaborate exposition (which is celebrated in other contributions to this volume) occurred in Thomistic elaborations of Aristotelian ethics. Enlightenment thinkers also made ethical conduct a central feature of their political economy. David Hume explained why: "The same age, which produces great philosophers and politicians, renowned generals and poets, usually abounds with skillful weavers, and ship-carpenters. We cannot reasonably expect that a piece of woollen cloth will be wrought to perfection in a nation, which is ignorant of astronomy, or where ethics are neglected."[1]

By the beginning of the twenty-first century, however, these older approaches appeared to have become largely extinct. New sorts of institutional answers— legal and corporate—had evolved to the questions once addressed by the ethical tradition. It is possible that the institutionalization of business education through the establishment of business schools played some part in this erosion. Today, business schools are widely blamed for the ethical failures of business, and anniversaries such as the forthcoming 2008 centenary of the Harvard Business School (HBS) are seen as much as occasions for self-examination and self-criticism as for unencumbered and unreflective celebration. Why is it that according to many ratings Harvard seems to have lost its way? According to the *Economist* Intelligence Unit's latest (2006) ranking of world business schools, Harvard was only at seventh place, while the top spot was occupied by the much younger IESE, celebrating its fiftieth anniversary in 2008.

The current criticism should lead to a sustained reflection on the purpose of a business education. Many observers, including some within the business school community, think that the unstated purpose was simply to make their students and alumni feel good about themselves and about their school. But in fact the problem lay in the explicit purpose of many business schools: as they had evolved in the twentieth century, the schools tried primarily to find ways of helping business leaders understand how the legal and managerial world of what might be termed the "modern economy" functioned. The new answers reflected the shift toward a managerial economy. In this world of functionally integrated and interdependent agents, the task lay in solving logistical problems. Solutions were exclusively technical. Much of Hume's formulation in consequence became for a modern audience quite unintelligible, perhaps even wholly absurd.

In particular, a strong ethical framework had once answered a critical and quite practical question that is central to the operation of a market economy: how can I trust the person with whom I am conducting business? Markets depend on promises about future conduct, but promises can be broken when circumstances are not conducive to keeping them. If the contract is one that is often repeated, between partners who know each other, the partners have an obvious self-interest involved in not reneging on it. They do not have such immediate self-interest in the case of once-only transactions, especially if they are separated by a long distance. Then there is a multiplication of the incentives to cheat.

On these grounds, Aristotle was skeptical about the possibilities of long-distance trade, which he thought provided temptations for immorality and abuse. In the Aristotelian tradition, businesses developed simply as an extension of the household, the *oikos,* and the kind of trust that was required for business dealings developed simply as an extension of personal honesty and reputation. There was no distinction between personal and business behavior.

Later, in the Enlightenment, a highly influential school of thought developed according to which commerce was the originator of a civilizing impulse. This tradition also tended to celebrate local commerce, which brought people into regular contact and thus educated them, and to disparage commercial contacts with very different types of people a long way away, which were necessarily much more occasional. For both Aristotle and this Enlightenment school, the market was far from an abstraction, but rather a daily education in civics.

In the course of modern economic development, the traditional approaches were overtaken by two developments that appeared to hold out the possibility of faster economic growth: the regulation of business conduct through legislation emanating from states which had a new kind of legitimacy founded on popular sovereignty, and the growth of the modern notion of a business corporation which could internalize its ethical problems and could appear to be fully rational. These provided the foundation of the modern managerial economy. But this managerial economy was constantly evolving, and in the course of the evolution major flaws and weaknesses were exposed.

I

Let us take up first the state regulation of business conduct. Modern economic development brought an answer to the problem of trust that did not depend on personal honesty. It was institutional innovation (rather than personal behavior) that allowed the establishment of relations based on confidence over a long distance. In consequence, business conduct became quite separated from personal conduct. It was correspondingly judged by different measures. Different spheres of human activity carried expectations of different behavior, or even multiple personalities. A businessman would be calculating and aggressive in his firm, and then come home to be warm and emotional in his family. (This was a contrast to the Old World, in which there was often no physical separation between home and work, and in which—incidentally—in consequence women would play a much more prominent role.)

The primary cause of a new confidence about business dealings came from changes in the legal environment. It was the law rather than an advanced ethical sensitivity that made for a newly enhanced sense of security in commercial transactions, and allowed for an explosion of economic activity. An influential interpretation ("law and economics") of British and American developments sees in the common law a legal form that made these societies uniquely and unprecedentedly successful. According to Morton Horwitz, the crucial breakthrough came in the eighteenth century and early nineteenth century, when contracts were no longer annulled by courts when they might be held to violate some rather vague concept of natural justice. Business figures no longer needed to fear that some objection might make their business calculation obsolete. Unfettered property rights made it possible to expand almost infinitely the areas of life that were subject to contracting. As a result, the factors of production could be combined much more efficiently, and a colossal wave of increasingly shared and universal prosperity followed.[2]

Almost every modern interpretation of the preconditions for successful economic development emphasizes the importance of the effective enforcement of property rights. For this reason, states should refrain from destroying expectations of stability by simple expropriation or by monetary experimentation. Where there is no legal security, or the legitimacy and dependability of the political system is eroded by widespread corruption, potential entrepreneurs will have no faith that their property rights will be respected, and in consequence will hold off from entrepreneurial activity.

The rise in government and legal regulation was in the first instance the great facilitator of market transactions. Early modern European states in general were quite weak, and found mercantile ventures quite threatening, especially when they crossed state borders. Some companies or corporations behaved like states without actually being territorial states. The Teutonic Knights and the Knights of Malta organized defense systems, fostered commerce, provided social networks and services (such as hospitals or schools), and of course did a great deal of fighting. These proto-NGOs were dedicated to a cause that was overwhelmingly important to their adherents (a religious crusade). But larger companies had to act in an analogous way.

The great merchant companies of early modern Europe indeed had their own armies: the most notorious examples are the French and the English East India Companies. The British East India Company had an important army at a time when the crown (i.e., the state) did not have a standing army at all. The companies took on regulatory and quasi-state powers with which they could exclude any competition: they were conceived as monopoly corporations. Political pressure flowed from protests against such privileged private corporations, and erupted in the American and French revolutions.

The debate produced a new type of state: a state that, because it derived its legitimacy from popular will ("We the people"), would deal with companies and non-state actors in a very different way. The state after the French Revolution would claim moral superiority in dealing with business corporations, instead of seeing itself as simply a party to a transaction that could be more or less cynically calculated (as Jakob Fugger had dealt in his lending operations with the Emperor Charles V).

It is a crude fallacy to think that the development and growth of the state necessarily brings disadvantages for enterprise or business culture. On the contrary, to the extent that the strengthening of the state made business life much more predictable, wealth-generation became easier. If the competition between European states made for more dynamic business life, the constitutional ordering of the popular will made life more certain. Previous monarchical borrowers had been prone to sudden bankruptcy, and the Habsburg and Valois dynasts had regularly turned on their creditors and used force (the threat of execution for usury) to renegotiate on better terms.[3]

The business response to this was one of grateful relief. As long as conditions were stable, it made sense to respect the will of the people as expressed in a systematically and constitutionally ordered way in whatever state a company did business. By the early nineteenth century, some large-scale lenders such as the Rothschilds began to insist that their customer states introduce constitutions or representative assemblies, because this made the repayment of credit more secure.[4] This was a foreign policy driven entirely by self-interest, but it was of course also a highly enlightened one. This point that businesses should be "good citizens" in response to the institutional environment in which they function has actually become something of a modern platitude.

This leads us to the second development that appeared to hold out the possibility of faster economic growth: the growth of the idea of a business that could internalize its ethical problems. The introduction of the modern limited-liability joint-stock corporation made possible a much broader range of contracts: with the providers of finance (thus solving a finance issue that had previously restrained economic development); with suppliers and customers; and with workers. Corporations in medieval and early modern Europe were highly restricted in what they might do. Especially after the big, speculative bubbles of the second decade of the eighteenth century, associated in England with the South Sea Company and in France with John Law's Mississippi scheme, joint-stock companies were treated as abuses, in which privileged insiders could exploit the ignorance and greed of gullible outsiders. Such a theme characterizes not only much of the literature of classical political economy, it appears with remarkable force in Adam Smith's *Wealth of Nations*. It is also echoed in a great part of the imaginative literature of the eighteenth and nineteenth century dealing with business, such as Anthony Trollope's *The Way We Live Now* and Theodore Dreiser's *The Financier* and *The Titan*, a lightly fictionalized account of the rise and fall of the Chicago and London municipal transport pioneer.

British legislation of 1844 and 1855 allowed the creation of joint-stock companies with limited liability. Belgium also had a liberal company law, and the rest of continental Europe followed in the 1860s and 1870s. Large corporations were now capable of raising the large amounts of capital required in the Industrial Revolution. Legal changes also made it possible to substitute power (in the hierarchical organization of a company) for the market, with its problematical dependence upon ethical behavior by others and the still partly uncertain and constantly costly legal enforcement of contracts. A company is a way of providing a substitute for the market where the market is too costly and uncertain: it allows, for instance, much easier enforcement of standardized measures and the maintenance of quality.[5]

Companies acquired a legal personality, and this was to have unexpected ethical implications for its employees. They could clearly be held to be legally accountable for their actions. When a company does something wrong, it—rather than the individuals who made the error—is responsible for the consequences of the decision. At the same time, new techniques of branding helped to give the impression that there also existed a corporate personality, a corporate culture, and a corporate social role. Companies began to think that they needed corporate biographies that told the story of how their structure and image molded the personalities of their employees. A strong corporate culture was widely thought to be important in motivating employees as well as customers.

In the twentieth century, the corporate image played a central role in the creation of consumer culture. Particularly companies that dealt with large numbers of customers needed to cultivate a personal image: either by the adoption of an animal or a human emblem, such as the Esso/Exxon tiger, or by naming the firm after a real or fictitious person, such as Martha Stewart or the fictitious

Ann Taylor and Thomas Pink. In the last quarter of the twentieth century, especially in the United States, the celebrated CEO became an easy path to establishing a corporate identity. The path was pioneered by Lee Iacocca's charismatic use of his own personality to rebrand the staid image of Chrysler. By the 1990s, CEOs such as General Electric's Jack Welch or Hewlett-Packard's Carla Fiorina became a standard part of the new American way of doing business. They found imitators elsewhere, such as Vivendi's Jean-Marie Messier, whose extravagant megalomania led him to style himself J6M (Jean-Marie Messier, *moi-même maître du monde*).

Out of the belief in a corporate personality developed the concept of Corporate Social Responsibility. In many cases, at least in the initial phases, it arose out of a desire to rectify an unfortunate or unpleasant image, as a simple marketing ploy. The United Fruit Company, notorious for its exploitative behavior in Central America, started to use the term "corporate responsibility" in the 1970s, in the aftermath of the Nicaraguan earthquake, which its chief executive Eli Black saw as an opportunity for the company to make some favorable publicity. Large petroleum companies, notably the British Royal Dutch Shell and British Petroleum, found an emphasis on corporate good deeds a way of compensating for the petroleum giants' bad reputation.

In consequence, in part as a response to legal and regulatory issues of corporate responsibility and in part as an extension of a motivational and marketing device, the analysis of behavior and personality moved from the individual level to that of the corporation. The analysts of this development often used medical and psychological language: companies could be healthy or sick, complacent or neurotic, or even psychotic. The result was that, if the company was a real personality, the individuals working in it did not need to behave like real or ethical people.

II

The personalization of the corporation and the notion that it had a moral as well as a legal status went hand in hand with the rise of the managerial economy. But it was paralleled by the way in which by the last decades of the twentieth century academics—especially business school academics—came to view the role of individuals within a corporation. A remarkable movement took place away from thinking of business behavior in terms of character, toward a notion of a "profession" detached from everyday life and everyday concerns.

In the early stages, many business school leaders, and especially many of the business owners and executives who helped establish the new institutions, saw the task of a modern higher-level business school primarily in terms of building character. Owen D. Young, the founding chairman of Radio Corporation of

America and then chairman of General Electric—the businessman of the 1920s who made the greatest contribution to American foreign policy, in attempting to devise a solution to the politically fraught question of German war reparations—was acutely conscious of a sense of moral obligation. He made this the point of his address in 1927 at the dedication of the new campus of the Harvard Business School: it is vital, he said,

> that the ministers of our business, like the ministers of our churches, should appreciate their responsibility. . . . We need today more than ever before men to administer this trust, who are not only highly skilled in the technique of business—men who have not only a broad outlook in history, politics, and economics—but men who have also that moral and religious training which tends to develop character.[6]

This sounded deliberately old-fashioned: it echoed the arguments given for setting up colleges in general; and in particular it fitted perfectly with the Puritan tradition of the business calling or vocation. In other words, the founders of the business school reverted easily, when they thought of the mission of their institutions, to the older language of ethical and moral responsibility that went back to Aristotle and Aquinas, as well as to the Enlightenment. There needed to be a calling that did not emanate from a perception of individual self-interest.

But as they developed in the course of the twentieth century, graduate business schools aimed at professionalizing management. Especially in the United States, they were designed to give modern managers a new status that would be commensurate with a changed and enhanced role in an evolving and improving economy. The new institutions were sharply distinguished from the older commercial schools, which had emphasized practical and vocational training. Their founders wanted a higher prestige and a more abstract and academic education for managers who would form an elite.

For much of the twentieth century, business schools instructed their pupils in how to deal with government and regulation. Indeed, many business school leaders saw the idea of creating a modern management as inseparable from the development of a modern planned society, in which government would play a vital role and in which the critical development was that of a scientific managerial elite. Business would simply fit into a policy-making group whose task was to resolve problems. As the second dean of the HBS, Wallace Bonham, explained: "Our objective . . . should be the multiplication of men who will handle current business problems in socially constructive ways."[7]

The experience of the Great Depression strengthened this view, according to which economic catastrophe had been the consequence of short-sighted greed and individualism. Conversely, planned collective action, involving an association of business and government looked to be the only way of over-coming the Depression. The program on business and international govern-ment (or "BIGI") remained a critical component of the HBS approach in the second half of the twentieth century. Big government and big corporations went hand in hand.

In the world of mundane practice, however, business schools found it impossi-ble to devise a curriculum that adequately reflected the founders' ideals. A widening gulf opened between a language of vocation that looked increasingly outdated and irrelevant and a practice aimed simply at producing new higher-status managers. Indeed, as Rakesh Khurana has pointed out in a new book, *From Higher Aims to Hired Hands,* the need to professionalize was intimately associated—as in medicine or engineering—with the need to transmit a partic-ular and specialized knowledge that would serve as a boundary to the profes-sion and exclude the amateurs. Unlike in medicine or engineering, it was never quite clear what the basis of that specialized knowledge was, since accounting, finance, and marketing might just as well be taught by the older commercial schools. That problem was not solved until the 1950s, when the Ford and Carnegie foundations used their resources to mold "New Look" business schools, modeled on the Carnegie Institute of Technology's Graduate School of Industrial Administration. In this new approach, mathematized social sci-ence would make business schools academically respectable. Faculty would be recruited and tenured on the basis of published scientific work.

Khurana points out the irony that from the 1970s on this scientific turn pushed innovative business schools to adopt a particular version of neo-classical economics, which emphasized "agency theory." The widespread adoption of its powerfully attractive language—it is an appealing model for understanding a world in which corporations are in flux, and ownership, markets, and techno-logies are constantly changing—led to a disintegration and erosion of tradi-tional notions of responsibility. This development brought the business school community even further from the original vision of the founder-generation. According to the new academic approach, pioneered by Michael Jensen, Wil-liam Meckling, and Eugene Fama, managers were agents whose interests were not necessarily aligned with those of the principals, the owners of a corpora-tion, or the shareholders. The company was nothing more than a legal fiction, a network of contracts, as Oliver Williamson put it. In this network, there was no place for a corporate ethos or corporate responsibility. Managers sought primarily their own advantage, which was not that of the company, let alone the community. For instance, managers had incentives to increase their remu-neration by expanding the size of the enterprise and increased their responsibil-ity, even when there was no profit to be found in such an expansion.

Agency theory focused on the identification of methods for monitoring managerial performance and for providing incentives for managers to improve business performance. The financial innovations of the 1970s and 1980s, in particular the use of leveraging and debt to restructure corporations, had a powerful justification in terms of increased efficiency.

Business schools and their modernized curriculum were thus in at least some measure responsible for the corporate scandals that reached a dramatic height with the collapse of Enron and WorldCom. As Khurana sums up the discussion:

> That business schools might have actively fostered misconduct by instill-ing in their students, over the course of a generation, the idea that markets provide an adequate mechanism for motivating, monitoring, and disci-plining managers and boards of directors who are not susceptible, in any case, to appeals to anything beyond self-interest was a distinctly minority view, but one that appears compelling in the context of the abandonment of the professionalization project in business education. . . . By demoting managers from professional stewards of the corporation's resources to hired hands bound only by contractual requirements and relation-ships, business schools thus helped create the conditions and standards of behavior through which the market-based mechanism of stock options was turned into an instrument for defrauding investors, jeopardizing the livelihoods of employees, and undermining public trust in managers and corporations.[8]

The business school thus literally demoralized its students. But the idea of the rationally managed corporation was also being eroded at the same time, for technological and organizational reasons.

III

It is helpful to place the transformation of the business school curriculum in a broader context of the rise and then, in the last decades of the twentieth cen-tury, the fall of managerial capitalism and the changing answers to the problem of trust with which we began.

Since the Industrial Revolution, three developments have made the classical modern institutional answer to the problem of trust in economic transactions—namely the corporation as regulated by a sovereign state—more and more problematic. First, business increasingly is not confined to national frontiers. Second, innovative businesses are often good at anticipating and circumventing attempts at regulation: especially in financial services, there is a constant race between regulatory responses to perceived problems and innovation that makes the regulation obsolete or inappropriate. Third, the character and structure of a company is constantly changing with new technologies (especially information technology) and is as a consequence less subject to hierarchical control. Taken together, these developments make more and more problematic the idea that a particular sort of institutionalized corporate culture can by itself produce good behavior.

I will take the developments in order. First, the question of the citizenship of business corporations became deeply problematic in the course of the twentieth century, because they were increasingly operating across national boundaries. Anxious executives expressed over and over the idea that a responsible multinational or transnational corporation should be a good citizen not just in its country of origin but also in the host countries in which it operates. Here are quotations from two twentieth-century business leaders that may strike the reader as utterly unremarkable.

The first quote is:

It is evident that a company which operates in a country where it is accepted and whose laws guarantee its protection has to be [unconditionally] loyal to that country and has to conscientiously comply with its wishes.[9]

The second is:

Now I believe that if an international business, such as General Motors, engages in the commercial activity of any country with the idea of making a profit . . . it has an obligation to that country, both in an economic sense as well as in a social sense. It should attempt to attune itself to the general business of the community; make itself a part of the same; conduct its operations in relation to the customs, and design its products so as to meet the needs and viewpoint of each community, so far as it can. I believe further, that that should be its position, even if, as is likely to happen and particularly as was the case during the past few years, the management of the Corporation might not wholly agree with many things that are done in certain of these countries.[10]

The first comes from Max Huber, the chairman of the Supervisory Board of a Swiss company, the Rheinfelden aluminum works (AIAG), with substantial production facilities in Germany, writing in the introduction to an official company history in 1942. The second comes from a letter of Alfred Sloan, the chief executive of General Motors, to an angry shareholder worried about the company's German subsidiary in the Nazi era. Perhaps these are both exceptional circumstances, but if so, they are extreme versions of a more common dilemma: that states cannot be relied upon to be "good." The greatest problem of today is how and by what standards companies, or indeed NGOs, can criticize and intervene in the affairs of states, which when under attack like to remind critics of the international law notion of "sovereignty." Is there a broader or more universal law (of humanity) that businesses should have to obey? If so, who is in the position to explain or codify that law?

The second development—that each new regulation soon produces as a response a technology that makes it obsolete—means that businesses often cannot have any significant or effective guidance from governments in their day-to-day decisions because the subject matter is too complex. Governments are forced to rely on self-enforced and even self-formulated standards. This problem is quite well understood in some technical areas, such as the regulation and supervision of financial sector risk, where a modern international consensus has left large parts of regulation to the banks' own risk models. But it applies equally to areas where businesses need to make judgments about the kind of government they are dealing with when they extend their operations globally: should companies ignore poor human rights records that may be responsible for some of the attractions (reduced labor costs, for example) of a particular production location?

The third development—that new technologies make companies less subject to hierarchical control—provides greater possibilities for entrepreneurial action, but also frequently makes it impossible for top management to understand what is going on throughout the corporation. The complex hierarchical structures of classical companies as they developed in the nineteenth century, with layers of management controlling and transmitting instructions to inferior layers, while information was passed up the other way, have become much flatter. Improved information technology (IT) has made the control function of the classical company easier to implement, supplying up-to-date sales information, to which the central executives can respond immediately: they no longer need the buffer of an enormous management hierarchy. But it also provides much more room for autonomous action at all levels of the business. The emphasis is on flexibility rather than action in accordance with predetermined guidelines. A considerable role in the flattening of the corporate hierarchy is also played by changing philosophies, especially the popularization of agency theory, which has led individual businesspeople to internalize a mode of analysis as a norm for behavior.

The remodeling of the corporation and a new self-understanding of behavior within the enterprise make their reputations vulnerable. In the absence of very clear hierarchies, and with much more initiative and responsibility delegated to distant and junior employees, it is much easier for the action of a single employee to damage a company's reputation or even to cripple it. It may be a question of inappropriate financial risk, combined with unauthorized and dishonest behavior to alleviate the consequences of that risk, as in the case of the old London banking house of Barings brought down by the actions of a Singapore manager Nick Leeson. It may be an issue of catastrophic negligence, as in the oil spill of the Exxon Valdez or the Texas oil refinery explosions of British Petroleum. In such cases, apparently isolated examples of bad behavior have profound impacts on corporations which have a global reach.

Cases such as these demonstrate the need for an ethic of personal responsibility that cannot simply be subsumed into some vague sense of corporate culture. Ethical questions become again absolutely central to a firm's reputation, and to its ability to do business. We are back in a world in which trust is a virtue that is required as a logical precondition of being an effective participant in markets.

IV

In a flattened business structure, where the corporation cannot be effectively controlled hierarchically, the individual personality matters much more. The individual is a whole person, whose activities cannot easily be broken up between business and private. In addition, where national regulation is increasingly ineffective or impotent as a result of the pace of technical change and of globalization, differences between systems of values and cultural norms become much more apparent. In consequence, there is more and more of a search for ways of guiding individual behavior so that it is trustworthy and constructive.

Some forms of enterprise that were largely ignored or discredited in the twentieth century have helped to fill the demand for true business personalities. Family firms have often been seen as relics of a pre-corporate age. But in fact, they play a vital part in the dynamism of many of the fastest growing regions of the world, in Asia and in Latin America. Family values can provide a basis of trust, of a long-term commitment of owners to their employees, their suppliers, and their customers. They make for an expectation of a particular kind of (trustworthy) behavior. They are one attractive answer—but not the only answer—to the question of reinserting commitment and values into business life.

There is a general malaise about what business schools teach, but it would be a mistake to treat this as simply a phenomenon of U.S. business life and the aftermath of the corporate scandals of the millennium and the attempted remedy in the form of the Sarbanes-Oxley Act of 2002. The problem cannot simply be unloaded onto governments and regulatory agencies, which are in no position to grasp the complexities of the problems they are required to solve. It is in these circumstances that a much older tradition, the tradition that demonstrates the necessity of ethics to efficient and just business, has a crucial part to play in a quickly changing and very modern world.

Notes

1. David Hume, "Of Refinement in the Arts," in *Essays, Moral, Political, and Literary,* ed. Eugene F. Miller (Indianapolis, Ind.: Liberty Fund, 1987), 270–71.

2. Douglass C. North and Barry Weingast, "Constitutions and Commitment: Evolution of the Institutions Governing Public Choice in Seventeenth-Century England," *Journal of Economic History* 49 (December 1989): 803–32; Morton J. Horwitz, *The Transformation of American Law: 1780–1860* (Cambridge, Mass.: Harvard University Press, 1977).

3. See Carmen Reinhart and Kenneth Rogoff, "Serial Default and the 'Paradox' of Rich-to-Poor Capital Flows," *American Economic Review* 94 (May 2004): 53–58.

4. See Niall Ferguson, *The House of Rothschild: Money's Prophets 1798–1848* (New York: Penguin, Viking Press, 1998): 231–56.

5. This is the way that Ronald Coase formulated the modern view of the function of the firm in his celebrated article "The Nature of the Firm," n.s., *Economica* 4 (November 1937): 386–405.

6. Quoted in Rakesh Khurana, *From Higher Aims to Hired Hands: The Social Transformation of American Business Schools and the Unfulfilled Promise of Management as a Profession* (Princeton, N.J.: Princeton University Press, 2007), 118.

7. Ibid., 116.

8. Ibid., 375.

9. Max Huber, quoted in Independent Commission of Experts Switzerland—Second World War, *Switzerland, National Socialism, and the Second World War: Final Report* (Zurich: Pendo, 2002), 299. I have added the word "unconditonally" from the German original (German original: "selbstverständlich, dass das Unternehmen seine volkswirtschaftliche Aufgabe in jedem Lande, desses Staat ihm Aufnahme und dessen recht ihm Schutz gewährt, in unbedingter Loyalität und mit dem Willen zu verständnisvoller Einordnung erfülle.")

10. Quoted in Henry A. Turner, *General Motors and the Nazis: The Struggle for Control of Opel, Europe's Biggest Carmaker* (New Haven, Conn.: Yale University Press, 2005), 27.

Chapter Two

VIRTUE AND PROFIT: A CRITIQUE
OF MANAGERIAL REASONING

Roger Scruton

IN A FREE ECONOMY people give freely of their energies, talents, and knowledge. They do this because they wish the best for themselves and their families. And at the same time, "by an invisible hand," as Adam Smith famously put it, they do the best for the economy as a whole, freely generating a productivity that dwindles just as soon as people are coerced into maintaining it.

The reasons for this have been much rehearsed, and perhaps by no one so thoroughly as F. A. Hayek, who drew on the work of Eugen von Böhm-Bawerk, Ludwig von Mises, and other members of the Austrian school in showing to a world corrupted by socialism and Keynesian mumbo-jumbo that there is a crucial flaw in all policies that propose state edicts in the place of the solutions spontaneously hit upon by our social instincts.

As the Austrian economists showed, a free economy sustains itself by generating the signals that enable individuals to make rational use of their powers.[1] In a free market price is a reliable guide to the utility and scarcity of goods, wages a reliable guide to the utility of a skill, and profit a reliable sign that a product is socially useful. In a free economy, therefore, individuals can plan to make the best use of their talents and skills, and to make money and spend it in the way that will bring the most reward. In short, individuals will be motivated to do what is best for themselves, and best for the strangers to whom they are bound in a network of mutual competition and support.

This does not mean that the motives that animate markets are merely self-interested, or that the invisible hand is nothing more than an impersonal corrective to personal greed. It was clear to Adam Smith that economic activity arises only among people who are guided by the moral sentiments, and therefore by conceptions of justice, responsibility, and obligation. And more recently, following Max Weber's celebrated work, *The Protestant Ethic and the Spirit of Capitalism,* published in 1921, it has been commonplace to connect the free economy with the Protestant, and specifically Calvinist, ethic. The Protestant posture of accountability toward God inculcates a spirit of honest dealing and accountability toward mortals too, and from this spirit there emerges a market economy and a habit of saving.

Weber's thesis is no longer credible—not because there is no connection between capitalism and the Protestant ethic, but because the connection is both wider and deeper, between the free economy and the religious frame of mind. Thus Peter Berger in a series of books, beginning with *Pyramids of Sacrifice*, has shown how religious beliefs promote the trust and entrepreneurship required by a free economy, and how wealth creation, far from being always an expression of "materialist" values, may sometimes be a spiritual exercise, with a deeply theological meaning.[2]

Berger writes from a Protestant perspective, but his thoughts are echoed by the Catholic theologian and philosopher Michael Novak, who in *Business as a Calling* showed how the Catholic theological tradition, rightly understood, not only condones business, but sees it as a calling in which we can fulfill our duty to God and to our fellow human beings.[3] For Novak, the capitalist economy is one part of a comprehensive social enterprise, the other parts of which are democracy and the rule of law. Between them these create the conditions in which individual initiative can be released and the creative potential of all members of society be given the opportunity to express itself and find fulfillment.

There is certainly an element of exaggeration in Berger and Novak, though this exaggeration is understandable, given the widespread contemporary view that businesspeople are somehow outside the fold of redemption, and that the "profit motive" is both the engine of business and its disgrace. In this paper, however, I shall argue that the "profit motive" is not the simple thing that appears either in the popular criticisms of business enterprise or in the microeconomic analysis that purports to show how business works.

Profit as By-Product

The old view of markets as driven by self-interest, and self-interest as the pursuit of profit (whether maximum, optimal, or satisfying), arises from a priori assumptions that are known to be empirically false. As Jim Collins and Jerry Porras showed in their celebrated study, *Built to Last*, the "visionary" company—the one that succeeds in circumstances where its rivals falter or go to the wall—is not the kind of "profit machine" envisaged by the opponents of corporate capitalism.[4] On the contrary, although it aims to be profitable, the visionary company understands profit in the way that a biologist understands oxygen—not the goal of life, but the thing without which there is no life. A corporation may be motivated by an ideology of group membership and consumer satisfaction, like Wal-Mart, or it may be fired by a desire to make a real contribution to society, like Hewlett-Packard (HP). It may even impress upon the world and its workforce that its primary purpose is to honor God (Chick-fil-A, for instance, or Dacor).

The point is that however the company describes its motivating principles, profit does not usually appear among the goals, but is more often construed as a side effect of pursuing them. In this connection it is worth quoting the words of John Young, CEO of HP from 1976 to 1992:

> Maximizing shareholder wealth has always been way down the list. Yes, profit is a cornerstone of what we do—it is a measure of our contribution and a means of self-financed growth—but it has never been the *point* in and of itself. The point, in fact, is to *win*, and winning is judged in the eyes of the customer and by doing something you can be proud of. There is symmetry of logic in this. If we provide real satisfaction to real customers—we will be profitable.[5]

What Young is saying is clear: by aiming exclusively at profit you risk losing your sense of purpose; by pursuing your sense of purpose, profit comes to you as a by-product. The very same "invisible hand" that, according to Mandeville and Smith, produces public good from the pursuit of private profit, produces private profit from the pursuit of public good. Moral and economic values are not in competition but, in the right context, to pursue the one is to obtain the other: and the dependency goes both ways. Moreover, as Collins and Porras show through the telling contrast between HP and Texas Instruments, the firm that puts profit at the top of its agenda, and regards all else as subservient to that goal, very soon begins to lose its competitive edge.

A team of researchers under the direction of William Damon, Howard Gardner, and Mihaly Csikszentmihalyi has shown the close connection, in particular cases, between moral conviction and business success. Through the exercise of "moral imagination," Damon argues, a firm can further the moral goals of its members, providing them with the personal satisfaction that comes from doing good, without sacrificing profitability.[6] Csikszentmihalyi goes further, in suggesting a kind of secular basis for the moral dimension of business, as people enter through business into moral relations with their fellows and work comes to function as the foundation of social harmony—performing the role that religion once performed, in imbuing life with purpose.[7] These studies take us far along the road to understanding the moral basis of capitalism, and the resources on which it draws. But they also point to interesting features of practical reasoning that get noticed by economists, as a rule, only as part of the amorphous idea of "social capital."

Social Capital

Social capital denotes the resources that are used in managing the day-to-day affairs of social existence, including customs, language, manners, and morals—in short, all the practices that are taught to us by our parents in order to make us fit members of society.[8] These things cannot be invented anew by each generation, since they are the distillation of a long process of accommodation. As Hayek and others have shown, the rules, customs, and traditions that enable people to live together in a great society are also products of "the invisible hand."[9] They are the beneficial results of cooperation and competition between neighbors, and the spontaneous byproducts of our attempts to live in peace. The very same freedom that produces the capitalist economy also produces the social capital that is needed if it is to run successfully.

Like economic capital, social capital can be accumulated and invested. It is built through creating networks of trust and goodwill, which enable people spontaneously to pool their intellectual and physical resources in a common enterprise. As Francis Fukuyama has shown, communities in which there prevails a culture of trust and accountability are able to prosper in adverse circumstances and to create wealth seemingly ex nihilo.[10] Western societies have accumulated a great stock of social capital in the form of culture, networks, institutions, and laws. In each area of human endeavor they have added to this stock, accumulating works of art and music, games and sports, festivals and competitions, through which individuals rehearse their social feelings and refresh their commitments.

Social capital can be wisely invested, as when we found a school or a university and endow it with good teachers, good books, and good facilities, so helping the fund of knowledge and skills to grow. It can dwindle, as Robert Putnam shows, through the gradual retreat from social contacts.[11] It can also be wasted, and the conspicuous waste of social capital is one of the most unhappy features of our societies today. This waste has been documented by several authors, notably by Charles Murray and James Q. Wilson, who have shown the way in which, by throwing economic resources into the welfare system, we do not merely waste those resources; we also waste social capital, producing the welfare-dependency that prevents people from learning how to be on equal and responsible terms with others, subsidizing indolence and exhausting our teachers, social workers, and doctors with the thankless task of caring for people who are often unwilling to care for themselves.[12]

The social capital on which a business draws is in part its own creation. Among the "savings" of a business we should count the activities devoted to building trust, commitment, and mutual respect among its employees, and to creating the social networks and goodwill that incorporate the firm into the feelings and plans of its members. And the theory of social capital goes some way to accounting for the fact that the "profit motive" does not mean the single-minded pursuit of profit. Many of the things necessary for the reliable generation of profit can be achieved only by pursuing something else— something which cannot be conceptualized in balance-sheet terms, even if it is valued, in part, as a means to improving the balance sheet.

Intrinsic Goods

Traditional econometric analysis can make the same place for social capital as it makes for any other kind of capital. However, there is a form of practical reasoning, every bit as important in business as in everyday life, which escapes the net of econometrics, and that is the rational deployment of intrinsic goods.

Consider friendship. The person with friends has help in his time of need, consolation in despair, and fellowship in rejoicing. In everything he attempts he is better off than the friendless person, and all his burdens are more lightly borne. But this does not mean that he values his friend merely as a means to achieving his own selfish goals. On the contrary, he values his friend for the particular person he is, and without thought for the benefit. The benefit is real, but it arises "by an invisible hand," from actions with another intention.

Moreover, the person who treats another as a means to his own goals, however gently, with whatever compunction, is not treating the other as a friend. And if you do not treat someone as a friend, he ceases to be one. From this we can derive a striking conclusion. Friends are useful, so long as you do not make use of them! Treat someone as a friend, value him for who he is, and he will repay your friendship a thousandfold. Treat him as useful, however, and he will soon cease to be so.

On the other hand, although the true friend does not aim at the benefit of friendship, he has that benefit *in view.* He must be sensible of the good that has come his way, and show it through gratitude, affection, and a measure of dependency. If he should ever lose sight of the benefit entirely then the result will be comparable to that of pursuing the benefit too purposefully: he will become careless of the friendship and so lose it. He must maintain in view an instrumental value that will vanish, just as soon as he explicitly pursues it. La Rochefoucauld wrote that "interest has many faces, including that of disinterest"; that is not what I have in mind. Rather the opposite: that disinterest has many faces, and one of them is the interest that we have in the benefits that flow from disinterest—an interest that must never be rewritten as a goal.

There is a simple model of practical reasoning, typical of the empiricist tradition in philosophy, but also recurring in sophisticated forms in modern decision theory and its offshoots, according to which practical reasoning consists in working out the means to satisfy our desires. In its modern form the theory goes as follows: we have certain preferences, and these are the data from which our practical reasoning begins. Preferences can be ordered—you prefer A over B and B over C—and also indifferent, as when everything preferred to A is preferred to B and A is preferred to everything to which B is preferred. Preferences for goods are also sensitive to time (how far they lie in the future), to probability (how probable is it that they will be obtained), and to risk (how probable are negative side effects and how negative will they be). And so on.

Enormous intellectual problems lie in the way of building a complete theory for the rational ordering of preferences, not least the problems of transitivity pointed out two centuries ago by Condorcet (it being relatively easy to construct cases in which an agent prefers A to B, B to C, and C to A). Nevertheless, the assumption in economics is that preferences are the raw material of rational choice, and that the rational person is the one who pursues as many of his preferences as possible to the point of fulfillment.

Against that picture I would put another, more consonant with the treatment of practical reasoning in Aristotle and Aquinas, and more consonant too with what we observe. People distinguish things they merely want from things they also value, and things they value instrumentally (either as a means to satisfy a want or as means to achieve some value) from things they value intrinsically. Wants can be weighed against each other and ordered in the manner of econometrics. Intrinsic values are more difficult to order, and sometimes impossible to weigh against each other. Yet things valued are also wanted, and usually have an instrumental value too. At the same time the condition toward which they are instrumental is something that we keep in view but do not pursue as a goal.

This condition, usually called happiness, self-fulfillment, or flourishing, comes, when it comes, as a by-product of other goals, and those goals can be pursued only by putting the benefit of obtaining them out of one's calculations. The example of friendship shows what it is, to keep in view the good things that follow from one's purpose, while not making them *part* of the purpose. It is plausible to suggest that this double intentionality is natural to self-conscious beings, and is also one of the roots—maybe even *the* root—of the moral life.

In friendship, therefore, people build up a capital asset by aiming at something quite different from a capital asset, even while keeping that asset in view. The same is true of the motive of virtue—and this lies at the heart of an ancient insight, that virtue and friendship are connected, and that only the virtuous have true friends (as opposed to companions and accomplices).

Courage, for example, is supremely useful. It is the characteristic that puts your goals within reach, and so helps you to attain them. But that is not the motive of courage. The courageous person is not simply motivated by what he wants: the coward too has that motive. The courageous person is motivated in another way. He sees his action from outside, as another would see it. And he is proud to act as he does; he feels that duty, honor, and his standing in the world require him to take the risk. And it is precisely because he sees his action in this way, as the right thing to do, regardless of consequences, that he obtains the reward.

Planning for Success

It is a failure to grasp this feature of practical reasoning that lies at the root of the suspicion of capitalism and the market economy. Neoclassical economics proceeds on the assumption that firms aim to make a profit, and that the market is a system in which individual firms, each acting to achieve its profit (either maximally, optimally, or sufficiently), coordinate their actions and achieve equilibrium. But neoclassical economics does not examine, because it cannot, the actual motives of the people who compose those firms, and the precise way in which the profit motive arises within them. To the critics of capitalism, therefore, it has seemed as if the whole system were built on ruthless self-interest, and that if anybody paused, for a moment, to consider the sufferings of others, it was only to study how to make efficient use of them.

If we look back at the founder of classical economics, however, we find quite another picture. Adam Smith's picture of competition in the marketplace was intended as an adjunct to his detailed description, offered in *The Theory of the Moral Sentiments,* of human motivation, in which the pursuit of profit is tempered at every juncture by sympathy, benevolence, and the posture of the "impartial spectator" forced on us by our moral nature. Human motives are never simple, Smith recognized. And what is, from one perspective, the pursuit of profit might be, from another and equally valid perspective, a gesture of benevolence. Often we achieve our goals by ignoring them, and the most profitable of our actions might be those in which we turn our backs on profit and act for the sake of honor, kindness, or compassion.

This is the kind of consideration that ought to lead us entirely to reject the caricature of capitalism that its critics love to reiterate. Private property, private initiative, private risk, and private profit are indeed all essential attributes of the capitalist system. But these things are economically effective only against a background of norms and values, in which profit may be kept in view, but seldom presented as the goal.

The Aristotelian position seems to be that happiness comes through virtue, but that the virtuous person does not aim at it, since his motive in all that he does is righteousness or honor (*to kalon*). Happiness, Aristotle makes clear, is not composed of fleeting sensations available equally to selfless and selfish people. It involves a settled contentment with one's lot, with oneself, and with others. It is not an experience but a condition, in which we flourish according to our nature, as a tree flourishes in healthy soil, or a fish in pure water. We teach our children to be courageous, wise, just, and temperate because we know that this will make them respected by their fellows, secure in their decisions, and able to take full control of their lives. That is the way to happiness. It is also the way in which the individual serves the community: the happiness of the individual and the prosperity of the community are both achieved through virtue.

Success in business is similar. It may come from a lucky accident. But lucky accidents cannot be planned. We prepare for success by acquiring virtues—dispositions that help us to take risks, to make decisions, to take responsibility for our actions, and to accept wise advice. These are the most important part of our human capital. But we do not invent them for ourselves. They form part of our collective inheritance. And through moral discipline we adopt them into ourselves.

The Pursuit of Virtue

Philosophers and moralists have tended to agree with Aristotle's list of the cardinal virtues—temperance, courage, justice, and prudence or practical wisdom (*phronesis*). By calling these virtues cardinal (from Latin *cardo*, a hinge), we emphasize that all else turns on them: that without them no other virtues can be reliably acquired or exercised.

But what is meant by calling them virtues? When I say that it is a virtue in a horse that it is steady in traffic, or a virtue in a chair that it is comfortable to sit in, I am relating the horse or the chair to the world of human interests. Being steady in traffic is an equine feature in which we, as riders, have an interest. From our point of view, the steadier the better. When I speak of the virtues of a human being, however, I mean something more far-reaching. I do not mean that he is useful to others. I mean that he has habits that contribute to human fulfillment and his own fulfillment first of all. We all have an interest in each other's character; but we also have a commanding interest in our own character, and what we do with it.

That is why we distinguish virtues from vices, recognizing that our most intimate self-conception will be affected by our habits, and that good habits bring not just success in our endeavors, but inner tranquility and peace of mind. Moral judgments are universalizable, and the qualities we love or hate in others we will also love or hate in ourselves. It follows that virtue is a necessary condition of happiness, since it is the foundation of the self-approval without which no one can be truly at peace with himself.

Aristotle also was of that opinion. The context in which he developed his argument—the context of the Greek city-state, existing in fierce commercial and military competition with its neighbors—was very far from the context enjoyed by a modern corporation. Nevertheless, his argument was aimed at what is permanent in human nature, with a view to identifying the qualities that people need in all the circumstances of life, if they are to achieve the fulfillment of which they are capable.

He saw virtues as dispositions, which we learn by imitation and habit, but which are something more than knee-jerk reactions. The virtuous person does not merely acquire new and more disciplined behavior; he acquires new and more fulfilling *motives*. To be genuinely courageous it is not sufficient to imitate the actions of a courageous person: in advance of the circumstances it is in any case impossible to know what those actions will be. To be courageous is to be moved as the courageous person is moved. It is to desire what is honorable and good, despite the cost in terms of personal discomfort and danger. The point about virtue is that it is reliable; and people become reliable when they are motivated in the right way. In a time of danger we look to the courageous person because we know that he will put the common good above his own personal safety, and therefore, through his leadership and example, create the best chance that the present danger will be overcome.

The Problem of Justice

The Greeks saw virtue as a unity. Each of the four cardinal virtues depends upon and amplifies the others. A courageous person must be temperate if he is not to overstep the mark. Intemperate courage is not courage but rashness, and temperance in turn needs courage if it is to face up to temptation and to the pressure of one's peers and still to say no. Prudence is involved in every virtue, and needs all other virtues if it is to be something better than a mean-minded refusal to take risks.

But one of the great difficulties that the Greek philosophers faced was that of integrating justice into their moral scheme. We can justify courage, temperance, and prudence as benefits to the person who possesses them—traits of character that bring success, and which make it maximally probable that the person who possesses them will overcome the difficulties that beset us in the trials of life. But justice is a much more "other-regarding" virtue, and the question "why be just?" troubled the Greek philosophers as it has troubled every thinking person since. It is the question that launches the argument of Plato's *Republic*. And it is the question dealt with by the Greek poets and tragedians in their most memorable bequests to us. It is also a question that bears directly on the conduct of business, since in so many contexts justice and profit seem to be at war. Indeed, for the Marxists, with their zero-sum vision of all market transactions, the war can be ended only when private profit is abolished.

Aristotle defined the virtue of justice as the disposition to give to each person his due: and this is the definition taken up centuries later by Ulpian in his digest of Roman law. All rational beings need justice, Aristotle argued, since all need the cooperation of their fellows, and the trust upon which this depends. Moreover, without justice there is no friendship, since the friend is the one who both gives what is due and receives it. The most interesting feature of Aristotle's discussion of justice is his recognition that it is a quality of the individual agent and of the individual action. Justice is something that we do, and which we are blamed for not doing. And it has its root and motive in the virtue of justice: the virtue displayed by the person who sees others as his equals and who responds instinctively to their rightful demands.

That ancient conception of justice has been overlaid in modern times by a rival idea, which sees justice as a feature of "society," rather than of individual actions. True, Aristotle already made a distinction between commutative and distributive justice, and this is often cited as authority by those who believe that social distributions can be assessed as just or unjust, regardless of their history. However, it is clear from his exposition that Aristotle believed that justice is a property of actions and agents, and that a distribution can be assessed as just or unjust only where people have collectively contributed to the production of a good, and thereby each established a title to some share in it. The idea—fashionable today, and indeed fundamental to the socialist-egalitarian world view—that distributions can be just or unjust simply as *states of affairs*, and without reference to the actions that brought them about, has no place in the Greek view of justice.

However, the socialist conception is not entirely new. The concept of "social or public justice" gained a hold during the nineteenth century, under the influence of Christian social thought. It has a large part to play in the Calvinist theories of Abraham Kuyper, the theologian who was briefly Prime Minister of the Netherlands at the turn of the twentieth century. And there is a powerful tradition within Catholic theology which also sees "social justice" as a primary obligation of the Church. The modern critics of the free economy make much of the "social injustices" it supposedly creates and sustains. And they often frame their demands in terms of a distributive conception of justice, as in the celebrated work of John Rawls, *A Theory of Justice*. It seems that the conception of a *purely* distributive justice has been gaining ground, and sidelining the kind of reasoning about the virtue that Aristotle thought gave sense to the concept.

Social Justice

According to the Christian tradition, "social or public justice" means a proper regulation of society, so that people can deal justly with each other in the *several* communities to which they belong. Social justice requires that we maintain the separate spheres of social interaction, so that each can be guided by its own spontaneous form of order: the order of the family, the club, the firm, the regiment, the school. That was what Kuyper understood by social justice: not the control of society by the state, but the retreat of the state from the self-governing spheres where it is not needed. A similar doctrine has been upheld by the Catholic Church under the name of "subsidiarity," meaning the freedom of social institutions to govern themselves. The Catholic doctrine was taken over by Wilhelm Röpke in order to show how a capitalist economy can be reconciled with social justice, by supporting the institutions of civil society, through which people help each other and relieve the stresses of competition.[13]

In the modern context, however, "social justice" has typically been held to require redistribution of goods by the State. In other words, it has come to mean the confiscation of property by bureaucrats who have no personal responsibility either in acquiring it or in giving it away. This use of the concept involves severing the idea of justice from that of individual accountability. And it condones the compulsory seizure of assets irrespective of whether they were justly or unjustly acquired. It is precisely this conception of social justice that authorized the great crimes committed in our day in the name of socialism and communism. And it is "social justice," understood in the socialist way, that has crippled the capitalist economies of Europe, to the great disadvantage of everyone, included those whom "social justice" is supposed to benefit.

Back to Aristotle

By seeing justice as a virtue of individuals, however, we help to reintegrate the demand for justice into a healthy and creative economy. Justice regulates and upholds contracts; it encourages respect in the workplace and accountability both to customers and to shareholders. It distinguishes the phony demands of interlopers from the rightful demands of those to whom something is owed. And it furthers the long-term relationships of trust on which a successful business, and the larger community, both depend.

By emphasizing the classical virtue as the core of justice, we once again put justice within our reach, and enable it to exert its benign influence over our actions. This does not mean that we can ignore the social conditions that surround us: evidently, where there is large-scale discrimination against minorities or blatant disregard of civil rights, justice demands that we take a stand on behalf of those who are being thus mistreated. But the important point is contained in that last word: for there to be injustice, there must be mistreatment. Someone must be *in the wrong*, and justice demands that the wrong be righted.

If we see justice in that way, however, we remove it from the frame of consequentialist reasoning that appeals to economists, and return it to the place where it belongs: among the motives and responsibilities of the individual agent. The just business is the one that treats others and its employees with respect, that takes responsibility for its faults, honors its agreements, and does not cheat on its rivals. And a business with such a disposition puts honor above profit in any conflict. Studies of virtuous companies have again brought home to us the empirical evidence for the view that justice, seen in this way, is not the enemy of profit, and that honesty remains the best policy—provided that it is not chosen as a policy.[14] At least this is so in the conditions of a free market, where profit is not arbitrarily confiscated and can therefore be openly declared, and where agreements are transparent and enforceable.

Virtuous Business and Its Enemies

However, there are two things that stand in the way of virtuous business: the state and the consultants. Both of them take a consequentialist view of justice, the state pursuing "social justice," in the form of a distributive pattern, the consultants advancing an agenda of "corporate social responsibility," which relegates justice to a sideline. State interference in the free economy, in order to secure some distributive pattern judged to conform to social justice, inevitably distorts the reasoning of private businesses. In a condition of enforced redistribution the virtue of justice begins to lose its appeal. Hence, in the state-monitored economies of France and Germany the black market accounts for nearly 20 percent of Gross Domestic Product, as the desperate attempt to maintain profits takes precedence over honest accounting. And, while doing their best to escape the grip of oppressive employment laws, businesses try to present a principled countenance to the world, by engaging in "social responsibility" projects of a kind that will coincide with the State's egalitarian agenda.

However, virtue is not "window dressing," and virtuous business is a long way from the kind of "grafted on" public relations exercise the consultants favor. Enron was quite good at Corporate Social Responsibility (CSR), giving money to fashionable causes, making the right noises about diversity, equal opportunities, care for the environment, and whatever else the activists were concerned to investigate. But CSR, conceived in this way, is simply a kind of protection racket, whereby a corporation buys off the busybodies among the Non-Governmental Organizations, wraps itself in a veil of political correctness, and gets on with the business of profit-taking.

It is only superficially related to the ethical heart of a business, and may indeed be nothing more than a systematic deception—like the advertisements for oil companies which present them as engaged almost exclusively in environmental programs, and which never mention fossil fuels, still less greenhouse gas emissions. This is not to say that oil companies should not be involved in environmental projects—of course they should. It is rather to emphasize that a virtuous company is an honest citizen, and its virtue not a public relations façade.

The considerations that might make us suspicious of CSR ought also to weigh against the current orthodoxies of "business ethics," as this is now taught in business studies courses and MBA programs, and as it intrudes into the political sphere. "Business ethics" as normally conceived too often consists in a set of rules—do's and don'ts—calculated to secure the approval of "stakehold-ers," and therefore of the activists who claim to represent them. It is all too often animated by a kind of political correctness which stems from the same suspicion of the "profit motive" as the socialist resentments that poisoned the heart of Europe in the twentieth century. Diversity, multiculturalism, environ-mental rectitude, and other agenda-driven prescriptions are made into absolute values, to be enforced without regard to the nature of the business or the condi-tions under which it can flourish. And business ethics, so conceived, prompts governments to devise ever-more-detailed regulations, and to appoint ever-more-meddlesome committees of people, often ignorant of or hostile to busi-ness, to enforce them.

Of course, there is such a thing as business ethics; but it is no different from any other kind of ethics. It consists in one simple injunction, namely: strive to do good—the first principle of natural law, according to Aquinas. We obey this injunction through the exercise of virtue, and not through public relations exercises designed to appease politically motivated activists. Ethics is not about conformity to a political agenda; it is about the internal character, the moral stature, in short the soul of the firm. The virtuous company does not need to be told how to treat its employees, its customers, or the environment: it knows from the outset that it is a steward of all that it touches, just as virtuous people are. If it enters the political realm at all it is not as a craven follower of some political ideology, but as a corporate statesman, taking its place on behalf of its shareholders and workforce in the shaping of our common future.

The Soul of the Firm

That view of the corporation conflicts, however, with the emerging "stake-holder" model. The stakeholder is to be sharply distinguished from the share-holder. The latter has risked his money in the firm, which is therefore bound to him by a fiduciary obligation not to waste or squander it. The former simply has a passing interest in the firm, whose obligation toward him is only that laid down by the general principles of morality and law.

Emphasis on the stakeholder should not be allowed to obscure the funda-mental nature of the corporation, as an association of individuals, bound to-gether by a shared risk and rewarded by a shared profit. The sharing of risk and profit creates relations of responsibility between management and workforce, owners and executives, and these endow the corporation with a soul of its own. Whatever the truth in the "stakeholder model" it must not be allowed to ob-scure this fundamental point: that corporations come into the world as distinct individuals, with souls that are shaped by the social capital which has been invested in them.

Readers might balk at the word "soul." Surely, they will say, corporations don't have souls in the sense that we have souls. There is no immortal essence to a corporation, nor does a corporation die and proceed to judgment. This talk of the corporate soul, they will say, is at best a metaphor. I would respond by saying that it is not a metaphor but a simile, and a simile grounded in real properties that are shared. For example, companies do things, they are blamed and praised for things, and they deliberate, take responsibility, and create bonds of loyalty and disaffection just as we do. And when you belong to a company you are acutely aware that it has its own way of proceeding, its own values, its own corporate culture, and its own ambient consciousness of how to conduct itself in business. The soul of the company is simply a special case of esprit de corps: the shared sense of belonging, following, leading, and obeying which unites the members around their common interests. Hence a company can be virtuous or vicious, just as an individual can be.

A virtuous company will be accepted in the economy not as a rapacious marauder but as a partner whose presence promises help, and which will conduct itself, wherever it might be, as a fellow citizen. Nothing is more valuable to a firm than its reputation for virtue. It is not enough to be "visionary" in the sense made familiar by Jim Collins: a visionary company can easily offend through its messages or its aggressive presence, as Exxon offended the Czechs after the fall of communism, by erecting gas stations surmounted by eye-catching and landscape-disfiguring tigers, or as Exxon offended just about everyone by attempting to evade responsibility for the 1989 Valdez oil spill.

The need for virtuous conduct, rather than CSR, is nowhere more apparent than in the global marketplace. A company like UPS, which is perceived as a responsible citizen wherever it goes, has a clear trading advantage. But it cannot secure this advantage by window dressing. It must be led by a genuine ethos of concern and service: something that we see in UPS's involvement, for example, in educational projects in Poland—projects which have radically enhanced its local standing precisely because they are seen to be an expression of concern for the Polish people, rather than a shallow exercise in CSR.

The Root of All Evil

There is a skeptical approach to business and its denizens which is as old as the Old Testament, and which is echoed by Aristotle, Jesus, St. Paul, the Koran, and a thousand other moralists and sages. According to this approach we must distinguish businesses that produce what people need—agriculture, industry, construction, and so on—from businesses that deal only in money. The idea that one can make money simply by dealing in money has been looked at askance by moralists from the beginning of recorded history. Such a way of making money seems too much like trickery to earn our respect, and it excites all those "zero-sum illusions" that inspired the nineteenth-century socialists. If someone is making money but selling nothing, someone else must be losing exactly that amount—and why isn't that theft?

This is not the place to mount a defense of the money market, of banking, of lending at interest, and so on. What is important is to recognize that banks too have souls, and that, in the normal case, it is by honorable conduct that they earn their place in the economy, and their opportunities for profit. To lend money at a market rate is to offer a service, and a firm can be entirely dependent on this form of business without sacrificing those other and higher goals which earn the trust of its customers and its own place in society. Think of the calamity that befell Baring's bank, in which the old and upright customs of the City of London were exploited from within by one of the new breed of self-centered nihilists. Or think of Lloyd's and its collapse, an episode that eloquently illustrates the distinction between honorable and dishonorable ways of using other people's money. Such examples remind us that it is as true of money as of any other business, that profit must come second to virtue, if it is to keep coming for long.

Of course, businesses have been radically changed by globalization, by out-sourcing, by asset-stripping, and other practices that affect their accountability to others and to their own employees. New opportunities for misconduct and vandalism arise every day, and there is no way of extracting from my argument some neat formula that will apply to all of them.

Nevertheless, I remain persuaded that the model of economic activity I am proposing, which sees profit as the by-product of morally admirable goals, is the only one that will deliver a coherent view of business ethics. The models currently entertained see businesses as profit-driven machines, and govern-ments as devices for redistributing the profit among those who did nothing to produce it. To this bleak vision I cannot help preferring the model that I have been defending. Instead of seeing business ethics as a compromise between two forms of immorality—self-centered profiteering and theft of the results—it recommends that businesses care for their souls as we should care for ours, so as to be upright citizens in a realm that we share.

Notes

1. See Ludwig von Mises, *Socialism: An Economic and Sociological Analysis*, 2d ed., trans. J. Kahane (New Haven, Conn.: Yale University Press, 1951).

2. Peter Berger, *Pyramids of Sacrifice: Political Ethics and Social Change* (New York: Basic Books, 1975) and Peter Berger, ed., *The Capitalist Spirit: Toward a Religious Ethic of Wealth Creation* (San Francisco: ICS Press, 1990).

3. Michael Novak, *Business as a Calling: Work and the Examined Life* (New York: Simon and Schuster, Free Press, 1996).

4. Jim Collins and Jerry I. Porras, *Built to Last: Successful Habits of Visionary Companies*, 10th ed. (New York: HarperCollins, Collins, 2004).

5. Quoted in ibid., 57.

6. William Damon, *The Moral Advantage: How to Succeed in Business by Doing the Right Thing* (San Francisco: Berrett-Koehler, 2004).

7. Mihaly Csikszentmihalyi, *Good Business: Leadership, Flow, and the Making of Meaning* (London: Hodder and Stoughton, 2003).

8. The idea has been applied in the context of modern business in Don Cohen and Laurence Prusak, *In Good Company: How Social Capital Makes Organizations Work* (Boston: Harvard Business School Press, 2001).

9. See especially F. A. Hayek, *Rules and Order*, vol. 1 of *Laws, Legislation, and Liberty* (London: Routledge, 1982).

10. Ibid.

11. Ibid.

12. James Q. Wilson, *The Moral Sense* (New York: Simon and Schuster, Free Press Paperbacks, 1993); Charles Murray, *Losing Ground: American Social Policy 1950–1980* (New York: Basic Books, 1984).

13. Wilhelm Röpke, *A Humane Economy: The Social Framework of the Free Market* (Chicago: H. Regnery, 1960; reprint, with a new introduction by Dermot Quinn, Wilmington, Del.: ISI Books, 1998).

14. See the examples in Damon, *Moral Advantage*, and Csikszentmihalyi, *Good Business*.

Chapter Three

ANTHROPOLOGICAL AND ETHICAL
FOUNDATIONS OF ORGANIZATION THEORY

Antonio Argandoña

THE FINAL YEARS of the twentieth century and the first few years of the twenty-first have been a time of uncertainty in management theory and the economic theories that for many years served as its primary basis.[1] We will not be able to say for some years whether we are seeing a deep crisis in management theory or mere growing pains, though I suspect the former. It is not my intention to make an in-depth analysis of the current model, as other social scientists have already done this effectively enough.[2] Instead, I want to offer some observations on how we can find a way out of the current crisis, if indeed such a crisis exists.

The aim of this article is as follows. First, we will revisit action theory, which is the starting point for the current economic model but based on an excessively restrictive anthropology, so we will turn to realist philosophy (Aristotle, Thomas Aquinas) for a broader conception of the characteristics of such action. We will thus be able to refer to more complex assumptions that can be used to explain human action within organizations and develop a more complex theory of organization. This broader-based anthropology will also allow us to discuss the role of ethics in organization theory, since ethics should originate from the same anthropology. This will in turn result in the natural integration of ethics into organization theory, in such a way that ethics becomes "the condition of stable equilibrium" for the behavior of individuals, institutions, organizations, and firms, as well as economic systems.[3]

My intention in this article is not to develop an entirely alternative theory of organization, but instead to indicate some of its initial stages.[4]

Action Theory

"Managing consists of leading a company from its current position to a future position that is better in relative terms."[5] Management is, first and foremost, action. We must therefore turn to action theory, which has traditionally been the preserve of economic science, as a first step in understanding the management of people.

Human action is intentional: a human being tries to achieve some end that he has set for himself, and his purpose or intention gives his action meaning.[6] In any action, the agent identifies a need and sees the possibility of meeting it, which is the action's end goal, or objective. There follows the deliberation, in which the subject then identifies the means and resources available, formulates the ways to achieve the end, analyzes the consequences of implementing them, establishes the criteria to appraise the means, and appraises them. Then the means to carry out the action are chosen and the action performed. Over time come the action's consequences or results—how and to what extent the planned end is achieved and other effects obtained, including unexpected or undesired effects—the evaluation of the consequences and results, and finally the correction of the decision, if the action is to be repeated in the future or forms part of a broader plan.

In neoclassical economics, the theory of action follows this model, with certain differences worth pointing out. The action's end is also the satisfaction of a need felt by the agent, in accordance with a function of preferences the agent takes as given. The deliberation consists of looking for alternatives (means) and appraising them. This process is usually carried out in terms of the subjective values attributed by the agent to the expected or anticipated results (objective values) of his choices, within a plurality of possible states. By inserting all preferences into a single function (utility function or order of preferences), under the assumption that the values are commensurable, it is possible to perform (mental) comparisons between the expected subjective outcomes using a single comparison unit (ordinal), which is the expected utility in each case. This establishes the decision criterion the agent will use, which is the maximization of his utility, in accordance with the "economic principle": the agent always tries to obtain the best result that can be obtained with the limited means available—or, alternatively, the agent always uses the lowest possible quantity of means to obtain a given result. (Certain hypotheses are added, such as that of continuity, to avoid lexicographic preferences; that of the preferences' internal consistency, to assure the decision's rationality; and that of the preferences' quasi-concavity and the infinite divisibility of goods, to guarantee the existence of a single optimal result when the range of feasible solutions is convex.)

The motivation for the action is the satisfaction of a need, and that alone is sufficient to start the process; no distinction is made between potential and actual motivation. The decision consists of choosing the means to maximize the expected utility. The economist usually does not consider the execution phase: the fact that the agent is considering acting implies the will to act and the capacity to do so, if he has the necessary resources. The action's results are also of little interest to the economist, at least in nonrepetitive actions or actions that do not form part of complex plans: the agent decides based on his appraisal (utility) of the action's expected consequences, in accordance with a given, unvarying function of preferences, and therefore the fact that the action's actual consequences do not match its expected consequences cannot influence the decision, which has already been made. In other words, either the agent does not learn from the consequences or such learning has no effect on the decision that already has been made. (Economic models for human action and, therefore, those that refer to organizations, with their well-defined utility functions and assumptions of perfect knowledge, work on the premise that agents will not learn and will therefore act like machines.[7] Given that agents do learn, these models are insufficient.) Therefore, the evaluation of the action's consequences is not relevant either, and neither is the correction of possible future decisions, at least in the case of nonrepetitive actions.

As we shall see, these differences indicate where action theory and organization theory should be changed.

The most interesting cases in action theory, particularly where this involves action within an organization (and therefore management action) are those in which a person (the "active agent," whom we shall assume is the manager) interacts with another person (the "reactive agent") and not with a nonhuman environment, when those actions form part of a series of repeated actions or plans. This means that to solve a problem the decision-maker must evaluate the action from three points of view: (1) how well it will satisfy the current need; (2) what effects it will have on the agent's ability to satisfy that same need when it recurs in the future; and (3) what effects it will have on the agent's ability to satisfy not only that need, but all her needs, now and in the future.

The agent will have to consider all the reasonably foreseeable results of the action: (1) the "extrinsic" result or the reactive agent's response (for example, when the employee complies with an order in such a way that the manager's wishes are satisfied and the manager gains prestige); (2) the "intrinsic" result or the effects on the active agent (for example, what the active agent learns on an operational level or the satisfaction he gets from performing the action); and (3) the "external" result or the effects the action has on the reactive agent (for example, what the reactive agent learns as a result of the action).[8] We are clearly looking at a range of results broader than the one found in conventional economics.

If this is the case, the active agent will have to assess three aspects of his or her decision, what Juan Antonio Pérez-López calls the effectiveness, the efficiency, and the consistency of the action.

1. Effectiveness: the extent to which the action contributes to achieving the specific purpose of the action. The action of giving an order is effective if the reactive agent complies with the order in the way the manager wishes. This corresponds with the result of the decision as analyzed by conventional

economics, in terms of a utility function subject to restrictions (preferences, resource availability, etc.).

2. Efficiency: the satisfaction and the learning the action brings the active agent, that is, the extent to which the action helps to develop the skills (operational habits) that will make it easier to satisfy those same needs when they recur in the future. The action of giving the order will be efficient if the agent learns to give better orders in the future and is also motivated to do so.

3. Consistency: the value for the active agent of the learning that takes place in the reactive agent as a result of the experience of the interaction. The action of giving the order will be consistent if the employee learns to comply better in the future, or is more disposed to comply, or is in a better position to understand the orders received, etc. The active agent must take into account the fact that the interaction with the reactive agent will change the reactive agent's behavior and make future interactions either easier or more difficult, and so will affect the active agent's ability to satisfy future needs with that same reactive agent.

As a result, organization theory should be based on an action theory that is not confined to the response of the reactive agent and the satisfaction it gives the active agent, that is, the effectiveness of the action. In the evaluation of the action, the agent must take into account not only the direct effects deriving from the reactive agent's response, as does traditional theory, but at least two other realities:

1. Operational knowledge: what the active agent herself learns about the action. Any analysis of an action is incomplete if it ignores this type of learning, that is, the impact the action has on efficiency. (This type of learning is taken into account in sociology and economics, and is included in some decision theories.[9])

2. Evaluative knowledge: the ability to recognize other people's inner states, that is, to assess the consistency of an action. An action is consistent if, after the first "transaction" (action-reaction cycle), the other party is more motivated, or at least not less motivated, to engage in a new cycle than she was previously. Any analysis of an action will be incomplete if this point is omitted. That is so for two reasons:

a. It may be that, as a consequence of the first interaction, the reactive agent becomes less interested in participating in further interactions ("negative learning" occurs). For example, the manager who abuses an employee's confidence is unlikely to obtain this employee's future collaboration.

b. Depending on the active agent's evaluation of his action's effects on the reactive agent, he will change, and that change may make satisfying other needs and developing beneficial interactions with other agents in the future more difficult.

Thus, action theory offers a dynamic decision theory that considers not only a decision's direct impact (the dimension of effectiveness), but also its other effects on the planes of efficiency and consistency. This is important for organization theory, because a manager's inconsistent decisions will eventually affect the effectiveness and efficiency of her actions and therefore the possibility of achieving the goals set by her organization (as well as her own personal goals).

Action theory is also the most suitable way of introducing ethics into the decision-making process, because "evaluating human acts according to how much they improve the person who performs them is the very substance of ethics."[10] Furthermore, it offers a solid base for ethics, one resting not on abstract rational principles or extrinsic results (consequences), but on the very reality of the decision process.

Organization Theory

An organization is "a group of people who coordinate their actions to achieve objectives in which they all have an interest, albeit for different reasons,"[11] objectives they would not be able to achieve, or would find it more difficult to achieve, without the combined actions of the group's members.[12] Organizations therefore exist to achieve certain common aims in a way that is compatible with the "different reasons" of their members, at least as far as the available resources allow. Organization theory must therefore be based on sound action theory. The reasons are the same as were given earlier: actions inside the company change the decision rules of the people who take part in them, and therefore also change the organization itself. Thus, the immediate consequences of those actions will not coincide with their long-term results, and an organization must strive not only to achieve immediate results, but above all, to build the capacity to continue to obtain results in the future and ensure that the results are the best ones possible.

Whatever the aims of an organization may be, managers must achieve them, and to do so they must secure the cooperation of the members of the organization, i.e., the people who possess the human and material resources that the company needs (owners, employees, and, to a certain extent, suppliers, customers, and other stakeholders as well). For that, the managers must monitor three "state variables," similar to effectiveness, efficiency, and consistency on the personal plane:[13]

1. For an organization, "effectiveness" represents the difference between the economic results obtained by providing a service to people (the consumers) and the resources employed, roughly equivalent to the profit obtained.

2. The equivalent to efficiency is "attractiveness" in an organization. An organization is attractive when it develops skills in its members that increase satisfaction or reduce the cost of doing something the organization requires of them, i.e., when it develops distinctive abilities which will allow it to learn how

to resolve problems more effectively or how to resolve more complex problems, because its members have a better knowledge of the needs to be addressed and are more capable of addressing them.

3. The equivalent to consistency is "unity." Unity is achieved when members of an organization identify with the organization and trust develops among members and between members, the management, and the company.

Effectiveness expresses the company's success in managing material resources. It is a necessary condition for its survival, but it is not its purpose. "The necessary and sufficient condition for an organization to really exist is that there be a group of people who are motivated to belong to that organization, with all that such belonging implies for them. The organization's objectives must be oriented to conserving and increasing those motivations, as otherwise the organization would disintegrate."[14] In order to achieve this, the organization fulfills at least some of the requirements which motivate people's contribution, in terms of effectiveness (for example, it does not give rise to costs in excess of revenues) and attractiveness (for example, it is not unpleasant for people who have to contribute to it). Nevertheless, these necessary conditions are not, on their own, sufficient, because an organization must also take into account the consequences for attractiveness and unity, which could modify the results achieved, probably in the long term.

Effectiveness is therefore necessary to the company as an economic institution, but it does not guarantee its survival or continuity. Survival depends on unity. And, contrary to what the economic literature says on the subject, this is not an economic problem that can be resolved by designing a control system that provides incentives to use the organization's operational capabilities to satisfy the needs of its members, because designing any such system

> is absolutely impossible if organizational members learn—operationally or morally—as a result of their actions within the organization. . . . Achieving optimal economic values is not an economic problem; it cannot be solved by manipulating economic variables alone. It depends on psychological and ethical variables. Only if these latter variables were fixed and could not be altered by learning processes . . . could the optimal economic value be achieved through purely economic processes.[15]

Maximizing effectiveness (profits) in the short term, conditional upon there being no learning (i.e., as if the other variables were constant), is meaningless, because learning will obviously occur, in which case the conditions for maximum effectiveness will no longer be met. Nor is it possible in advance to "maximize in the long term" and anticipate all the learning that will take place, because, although we know that the agents will learn, we do not know what they will learn, how they will learn, or how and when their decision-rules will change.

Which Ethics?

What is this kind of ethics, built on action theory, that we have proposed? If this action theory is based on the realist philosophy of Aristotle and Thomas Aquinas, ethics must be what these writers proposed: virtue ethics, aimed at creating conditions that will allow the agent to develop as a person, i.e., to be in a position not only to make correct decisions in the present (effective) but also, and above all, to make better decisions in the future (efficient and consistent). Ethics, writes Pérez-López, "analyzes the process by which people may develop their ability to perceive reality, the whole of the reality that affects them, not just the small part of reality that attracts them or that they happen to observe at a particular point in time."[16] That whole reality includes the external results of action (the reactive agent's response to the active agent's action), which are that readily observable and more attractive reality; but it also includes what the agent himself learns, and, above all, the results her actions have for others.

This also can be explained another way. Decision-making is the result of a set of motivations, some spontaneous, others rational. Spontaneous motivations demand a decision based on the expected extrinsic results (effectiveness). However, considerations of efficiency and consistency may prompt the agent to resist the attractiveness of the spontaneous motivations and make rational decisions. The moral virtues allow a person to choose "an alternative that will bring her less economic benefit [a less-effective alternative] than another, or various others, which she could have chosen instead."[17] Without the virtues, the attractiveness that immediate recompense holds for the individual in terms of extrinsic results will probably be so strong that she is not able to understand that it is preferable to make another decision which, though less effective, may be more efficient and consistent (i.e., offers the expectation of intrinsic and external results that may lead her to change her choice), and to exert the will-power to overcome the attraction of the extrinsic results.

Virtues are operational habits acquired and developed through the deliberate, effortful repetition of acts aimed at developing them, when the agent makes an effort to achieve what is good both for himself and for another person, "precisely because they are 'good' for others (and not because of any other consequences of the action)."[18] What moral virtues facilitate is not "doing things," but "wanting things," learning to desire what is best for us, that is, developing the quality of the motives behind actions.

The vast majority of human actions cannot be analyzed on the assumption that people are capable of correctly evaluating in advance the results of their actions, because the real value of those actions can only ever be fully known after the fact, when the decision-maker has already experienced all the effects the action has on her satisfaction. Then, the real problem is not making good decisions, but acquiring the abilities (moral virtues) that will make it possible always to make good decisions.[19]

Virtues, in short, allow people to develop and strengthen their moral growth and increase their capacity to make decisions that are ever more effective, efficient, and consistent, thus overcoming the temptation for spontaneous motivation, i.e., agreeable results in the short term. As Pérez-López writes: "Every time a person freely chooses something that he knows is better, even though it is less attractive than another thing that is worse, he is training, building up the strength that will free him of any pressure that might deflect him."[20] In a word, once fully developed, the moral virtues create a state in the agent "that makes all interactions possible."[21] "Why be ethical? The simple answer is, in order to learn how to build fully satisfactory relationships with other people. Being ethical means learning to value people as people; it means learning to love."[22]

In an organization, ethics allows each member to develop her capabilities to carry out the optimal plan, so that if an agent acts accordingly, her actions will be consistent, and she will be in a position to contribute to the organization's optimal plan. Hence, the contribution of ethics to the development of the organization consists essentially of "maximizing the set of feasible interactions."[23]

Virtue ethics is generally associated with a "good life" or a "fulfilled life." It should therefore be a necessary part of "good management," because this represents part of the "good life" of both manager and company. In other words, a good manager is an ethical manager, a manager with virtues, a manager who tries hard to achieve excellence.[24] "Perfection is achieved through action in both its aspects: internally (the agent himself) and externally (the product or service offered)."[25] A manager who lacks virtues may obtain excellent financial results in terms of profits or stock value, but he cannot be a "good" manager, even in the technical sense, because he will lack the ability to understand all the consequences of his actions, particularly the consequences affecting attractiveness and unity. This ability does not depend solely on his intellectual capabilities, but also, and above all, on his analytical knowledge, his capacity to know the internal state of other people. This can only be acquired through the practice of the virtues.

Conclusion

All social sciences are based on an explicit or implicit anthropology. The anthropology on which economics is based (the anthropology of *homo economicus*) was, in its day, a very useful simplification suited to many applications, such as explaining the way the markets work in a context in which a large number of agents establish impersonal relationships in which the motivations and learning that result from human interaction are more or less entirely unimportant. However, when this anthropology was applied to organization theory, its limitations became very clear.

It is easier to criticize than to construct, which is why we lack reliable proposals to overcome the limitations of the dominant model. We are also unable to create a broader theory that not only explains what the current theory already explains well but also overcomes its limitations, while allowing us to tackle new problems, thus creating a new and more promising tool for research.

This article represents an attempt to do just that. Using the theories of Pérez-López, I have tried to show that the extension of action theory, using elements of realist philosophy mainly from Aristotle and Thomas Aquinas, could help revamp the current model. I have also shown how these theories of action and organization can be combined with virtue-centered ethics inspired by the same writers. Economics is a positive science of human action, while ethics is a normative science of human action. Therefore, economics and ethics should share their model of humankind, even if they then differ in the methodology and scope of their propositions. There can then be a productive exchange between these two sciences.

The various ethical theories usually focus on one of the three anchor points of the theory of action: the agent, the action itself, and its consequences.[26] This gives rise to theories based on intention or motivation (virtue ethics), on duties or rules (deontology), and on consequences (consequentialism). However, our reflections lead us to conclude that an ethical theory must include all of the elements of action, that is, one that encompasses goods, norms, and virtues,[27] not by adding recommendations but by developing a comprehensive explanation of what human action is and what its normative consequences are. This is by no means an easy task, given the plurality of viewpoints on ethics, but would no doubt be made easier by a deeper study of human action.

In fact, since human action seeks what is good for humankind, ethics should study those things that are good and that are the intended result of this action. Economics assumes that the agent has sufficient knowledge of her preferences and is better qualified than anyone else to act in accordance with her own interests. However, this is not always achieved. This raises the role of ethics as a long-term "equilibrium condition" for the agent and for all human systems.[28] Ethics has a primarily negative role: do not make immoral decisions because you will deteriorate as a person, you will harm the communities and society to which you belong, and you will limit your opportunities for future action.

This is the first role of the ethics of norms: to place limits on human action, insofar as it can lead to negative learning—voluntary limits, of course: moral standards may or may not be abided by, but this does not detract from their normative content. However, ethical standards are above all positive: do good, try to do all that you can, and do it well, a message consistent with the economic viewpoint of human action. To do this, the agent must develop human capabilities for ethically correct action—that is, virtues—and their rational component, because virtues enable agents to improve their capacity for analysis, judgment, and appraisal.

Notes

1. This article forms part of the work of the "la Caixa" Chair of Corporate Social Responsibility and Corporate Governance, IESE Business School, University of Navarre.

2. For example, Lex Donaldson, "Damned by Our Own Theories: Contradictions between Theories and Management Education," *Academy of Management Learning and Education* 1 (September 2002): 96–106; Fabrizio Ferraro, Jeffrey Pfeffer, and Robert Sutton, "Economics Language and Assumptions: How Theories May Become Self-Fulfilling," *Academy of Management Review* 30 (January 2005): 8–24; Sumantra Ghoshal, "Bad Management Theories Are Destroying Good Management Practices," *Academy of Management Learning and Education* 4 (March 2005): 75–91; and Hector O. Rocha and Sumantra Ghoshal, "Beyond Self-Interest Revisited," *Journal of Management Studies* 43 (May 2006): 585–619.

3. Antonio Argandoña, "¿Qué es la economía?" in *Enciclopedia Práctica de Economía*, vol. 8, eds. Antonio Argandoña, V. Pou, and F. Segura (Barcelona: Editorial Orbis, 1985), 298.

4. As in some of my earlier works, I have substantially drawn on the work of an IESE Business School colleague, Juan Antonio Pérez-López, who died a few years ago and who broadly explained and demonstrated what I will attempt to show in this article. See mainly his *Teoría de la acción humana en las organizaciones. La acción personal.* (Madrid: Rialp, 1991); *Fundamentos de la dirección de empresas* (Madrid: Rialp, 1993); and *Liderazgo y ética en la dirección de empresas* (Madrid: Deusto, 1998). See also J. M. Rosanas, "Beyond Economic Criteria: A Humanistic Approach to Organizational Survival," (working paper, no. 654, University of Navarre, IESE Business School, October 2006).

5. Antonio Valero and José Luis Lucas, *Política de empresa. El gobierno de la empresa de negocios* (Pamplona, Spain: Ediciones Universidad de Navarra [EUNSA], 1991), 28.

6. The action theory explained here draws its inspiration from Pérez-López, *Teoría de la acción humana*; Joseph Pilsner, *The Specification of Human Actions in St. Thomas Aquinas* (Oxford: Oxford University Press, 2006); and Ricardo Yepes, *Fundamentos de Antropología. Un ideal de la excelencia humana* (Pamplona, Spain: Ediciones Universidad de Navarra [EUNSA], 1996).

7. Rosanas, "Beyond Economic Criteria," 16.

8. Pérez-López, *Teoría de la acción humana*, 28.

9. See Antonio Argandoña, "Preferencias y aprendizajes," in *De Computis et Scripturis. Estudios en homenaje a Mario Pifarré Riera* (Barcelona: Real Academia de Ciencias Económicas y Financieras, 2003); Antonio Argandoña, "La teoría de la acción y la teoría económica," in *Estudios de teoría económica y antropología*, eds. Rafael Rubio de Urquía, Enrique M. Ureña, and Felix Fernando Muñoz Pérez (Madrid: Unión Editorial, 2005); Antonio Argandoña, "Economics, Ethics, and Anthropology," in *Moral*

Foundations of Management Knowledge, eds. Marie-Laure Djelic and Radu Vranceanu (Cheltenham and Camberley, United Kingdom: Edward Elgar, 2007); and Antonio Argandoña, "Integrating Ethics into Action Theory and Organizational Theory," *Journal of Business Ethics* 78 (March 2008): 435–46.

10. Juan Antonio Pérez-López, "Moral, ética y negocios," (technical note, FHN-113, University of Navarre, IESE Business School, January 1977), 5. The consequences of an action, in each of the three facets mentioned (effectiveness, efficiency, and consistency), will occur whether the agent takes them into account in his decision or not and whatever his intentions may be. Note that this action theory is symmetrical: the problem can, and must, be analyzed from the standpoint of both the principal and the agent (Rosanas, "Beyond Economic Criteria"). The three dimensions of the decision that I go on to mention must be analyzed from the perspectives of both the company manager and her subordinates, and problems of ineffectiveness, inefficiency, and inconsistency may arise on both sides of the relationship.

11. Pérez-López, *Fundamentos de la dirección*, 13.

12. Rosanas, "Beyond Economic Criteria," 2.

13. Pérez-López, *Fundamentos de la dirección*, 115.

14. Juan Antonio Pérez-López, "Dimensiones de la responsabilidad social en la empresa," (research paper, no. 49, University of Navarre, IESE Business School, January 1981), 5. Reprinted as "Dimensiones de la empresa," chap. 1 in Juan Antonio Pérez-López, *Liderazgo* (Barcelona: Folio, 1997) and as "Dimensiones de la responsabilidad social de la empresa," chap. 2 in Pérez-López, *Liderazgo y ética*.

15. Juan Antonio Pérez-López, "El desarrollo de la calidad ética de las personas y su influencia en los logros económicos de la empresa," (mimeograph, University of Navarre, IESE Business School, May 1987), 12–13.

16. Pérez-López, *Fundamentos de la dirección*, 6.

17. Juan Antonio Pérez-López, "El logro de la eficacia social a través de la libre iniciativa individual," chap. 2 in Alfredo Pastor, Juan Antonio Pérez-López, and Domènec Melé, *La aportación de la empresa a la sociedad* (Barcelona: Folio, 1991).

18. Juan Antonio Pérez-López, "Should Businessmen Behave Ethically?" (technical note, FHN-188-E, University of Navarre, IESE Business School, December 1986). Reprinted as "¿Deben los empresarios y directivos comportarse éticamente?" chap. 7 in Pérez-López, *Liderazgo y ética*.

19. Juan Antonio Pérez-López, "Ética y dirección de empresas," (technical note, FHN-111, University of Navarre, IESE Business School, January 1993), 6–9.

20. Juan Antonio Pérez-López, "Libertad y economía," (technical note, FHN-117, University of Navarre, IESE Business School, December 1977), 10. Reprinted as chap. 5 in Pérez-López, *Liderazgo y ética*.

21. Pérez-López, *Teoría de la acción humana*, 85.

22. Juan Antonio Pérez-López, "I Am the Boss. Why Should I Be Ethical?" in *People in Corporations: Ethical Responsibilities and Corporate Effectiveness*, eds. Georges Enderle, Brenda Almond, and Antonio Argandoña (Boston: Kluwer Academic, 1990), 187. If this is the case, action theory relies on virtue ethics and does not require other forms such as deontological, consequentialist, or dialogical ethics. It receives no support from them (A. Rodríguez, "Lugar y desarrollo de la ética en la empresa. Una fundamentación antropológica," [mimeograph, University of Navarre, IESE Business School,

1998], 27). In particular, there is no point in including ethical criteria that have been imposed from outside the action itself in the decision-making process, in the way that exogenous restrictions are placed on economic decisions. See Antonio Argandoña, "From Ethical Responsibility to Corporate Social Responsibility," and Stefano Zamagni, "The Ethical Anchoring of Corporate Social Responsibility and the Critique of CSR," both given at the 6th International Symposium on Catholic Social Thought and Management Education on "The Good Company: Catholic Social Thought and Corporate Social Responsibility in Dialogue," Rome, 5–7 October 2006.

23. Pérez-López, "I Am the Boss," 181.

24. Robert C. Solomon, *Ethics and Excellence: Cooperation and Integrity in Business* (New York: Oxford University Press, 1992).

25. Rodríguez, "La ética en la empresa," 27.

26. Robert C. Solomon, "Normative Ethical Theories," in *Economics, Ethics, and Public Policy*, ed. Charles Wilber (Lanham, Md.: Rowman and Littlefield, 1998).

27. Leonardo Polo, *Ética: Hacia una versión moderna de los temas clásicos* (Madrid: Unión Editorial, 1996), 112.

28. Argandoña, "¿Qué es la economía?" 298.

Chapter Four

NATURAL LAW, HUMAN DIGNITY, AND
THE PROTECTION OF HUMAN PROPERTY

David Novak

Ethics and Business

Being a major component of social life, where so much power is exercised over all of us, business and commerce present great opportunities to do right and equally great temptations to do wrong. Here the ethical issues are ubiquitous. I shall get to the current ethical crisis in the business world shortly, but first let me tell you how I see the general relation of ethics and business or commerce, which is to my mind anyway, the theoretical aspect of today's crisis. Some very unethical ideas (the stuff of theory) have led and still do lead to some very unethical acts. Our right acts and our wrong acts most often begin in our heads. "Learning God's law is greater than practice of it, since learning brings one to practice," states the *Babylonian Talmud*.[1] Here is where concern with business ethics begins.

To my mind, the most basic ethical terms are "right" and "wrong," or "just" and "unjust." Most other ethicists, though, consider "good" and "bad" (or "evil") the most basic.[2] "Good" and "bad" are primarily aesthetic terms, which are then transposed into ethics by analogy.[3]

So, for example, I can call a picture "good" *because* its harmonious form gives me pleasure by looking at it. Thus the picture is *good for me*. It is hard to imagine anyone calling an *experience* "good" if it did not give him or her pleasure, whether tactical, visual, audible, or intellectual. Furthermore, one can call an *act* "good" if it is done well, that is, if it seems to accomplish what its agent intended it to accomplish.[4] So in business, for example, one can speak of a "good deal" as being a transaction skillfully performed, but one could also say this about the deals of thieves, embezzlers, and swindlers.[5]

Thus judgments of "good" and "bad" do not in and of themselves involve *ethics* per se. When used in ethical discourse, an aesthetic term like "good" presupposes an often unstated analogue.

Many people seem to think that the legal level will give us a more satisfactory plane for genuine ethical judgment. I disagree.

The basic legal terms are "legal" and "illegal," or "correct" (that is, "according to law") and "incorrect" ("contrary to law"). One can speak of a "good law" or a "bad law," yet that can simply mean either a law (or a whole legal system) that pleases or displeases me, or a law that is consistent or inconsistent with the legal system (or constitution) from which it derives its authority.[6] I could be speaking of a law within the Nazi or the Soviet legal system (or, maybe, the Iranian legal system today), or that system in toto. Very unethical acts—indeed, very horrendous crimes—have been justified (or rationalized) by the standards and procedures of such legal systems and the political regimes who have authorized them.[7]

One could say that importing other modes of discourse into business or commerce is artificial, and will probably not affect the people it is supposed to guide. Such importation is what many philosophers would call a "category error." To many businesspeople, it seems the equivalent of applying the principles of German grammar to English speech. It seems like foreigners telling them how to run their own country.[8]

We can avoid this problem, I think, when we see that the most basic ethical terms are "right" and "wrong," or "just" and "unjust." When we say that a transaction is "right," we are not saying that it necessarily benefits or pleases me or you. Instead, we are saying: *a right transaction satisfies the justifiable claims of the parties of the transaction, and the justifiable claims of the society that justice be done.* So, for example, when A is to render services to B in return for payment, the transaction is "right" when A renders his or her services properly and when B pays for these services properly.

The likelihood of the transaction being performed rightly or justly will be far greater if it is performed well—that is, if it is performed harmoniously and if the parties in the transaction see their own respective interests benefited— but the pleasure taken in the transaction does not ethically ground the transaction. A may get pleasure out of being well-serviced by B, and B gets pleasure out of enhancing his or her reputation as a *good* credit risk, but the pleasure each party gets from the transaction itself, which includes the pleasure of personally dealing with competent and honest people, is a secondary accompaniment to the rightful transaction itself.[9] This pleasure, which at best becomes the mutual pleasure of commercial friendship, enhances the rightful transaction.[10] Therefore, pleasure taken in a rightful transaction is right, and pleasure taken in a wrongful transaction is wrong.

Business ethics is not a set of criteria from another discipline that is imported into or imposed upon the business world. It employs general ethical criteria that apply in other areas of human interaction, but the formulation of business ethics arises from within commercial experience itself. One could compare business ethics to biomedical ethics. In biomedical ethics, the questions to be addressed arise from within the whole biomedical enterprise, which leads to the constant search for cogent principles of ethics or "practical" (as distinct

from "technical") reason. The fact that these principles are usually quite similar
to those arising in other areas of human interaction only confirms the truth
that universal principles always function within specific situations, and their
particular application is *to* and *for* these situations, yet they are not produced
by these situations.[11] They are discovered, not invented. Were they discovered
in only one area of human interaction, they might be rationalizations for particular practices. If business ethics had nothing in common within any other
manifestation of ethics, we could suspect that business ethics is only a rationalization for certain business practices, rather than being a set of principles that
can guide these practices and even be employed to judge them, that is, to
conclude whether they are right or wrong.

Natural Law Ethics

Natural law is a kind of ethical formulation. To my mind, it is the most philosophically astute kind of ethics. Since it includes those norms that can be seen
to pertain to all humans everywhere at every time, it is discoverable by human
reason anywhere at any time, even though the method of such discovery will
vary from one culture to another.[12] The "nature" in "natural" law is universal
human nature; the "law" in natural "law" is an imperative that does not depend
upon the act of a particular human judge or human ruler to be known or
enacted.

Thus "universal ethics universally knowable"—for example, the type of ethics human rights activists employ (whether they know it or not)—and "natural
law" are interchangeable terms. That equation of universal ethics universally
knowable and natural law becomes apparent once we see that the "universal"
here pertains to the humanly inhabited universe or human society per se, and
the "natural" here pertains to what enables human beings to make rationally
justifiable, uniquely human, claims upon one another in that society.

We could say that ethics is to business practice what mathematics is to physics.[13] Physics is not deduced from mathematics; instead, mathematics is suggested by physics in the sense that the language of physics, beholden as it is to
material objects, cannot deal with its *formal* considerations adequately. That is
the job of mathematics as theory. Mathematics *informs* physics, giving it an
intelligibility it cannot give itself. Although suggested by physics, perhaps even
called for by physics, mathematics is brought *to* physics; it does not come down
from physics any more than physics is deduced from mathematics. (Even Einstein's highly mathematical physics needed experimental validation.)

Just as physics is not deduced from mathematics, so just business practices
are not deduced from natural law. Instead, natural law reasoning is called for
by the type of ethical problems that the language of commerce itself, beholden
as it is to particular cases, cannot answer, because it cannot provide adequate

concepts to deal with their universal or rational considerations. That is the job of natural law as theory. Just as mathematics provides physics with its formal language, natural law provides business practices with their reasons.

Therefore, just as one would not speak of "*the* mathematics" but simply "mathematics," one should not speak of "*the* natural law" as if it were some sort of object, but of "natural law," as a form to be applied to any positive human situation. Yet that cannot be done before one is already engaged in that situation. One lives natural law *through* positive human situations, not apart from them. It is a method for clarifying and deepening the moral meaning of these human situations.

This relation *between* ethics and these positive human situations is important to bear in mind when natural law advocates are accused of "imposing" their philosophical or even their "religious" views on situations many assume are "none of their business." The answer is that we are only using natural law concepts to bring out whatever moral meaning is already latent within these situations themselves. Natural law is not a positive substitute for anything.

The Political Culture of Thieves

Now, what does all this theory have to do with the current crisis of criminal misconduct at the highest levels of American and global business? Do we really need this theoretical background to discern that theft is wrong and thieves should be forced by the law to make civil restitution to their victims, plus have criminal penalties imposed upon them? We do need to think about something deeper. We need to think about a relatively new political culture from which too many of us get our ethics or moral principles. (I use the terms "ethics" and "morality" interchangeably here.)

The political culture of which I speak is one that encourages immoral conduct even when it doesn't explicitly mandate it. That encouragement is often a form of implied or tacit approval.[14] It provides no good reason to judge these acts to be immoral rather than just stupid—that is, the stupidity of being too greedy, so that one gets caught for the stupid (in some cases, flamboyant) exercise of greed. This political culture of economic opportunism is antithetical to the political culture that looks to natural law ethics for the formulation and reformulation of its standards, or, if you will, its "values."

Some of our corporate thieves have internalized this political culture and rationalize their immoral acts by its values or standards. Some sympathize with them, perhaps hoping to learn what not to do from their error in getting caught. And others can't summon up any genuine outrage at what they have done. So we need to examine the political culture that has encouraged and rationalized executive thievery, for those who have actually engaged in it, for a larger number who might want to do it more cleverly, and for an even larger number who have no good reason to judge it to be wrong.

What is new is not what these thieves have done, or even how they have done it. What is new is the political culture that has deprived them of the capacity for any real agony before they steal, or the capacity for any real remorse after they have stolen, even after they have been caught. What is new is the political culture that has deprived too many of us, who are not thieves, of the capacity to demand any real regret from those who are thieves, because we have lost the capacity to judge thievery with any real opprobrium.

Executive thieves are not like the lone bandits who used to rob stagecoaches. The fact that they are outlaws does not mean they are social outcasts. Quite the contrary. They are very much social insiders. They could not possibly have done what they have done without being participants in a society called a "corporation," which functions within a larger civil society. These intricate social systems operate according to elaborate rules and procedures, which these executive thieves have had to convince others they fully endorse and subscribe to in order to gain their trust. Without that public affirmation of morality, these thieves could not have gained enough trust from others to be able to deceive them in the way they did. In the Talmud, lying to someone else for the sake of obtaining from him or her what does not belong to one is called *genevat da'at*, that is, "stealing somebody else's good opinion."[15] Such deceit enables one to be a thief rather than a robber, because the deceitful thief has so disarmed the victims that they are oblivious to being "robbed blind," only noticing the theft after, often long after, it had taken place.

These thieves fully endorse and subscribe to social rules in public, but violate them in private, and do so with a sociopath's lack of shame, even when their misdeeds are finally exposed and judged in public to be wrong. This type of bad human conduct is uninformed by the basic norms of natural law. We now need to look at the political culture that makes such a radical difference between the public and private realms, approving of acts in one realm that it condemns in the other.

Public Virtue, Private Vice

Nobody who has any stake in the successful functioning of their society could deny that society must have institutions to protect its citizens from harm to their bodies—and to their property as an extension of their bodies—and norms that prescribe punishment of those who violate the body or the property of a fellow citizen. This is what Isaiah Berlin famously called "negative freedom."[16] The punishment for the violation of this negative liberty is both civil and criminal: civil in terms of arranging for the payment of restitution for the loss of use of one's body or one's property, criminal in terms of incarceration (and, in some societies, even capital punishment) for the suffering caused by the violation of a body or its property.

That is society's duty to its citizens. (Whether society has some more positive duties to its citizens, what Berlin called "positive freedom," let alone what such rights are specifically, is a question every society must answer for itself.[17]) When society cannot exercise its duty to protect its citizens from crime (even if it fails unwillingly, because of lack of means), society—in the person of those who have authority in it and for it—cannot expect its citizens to dutifully respect that authority by obeying its laws. In other words, society has a claim upon its citizens that obliges them to accept its protection of their bodies and their property. But the citizens themselves have a prior claim on society that obliges it to protect the citizens' bodies and the citizens' property.

In this view, the claims of individuals upon society precede society's claims on individuals, even though historically speaking, society is there before any particular individual comes to it either by birth or by choice. Individuals' claims are, in this view, basically selfish: individuals require society to protect them and their bodies and their property, in return for which they promise to cooperate with it in its duty to protect the bodies and property of their fellow citizens. The sole reason for one's adherence to social norms is the promotion of what one believes to be one's own good. Citizens need society and its institutions (primarily, the police and the courts) for private self-interest. In this view, we are all private beings, only becoming public beings (law-abiding citizens) to enhance our private interests. This kind of society is primarily a collection of strangers. Nobody is there because he or she desires the friendship or even the company of his or her fellow citizens. One's interest only includes the members of one's own select interest group, and membership in that group is ephemeral.

There is no idea here of society being a communion of persons, one whose institutions are designed essentially to promote political communion or interpersonal interaction as an end in itself.[18] Without a notion of common purpose, which stands over and above individual interest (without obliterating individual economic interest, as was done by communism) and is more than the interest of the majority (as in utilitarianism), self-interest can be the only reason those having political authority could possibly want it. Their motive in seeking political power can only be that their own self-interest consists of wielding power over their fellow citizens. (All too often, power-seeking politicians loot public funds as a symbol of their political power; hence their misdeeds are more the result of the desire for recognition than of mere physical appetite.)

Politicians of this individualistic frame of mind convince their fellow citizens that their exercise of power is in the citizens' best interest. The citizens might want the government to work, in what they perceive to be their best interest, to protect them from criminals domestic and foreign by the use of its police power; or they might want the government to help them economically by striving to raise the GNP. The question is who has political power, how it is wielded, and why anyone would want to wield it. And this problem exists whether the official ideology of the society is socialism, or the unofficial ideology of the society is capitalism. Though at this level, it can indeed be said for the preferability of capitalism that a society with a robust private economy will have greater private scrutiny of public officials than a socialist regime where there is no such economic "balance of power." Nevertheless, when governmental scrutiny of the private sector is very much out of balance with private, we get an age of "robber barons."

In this notion of a contractual state, there is an exchange made between political authorities and ordinary citizens. That is an exchange between the rights and duties of each side: society's claims *on* its citizens and its duties *to* them, and individual citizens' claims *on* society and their duties *to* society, which is to obey its laws, and to follow the orders of the political authorities when they function in a lawful manner. This exchange becomes manifest at those times when each side has to *promise* to live up to its commitments to the other side.

I will now use the first person in the way a phenomenologist attempts to "get inside" the experience of which he or she is describing.

Who Can Be Trusted?

At the most basic level, the relationship between individuals and society requires trust. I must be able to trust the commitment or promise or pledge of others to me; others must be able to trust my commitment or promise or pledge to them. The question is then: "Why should I trust you, and why should you trust me?"[19] Following the self-interest theory we have been examining, one could say that I gain the trust of others in my own self-interest. Others would avoid me if they thought that I would steal from them once their backs were turned.[20] Nevertheless, couldn't I gain the trust of others to put them off-guard long enough to take more from them than I could if I suddenly and openly robbed them like the lone stagecoach bandit of the Westerns I thrilled to as a child? Thieves who operate this way, by betrayal of the trust others have placed in them, used to be called "confidence men."

But what about the law? I know quite well that I wouldn't be able to steal corporate funds if there weren't an elaborate system of law that enabled corporations to function in a lawful society. I am not an anarchist (most of whom live in the wilderness or on the streets, not in board rooms). I certainly do not want everyone to do what I am now doing. But the authority of my society and its laws serves my self-interest by doing two things for me: one, it protects my property from being stolen by others with impunity, and two, it enables others to accumulate more property than they could in an anarchic social situation, thus providing me with more to steal. So while I am grateful to society for providing me with such good opportunities to steal, and for providing me such good opportunities to spend and enjoy in public what I have been able to steal privately, I have to consider the fact that I might get caught by "the law," become impoverished by the fines levied upon me by the court, and lose my liberty by going to prison. When considering this possibility, my only deliberation consists of a cost-benefit calculation. What are my chances of getting caught? Is the gain I know I can get now worth the risk of the punishment I *might* get later?

The "remorse" that a number of convicted executive thieves have shown (usually between the time of their conviction and the time they are sentenced) seems to be little more than a ploy to get a lighter sentence, rather than an acceptance of true justice. We need to ask: If the remorse shown by those who have imbibed the political culture that judges self-interest to be right per se seems phony to us, what sort of remorse would be more genuine? If remorse is the proper expression of shame for having done something inherently wrong, what sort of political culture encourages people to be ashamed of what they have done and to be remorseful about it? And in what sort of political culture does the fear of being publicly shamed and personally *ashamed* become an incentive not to risk shame? My internalization of the fear of being ashamed of what I could do is what we call "conscience." What sort of a political culture encourages the development of conscience?

Conscience and Political Culture

A culture that cannot distinguish between neurotic "guilt feelings" and genuine shame cannot tell us why remorse is required of those who have done wrong. Lacking a good reason for remorse, it cannot provide the means for anyone who has imbibed its values to express his or her remorse and truly *mean*—that is, honestly *intend* to say—what he or she is saying. Such a culture cannot encourage the development of conscience by its adherents.

At this point, it might be helpful to remember the motto that introduced some of the great codes of Roman law: *Honeste vivere* ("to live with honesty or integrity"); *alterum non laedere* ("not to harm another"); *suum cuique tribuere* ("to grant each his own").[21] In other words, those who live dishonestly— affirming one standard in and for the public and acting upon an opposite standard with and for themselves—will usually have no qualms about harming others when that is in their self-interest, and they will usually regard everyone else's property as theirs potentially—that is, as grist for their mill.

The key, then, is to distinguish between a political culture that cogently encourages one to be ashamed of wrongdoing, and a political culture that only pragmatically judges the good or bad consequences resulting from the exercise of one's self-interest or actually approves of what one has done. That kind of culture only pities the criminal for his or her bad luck in getting caught, and especially for having to "do hard time" in prison. Such pity is born of the sympathy felt for the poor fool about whom it might be said: "There, but for my good luck, go I."

I remember a time about twelve years ago or so when my wife and I were invited to a party being hosted by a social acquaintance, a woman whose husband had just been released from prison. He had served a short sentence for having defrauded a large number of investors in his company, most of whom were barely indemnified for their losses, if at all. The invitation actually said that this party was a "celebration" of her husband's "homecoming," and that he had been "the victim of an unfortunate misunderstanding." Knowing him to have been quite civil, even charming, to us in our social interactions with him—and, fortunately, not having invested in any of his business ventures—our first reaction was to accept this invitation. After all, this couple had always hosted great parties in the past.

But my wife, being a better judge of character than I, quickly came back to her moral sense, and just as quickly brought me back to my moral sense. She said that were she this man's wife, she would get him and herself out of town, and maybe even change their name and try to assume a new, anonymous identity somewhere else. When we didn't accept this invitation, not giving our reasons lest we add to the embarrassment of this convicted felon and those nearest to him, we heard that we were criticized by some of his social circle for being "moralistic and judgmental." Apparently, we are adherents of a different culture than this man, his wife, and their friends.

Rights and Duties

Philosophically speaking, where does the error of this political culture of economic opportunism lie? And what is its obverse? I submit that the error lies in a false correlation of the idea of rights with the idea of duties. The political culture that has encouraged executive thievery has a skewed notion of the relation between rights and duties.

Rights are the justifiable claims one person (or persons) may make upon another person (or persons). Duties are the valid responses to the justifiable claims one person (or persons) is obliged to make to another person (or persons).[22] Rights and duties are correlative; that is, you can't have one without the other. Natural law is the set that includes all rights-duties correlations that can be taken as universal in scope and are universally intelligible. Thus an unjustifiable claim—such as "give me all your money," which I can tacitly take without your knowledge and consent—entails only one valid response, which is my duty to disobey (even though considerations for my own life and safety might well require me to obey such an unjustifiable command). That duty can be fulfilled before the fact by my strengthening my right to keep my own property away from thieves like you. And that duty can be fulfilled after the fact by my filing charges against you.[23] Even when you force me to give you my money (whether at gunpoint or more subtly, say, by economic threats), I can still disobey inwardly, in the sense of not recognizing your "claim" as a right I ought to honor. The question is: If rights and duties are correlative, which one has priority? Are duties created by rights, or are rights created by duties? Another way of putting the question is: Do *my* rights precede *your* duty to respond to them, or do *your* rights precede *my* duty to respond to them?

Logically speaking, a right as a claim creates the duty to respond to that claim. If, minimally, a claim is a request (maximally, a command), a request intends a response or an answer to it, even when there is no actual response in fact. (If it continually gets no response, it is futile but not unintelligible.) Thus a claim *initiates* a response, whether successfully or not. But a response when there has been no prior request is meaningless.

The question, though, is how one experiences the order of an exercise of a right and the exercise of a duty. I experience the exercise of your right, your claim upon me for a dutiful response, before I learn how to make my claim upon you for your dutiful response to me. That, of course, assumes that you are there in the world before I am. Hard as it is for children to accept, they come into a world that has been there before them. They must learn how to respond to the claims of those adults already there, waiting for them. Only then can they learn how to make their own claims upon those whom they encounter in the world.

And, as we know from child psychology, when children's basic experience of claims is the experience of unjustifiable, self-serving claims made by those who are supposed to care for them, they often never learn how to make justifiable claims upon others. Such children become adults who are convinced that making a rights-claim is the equivalent of screaming a threat. They become the type of adults who demand or take what they want because they want it, instead of asking and working for what they need because they deserve it and because they can justify—that is, rationally argue for—what they need.

At the most basic level, that just dessert exists not because of what a person has done to earn it, but because of who that person is in the world. Jews and Christians formulate the claims of human personhood best when they assert that human nature is most unique in being the *imago Dei*, "the image of God."[24] *What* the sanctity of human personhood is can only be positively constituted by revelation. But, even without revelation, we can discern *that* human personhood reflects a source beyond the world, and that is why human persons are deserving of respect.[25] This is what the Jewish tradition calls *kevod ha-beriyot*, "human dignity."[26]

I am a "me" who is addressed by another, before I am an "I" who addresses others. All such address is based upon need: You need something from me, I need something from you. And there is always a "you" in the world that becomes *my* world before there is a "me" cast into this world thereafter. When your rights and my duties, *then* my rights and your duties, are properly correlated, we can intelligently affirm a world that is *our* world. Yet this common world is not our possession. As the biblical story of the Tower of Babel teaches, when humans regard the world as their possession, it inevitably leads to the exploitation of one group of humans by another in the process of robbing God of what rightfully belongs to Him alone.[27]

Because of our mortality, we can only hold some possessions temporarily. And because of our mortality, even what we rightfully purchase (with our money or with our labor) is at best a long-term lease, not a permanent endowment. When we are truly honest with ourselves, we learn that we are just passing through this world, that we are tenants and not landlords. Yet, even as mere transient tenants, we ought to keep up the property as best we can, making it as comfortable for ourselves and the other tenants as possible.[28] Furthermore, when philosophy properly reflects on human nature from our perspective, it can teach us *that* we are transient tenants in the world. But when theology properly reflects on human nature from a divine perspective, from the perspective of the Master of the world, it can teach us *whose* guests we are in the world.[29]

When we have acted as ungrateful guests in the world, taking without giving in return, our place in the world restrains us and punishes us as it must—even if our subplace or "counterculture" in the world gives us its approval. Our counterculture has done us no favor when it deprives us of the ability to feel and express remorse, let alone seek an authentic expiation. How can I feel the moral outrage I want to feel at what somebody else has either done to me or is likely to do to me, when I felt no moral outrage, no shame, when I did the same thing or was likely to do the same thing to others?[30] How can I ask for forgiveness from my fellow guest in the world and from the host of the world, if I cannot believe myself to have really done wrong, to have acted against greater social communion rather than for it?

Despite all my action that presumes that I *begin* the world, the truth is that the world *began* long before me, and will endure long after me. Moreover, no matter how wretched my origins may have been, the world did welcome me by affording me the opportunity to survive, maybe even to flourish. That in all honesty I cannot deny. That is why I *owe* the world more than the world *owes* me. Thus I need the means to feel and express shame for my betrayal of my obligation to work for the common good (which can certainly include my own justifiable exercise of self-interest as in my rightful acquisition of private property).

And that means the world's claim on me to benefit it as much as I can is greater than any good I pursue for myself. Without the means to seek expiation from the Master of the world for my ultimate betrayal, I will die unreconciled to the world, which did more for me than I could ever do for it. A political subculture that denies me opportunities for the reconciliation and expiation that my being-in-the-world surely needs, has not only enabled me to harm others easily, it has harmed me by making me, in the deepest sense, "a restless wanderer on earth" (Gen. 4:14).

Notes

1. Babylonian Talmud *Kiddushin* 40b.
2. Note the commonality of three otherwise disparate modern ethicists on the primacy of the term and concept *good* for ethics: G. E. Moore, *Principia Ethica* (Cambridge: Cambridge University Press, 1903), 1–36; Germain G. Grisez, "The First Principle of Practical Reason," *Natural Law Forum* 10 (1965): 168–201; Emmanuel Levinas, *Totality and Infinity*, trans. Alphonso Lingis (Pittsburgh, Pa.: Duquesne University Press, 1969), 102–3, 304–7.
3. See David Novak, *Covenantal Rights: A Study in Jewish Political Theory* (Princeton, N.J.: Princeton University Press, 2000), 12–25.
4. See Aristotle *Nichomachean Ethics* 1.1.1094a1–18.
5. See Plato *Republic* 351D–E.
6. See Aristotle *Politics* 3.10.1286a9. Cf. John Finnis, *Natural Law and Natural Rights* (Oxford: Oxford University Press, Clarendon Press, 1980), 266–76.
7. See Leo Strauss, *Natural Right and History* (Chicago: University of Chicago Press, 1953), 1–8, esp. 4 n. 2.
8. See Alasdair MacIntyre, *Whose Justice? Which Rationality?* (Notre Dame, Ind.: University of Notre Dame Press, 1988), 1–11.
9. See Plato *Philebus* 63E; Aristotle *Nichomachean Ethics* 7.11.1152b1–24.
10. Aristotle *Nichomachean Ethics* 8.3.1156a15–20.
11. See ibid., 1.6.1096a11–b30.
12. See David Novak, *Natural Law in Judaism* (Cambridge: Cambridge University Press, 1998).
13. This is based on the insight of the German Jewish philosopher Hermann Cohen (d. 1918) that ethics functions as the logic of the human sciences (*Geisteswissenschaften*, or what we now call the "social sciences," which might very well include "business administration" as well as economics). See his *Ethik des reinen Willens*, 5th ed. (Hildesheim and New York: Georg Olms Verlag, 1981), 65, 227.
14. See Babylonian Talmud *Sanhedrin* 27b re Lev. 26:27.
15. Babylonian Talmud *Hullin* 94a; Maimonides *Mishneh Torah* 2.6.
16. Isaiah Berlin, "Two Concepts of Liberty," in *Four Essays on Liberty* (Oxford: Oxford University Press, 1969), 122–34.
17. Ibid., 131–34.
18. See Aristotle *Politics* 1.1.1253a9–40.
19. See David Novak, *The Jewish Social Contract: An Essay in Political Theology* (Princeton, N.J.: Princeton University Press, 2005), 205–12.
20. See Plato *Republic* 359D–360D.
21. Ulpian *Digest* 1.1.10.1.

22. See Novak, *Covenantal Rights*, 3–12.

23. See Babylonian Talmud *Baba Batra* 40a. Cf. Babylonian Talmud *Shabbat* 88a.

24. See Novak, *Natural Law in Judaism*, 167–73.

25. See David Novak, *The Sanctity of Human Life* (Washington, D.C.: Georgetown University Press, 2007), ix–xiv.

26. See Babylonian Talmud *Berakhot* 19b re Deut. 17:11.

27. See Gen. 11:1–11; see also Louis Ginzberg, *Legends of the Jews*, vol. 1 (Philadelphia: Jewish Publication Society of America, 1909), 179–81.

28. See Aristotle *Politics* 2.2.1263a25–b29.

29. See Lev. 25:6; see also Ps. 23:6.

30. See Babylonian Talmud *Shabbat* 31a.

Chapter Five

BUSINESS IN A DECENT AND DYNAMIC SOCIETY

ROBERT P. GEORGE

BUSINESS IS A CALLING, even a vocation. It is, to be sure, a way of making a living—sometimes a very good living indeed—but it is also a way of serving. In these dimensions it is like law, medicine, and the other learned professions. And the great schools of business are like the great law and medical schools. Like the other great professional schools, however, many business schools are going through something of an identity crisis. The *Wall Street Journal* recently published an article previewing a soon-to-be-released book by Rakesh Khurana, a professor at the Harvard Business School. Professor Khurana does not spare even his own school from the charge that, as George Anders of the *Journal* puts it, "M.B.A. training has deteriorated into a race to steer students into high-paying finance and consulting jobs without caring about graduates' broader roles in society." Anders quotes Khurana as charging that the "logic of stewardship has disappeared" from business education. "Panoramic, long-term thinking," Anders says, summing up Khurana's argument, "has given way to an almost grotesque obsession with maximizing shareholder value over increasingly brief spans."[1]

Business operates in the context of a larger society. It is affected by what happens in other dimensions of the society, and it in turn affects them. The broader society plainly has a large stake in what goes on in business, and business has a large stake in what goes on in society. Business depends for its flourishing on things that it cannot produce. These things are produced, if they are produced at all, by other social institutions. So business has a stake in the health, the flourishing of these institutions.

Decency's Pillars

So far I have been speaking very abstractly, as philosophers are inclined to do. Let me now speak a bit more concretely, in the mode of the sociologist, as it were.

Any healthy society, any decent society, will rest upon three pillars. The first of these is respect for the person—the individual human being—and his dignity. What I mean is that the formal and informal institutions of society, and the beliefs and practices of the people, are such that the human being is regarded and treated as an end-in-himself, and not a mere means to other ends. He is understood to be a subject of justice and human rights, and not an object, an instrument, or a thing. A society that does not respect the person will generally regard the human being as a cog in the larger social wheel whose dignity and well-being may legitimately be sacrificed for the sake of the collectivity. In its most extreme modern forms, totalitarian regimes reduce the individual to the status of an instrument to serve the ends of the fascist state or the future communist utopia. When liberal regimes go awry, it is usually because a reigning utilitarian ethic reduces the human person to a means rather than an end to which other things—including the systems and institutions of law, education, and the economy—are means. In cultures in which religious fanaticism has taken hold, the dignity of the individual is typically sacrificed for the sake of theological ideas and goals.

By contrast, a healthy liberal ethos supports the dignity of the human person by giving witness to fundamental human rights and civil liberties, and where a healthy religious life flourishes, faith provides a grounding for the dignity and inviolability of the human person by, for example, proposing an understanding of each and every member of the human family, even those of different faiths or professing no particular faith, as persons made in the image and likeness of God or bearing a divine spark that is evident in the human powers of reason and freedom of the will. The first pillar of a decent society is present when a society in its institutional commitments and social practices manifests the conviction that human beings as such possess a profound, inherent, and equal dignity, one that in no way varies according to factors such as race, sex, ethnicity, alienage, age, size, stage of development, or condition of dependency.

The second pillar of any decent society is the institution of the family.[2] It is indispensable. The family is the original and best ministry of health, education, and welfare. Although no family is perfect, no institution excels the healthy family in its capacity to transmit to each new generation the understandings and traits of character—the virtues—upon which the success of every other institution of society, from law and government to educational institutions and business firms, vitally depends. Where families fail to form, or too many break down, the effective transmission of the virtues of honesty, civility, self-restraint, concern for the welfare of others, justice, compassion, and personal responsibility is imperiled. Without these virtues, respect for the dignity of the human person, the first pillar of a decent society, will be undermined and sooner or later lost, for even the most laudable formal institutions cannot uphold respect for human dignity where people do not have the virtues that make that respect a reality and give it vitality in actual social practices.

Respect for the dignity of the human being requires more than formally sound institutions; it requires a cultural ethos in which people act from conviction to treat each other as human beings should be treated: with respect, civility, justice, compassion. The best legal and political institutions ever devised are of little value where selfishness, contempt for others, dishonesty, injustice, and other types of immorality and irresponsibility flourish. Indeed, the effective working of governmental institutions themselves depends upon most people most of the time obeying the law out of a sense of moral obligation, and not merely out of fear of detection and punishment for law-breaking. And perhaps it goes without saying that the success of business depends on there being reasonably virtuous, trustworthy, law-abiding, promise-keeping people to serve as workers and managers, lenders, regulators, and payers of bills for goods and services.

The third pillar of any decent society is a fair and effective system of law and government.[3] This is necessary because none of us is perfectly virtuous all the time, and some people will be deterred from wrongdoing only by the threat of punishment. More importantly, contemporary philosophers of law tell us that the law coordinates human behavior for the sake of achieving common goals—the common good—especially in dealing with the complexities of modern life.[4] Even if all of us were perfectly virtuous all of the time, we would still need a system of laws (considered as a scheme of authoritatively stipulated coordination norms) to accomplish many of our common ends (safely transporting ourselves on the streets, for example).

The success of business firms and the economy as a whole depends vitally on a fair and effective system and set of institutions for the administration of justice. We need judges skilled in the craft of law and free of corruption. We need to be able to rely on courts to settle disputes, including disputes between parties who are both in good faith, and to enforce contracts and other agreements and enforce them in a timely manner. Indeed, the knowledge that contracts will be enforced is usually sufficient to ensure that courts will not actually be called on to enforce them. A sociological fact of which we can be certain is this: where there is no reliable system of the administration of justice—no confidence that the courts will hold people to their obligations under the law—business will not flourish, and everyone in the society will suffer.

A society can, in my opinion, be a decent one even if it is not a dynamic one, if the three pillars are healthy and functioning in a mutually supportive way (as they will do if each is healthy). Now, some people believe that a truly decent society cannot be a dynamic one. Dynamism, they believe, causes instability that undermines the pillars of a decent society. So some people, such as the Southern Agrarians, opposed not only industrialism but the very idea of a commercial society, fearing that commercial economies inevitably produce consumerist and acquisitive materialist attitudes that corrode the foundations of decency.[5] And some, such as some Amish communities, reject education for their children beyond what is necessary to master reading, writing, and arithmetic, on the ground that higher education leads to worldliness and apostasy and undermines religious faith and moral virtue.[6]

Although a decent society need not be a dynamic one (as the Amish example shows), dynamism need not erode decency. A dynamic society need not be one in which consumerism and materialism become rife and in which moral and spiritual values disappear. Indeed, dynamism can play a positive moral role and, I would venture to say, almost certainly will play such a role where what makes it possible is sufficient to sustain it over the long term.

That is, I realize, a rather cryptic comment, so let me hasten to explain what I mean. To do that, I will have to offer some thoughts on what in fact makes social dynamism possible.

The two pillars of social dynamism are, first, institutions of research and education, in which the frontiers of knowledge across the humanities, social sciences, and natural sciences are pushed back, and through which knowledge is transmitted to students and disseminated to the public at large; and, second, business firms and associated institutions supporting them or managed in ways that are at least in some respects patterned on their principles, by which wealth is generated, distributed, and preserved.

We can think of universities and business firms, together with respect for the dignity of the human person, the institution of the family, and the system of law and government, as the five pillars of decent and dynamic societies. The university and the business firm depend in various ways for their well-being on the well-being of the others, and they can help to support the others in turn. At the same time, of course, ideologies and practices hostile to the pillars of a decent society can manifest themselves in higher education and in business, and thus these institutions can erode the social values on which they themselves depend not only for their own integrity, but for their long-term survival.

Threatening Forces

It is all too easy to take the pillars for granted. So it is important to remember that each of them has come under attack from different angles and forces. Operating from within universities, persons and movements hostile to one or the other of these pillars, usually preaching or acting in the name of high ideals of one sort or another, have gone on the attack.

Attacks on business and the very idea of the market economy and economic freedom coming from the academic world are, of course, well-known. Students are sometimes taught to hold business, and especially businessmen, in contempt as heartless exploiters driven by greed. In my own days as a student, these attacks were often made explicitly in the name of Marxism. One notices less of that after the collapse of the Soviet empire, but the attacks themselves have abated little.

Similarly, attacks on the family, and particularly on the institution of marriage on which the family is built, are common in the academy. The line here is that the family, at least as traditionally constituted and understood, is a patriarchal and exploitative institution that oppresses women and imposes on people forms of sexual restraint that are psychologically damaging and inhibiting of the free expression of their personality.[7] I believe that there is a real threat to the family here, one that must be taken seriously. The defense of marriage and the family in the public debate, including the debate within academia, is critical.

Some will counsel that business "has no horse in this race." They will say that it is a moral, cultural, and religious question about which business people as such need not concern themselves. The reality is that the rise of ideologies hostile to marriage and the family has had a measurable social impact, and its costs are counted in ruined relationships, damaged lives, and all that follows from these personal catastrophes. In many Western nations, families are often failing to form and marriage is coming to be regarded as an optional "lifestyle choice": one among various optional ways of conducting relationships and having and rearing children. Out-of-wedlock birthrates are very high, with the negative consequences of this particular phenomenon being borne less by the affluent than by those in the poorest and most vulnerable sectors of society. In 1965, the Harvard sociologist and later United States Senator Daniel Patrick Moynihan shocked Americans by reporting findings that the out-of-wedlock birthrate among African-Americans in the United States had reached nearly 25 percent. He warned that the phenomenon of boys and girls being raised without fathers in poorer communities would result in social pathologies that would severely harm those most in need of the supports of solid family life.[8] His predictions were all too quickly verified. The widespread failure of family formation portended disastrous social consequences of delinquency, despair, drug abuse, and crime and incarceration. A snowball effect resulted in the further growth of the out-of-wedlock birthrate. It is now 69 percent among African-Americans. It is worth noting that at the time of Moynihan's report, the out-of-wedlock birthrate for the population as a whole was almost 6 percent. Today, *that* rate is at 33 percent.[9]

And these figures are only a small part of the larger story. Many family scholars are observing with particular interest the relationship in Europe between social and legal changes pertaining to marriage and the family, on the one hand, and the decline of birthrates to the point of near demographic collapse on the other. There are fascinating and important issues here, issues of obvious social and economic significance, that deserve rigorous sociological study.[10]

You will have no trouble surmising the consequences for business of these developments. Consider the need of business to have available to it a responsible and capable workforce. Business cannot manufacture honest, hardworking people to employ; nor can government create them by law. Businesses depend on there being many such people, but they must rely on the family, assisted by religious communities and other institutions of civil society, to produce them. So business has a stake in the health of the family. It should avoid doing anything to undermine the family, and it should do what it can where it can to strengthen the institution.

As an advocate of dynamic societies, I believe in the market economy and the free enterprise system. I particularly value the social mobility that economic dynamism makes possible. At the same time, I am not a supporter of the laissez-faire doctrine embraced by strict libertarians. I believe that law and government do have important and, indeed, indispensable roles to play in regulating enterprises for the sake of protecting public health, safety, and morals, preventing exploitation and abuse, and promoting fair, competitive circumstances of exchange. But these roles are compatible, I would insist, with the ideal of limited government and the principle of subsidiarity. According to that principle, government must respect individual initiative to the extent reasonably possible, and avoid violating the autonomy and usurping the authority of families, religious communities, and other institutions of civil society that play the primary role in building character and transmitting virtues.

Having said that, I would warn that limited government—considered as an ideal as vital to business as to the family—cannot be maintained where the marriage culture collapses and families fail to form or easily dissolve. Where these things happen, the health, education, and welfare functions of the family will have to be undertaken by someone, or some institution, and that will sooner or later be the government.[11] To deal with pressing social problems, bureaucracies will grow, and with them the tax burden. Moreover, the growth of crime and other pathologies where family breakdown is rampant will result in the need for more extensive policing and incarceration and, again, increased taxes to pay for these government services. If we want limited government, and a level of taxation that is not unduly burdensome, we need healthy institutions of civil society, beginning with a flourishing marriage culture supporting family formation and preservation.

Business's Contributions

I will close with some brief reflections on the ways in which I believe that business has historically contributed to the strength of the other four pillars of decent and dynamic societies. While it is true that some business firms have exploited workers, many have enhanced the dignity of individuals by offering challenging and decently paid jobs, providing opportunities for further education, either on the job or in training programs, and encouraging workers to think creatively about how to improve the quality of products and services and the efficiency of production and delivery. Moreover, business has made upward economic and social mobility possible for countless persons. The free enterprise system has given many people the freedom to pursue fulfilling and remunerative careers that would have been unimaginable as options for their grandparents, and provided opportunities for them to become entrepreneurs and investors. Whole societies have been made better-off by economic growth produced by market economies. Businesses and successful business leaders and investors have helped to relieve poverty and have advanced many good causes through their charitable giving. Even when government rather than business supplies the money, it is business that is generating the wealth that government distributes.

While some business firms, it is true, have been involved in corruption and have even stimulated it, it is also true that business has in many places been in the forefront of demanding reform of corrupt courts and governmental agencies. Business leaders have helped to shape laws and policies that are suitable for modern systems of production and exchange, and that will enable us to meet the challenges of the globalized economy.

Notwithstanding the hostility to business in some sectors of academia and the elite intellectual culture, businesses and business leaders have been instrumental in supporting education at every level, especially higher education. This is particularly true in the United States, where the tradition of alumni giving is strong and where colleges and universities depend upon it, but it is true in Europe and elsewhere, too. Even where the overwhelming bulk of financial support is provided by governments, it is once again important to remember that governments obtain most of the money they spend through taxation, and taxation at the levels necessary to support modern universities is possible only as a result of the successful efforts of businesses.

So business is a pillar of decent and dynamic societies, it can and must support the other pillars, and it depends on them for its own flourishing. For these reasons, I hope that business leaders, entrepreneurs, and investors will turn their minds to the question of what they can contribute to the cause of upholding marriage and the family in the face of great threats. What business leaders have done in other domains, let them now do in defense of this distinctively human and uniquely humanizing institution. Just as the family has a stake in business, which, after all, provides employment and compensation, and which generates economic prosperity and with it social mobility, business has a stake in the family. This will be clear, I believe, if we adopt the "panoramic, long-term view," and follow out (if I may borrow Professor Khurana's phrase) the logic of stewardship.

Notes

1. George Anders, "Business Schools Forgetting Missions?" *Wall Street Journal,* 26 September 2007, Eastern Edition, sec. A, p. 1, The Economy; Rakesh Khurana, *From Higher Aims to Hired Hands: The Social Transformation of American Business Schools and the Unfulfilled Promise of Management as a Profession* (Princeton, N.J.: Princeton University Press, 2007).

2. On the profound and indispensable social role of marriage and the family, see Robert P. George and Jean Bethke Elshtain, eds., *The Meaning of Marriage* (Dallas, Tex.: Spence Publishing Company, 2006).

3. See John Finnis, *Natural Law and Natural Rights* (Oxford: Oxford University Press, Clarendon Press, 1982), esp. chaps. IX–XII; see also John Finnis, *Aquinas: Moral, Political, and Legal Theory* (Oxford: Oxford University Press, 1998), esp. chaps. VII–IX.

4. See Finnis, *Aquinas,* esp. chaps. VII–VIII.

5. On the thought of the Southern Agrarians, see John Crowe Ransom et al., *I'll Take My Stand: The South and the Agrarian Tradition* (New York: Harper, 1930; reprint, with a new introduction by Susan V. Donaldson, Baton Rouge, La.: Louisiana State University Press, 2006), xli–lii.

6. On the educational philosophy of the Amish, see John Andrew Hostetler, *Amish Society* (Baltimore, Md.: Johns Hopkins Press, 1968), 193–208; see also the Supreme Court's treatment of the case of the Amish in *Wisconsin v. Yoder,* 406 U.S. 205 (1972).

7. See, for example, Judith Stacey, "Good Riddance to 'the Family': A Reply to David Popenoe," *Journal of Marriage and the Family* 55 (August 1993): 545–47. See also Susan Moller Okin, *Justice, Gender, and the Family* (New York: HarperCollins, Basic Books, 1989), 183–86, wherein the author, who before her death was Professor of Political Science at Stanford University, argued in favor of "genderless" families.

8. U.S. Department of Labor, Office of Planning and Research, *The Negro Family: The Case for National Action,* by Daniel Patrick Moynihan (Washington, D.C.: Government Printing Office, March 1965), http://www.dol.gov/oasam/programs/history/webid-meynihan.htm.

9. Congress, House Committee on Ways and Means, *2004 Green Book,* 108th Cong., 2d sess., 2004, Committee Print 108-6, Appendix M, M-1 to M-4, http://waysandmeans.house.gov/media/pdf/greenbook2003/AppendixM.pdf.

10. On Europe's demographic challenges, see Allan Carlson, "Sweden and the Failure of European Family Policy," paper presented at the forum of Focus on the Family entitled "The Family as the Foundation for Social and Economic Development," Washington, D.C., 27 July 2005, http://www.profam.org/docs/acc/thc.acc.050727.fof.sweden.htm.

11. Seana Sugrue, "Soft Despotism and Same-Sex Marriage," in *Meaning of Marriage,* eds. George and Elshtain, 172–96.

PART TWO

Practical Challenges for Ethical Management

Chapter Six

MANAGEMENT AND THE CORPORATE STATE:

PRIVATE ENTERPRISE WITHOUT ENTERPRISE,

AND PUBLIC SERVICE WITHOUT SERVICE?

Anthony Daniels

HE WHO WOULD UNDERSTAND the current state of the British public administration must read three authors: Gogol for the absurdity, Kafka for the menace, and Orwell for the mendacity and distortion of language.

From the authors cited, it will be apparent that I will give a descriptive rather than a scientific analysis of the phenomena with which I propose to deal. In any case, it is one of the consequences of the managerialism that now dominates the public administration that the very statistics upon which a scientific account might be based have been deeply corrupted by the very process to be analyzed. The covering of its traces is one of the achievements of managerialism in the British public service.

I will start with a concrete example. In Britain, approximately 95 percent of healthcare, nearly 100 percent of emergency services, is funded by the government from general taxation. Thus, if the public expresses dissatisfaction with the healthcare it receives, the government is in a very exposed position. He who lives by an assumed responsibility dies by an assumed responsibility.

In the event of public dissatisfaction, therefore, the government can do one or more of several things: it can face the public down with counter-propaganda, it can abandon the whole government-funded system on the grounds that it caused the dissatisfaction in the first place, it can improve the system, it can engage in a lot of distracting activity that makes it very difficult to assess what is actually happening, or it can find a scapegoat. In practice, the latter two are the most expedient, because they are the easiest, though it is possible that they are engaged upon without conscious intention to deceive.

Here it is worth pointing out that successive British governments have become prisoners, as well as beneficiaries, of an historical myth: that before the institution of the National Health Service (NHS) there was no healthcare provision for the poor, or none to speak of. In fact, more hospitals were built in the economically depressed years of the 1930s than in the first thirty-three years of the existence of the NHS—during times, be it remembered, of general and sometimes unprecedented economic expansion. Shortly after the institution of the NHS, in 1952–53, capital expenditure on hospitals was less than a third of what it had been in 1938–39.[1] This is not the place to recall the often glorious history of Britain's voluntary hospitals, expropriated by the state in 1948; suffice it to say that the historical myth is the ultimate justification for the monopolistic state-run system in place today, a myth that has been swallowed whole by the population and that has therefore become an important political factor. In human affairs, you can never get away (even should you for some reason want to do so) from the role of ideas.

The government, wanting to demonstrate its paternal or avuncular concern for the well-being of its wards—the people—and aware that attendance at hospital in an emergency in Britain is a far more unpleasant experience than it need be or is in other, similarly developed countries—thanks to the long delays—decreed that henceforth no member of the public should wait more than four hours after his arrival in the hospital for a place in a hospital bed for further investigations or treatment, should he need it. Furthermore, hospitals and their managers would henceforth be judged, and financially rewarded or penalized, according to the degree to which they met this target.

The slightest familiarity, actual or theoretical, with the Soviet experience should have been more than sufficient for any sensible person to have predicted exactly what would happen next. In a highly centralized and bureaucratic system, with no possibility of external monitoring, the main product of targets is lies. Indeed, it makes of lying and all its variants the queen of the sciences, and the key to career advancement and even survival (though in practice a bureaucracy usually looks after its own, and a bureaucrat fired from one position can usually be found a niche somewhere else in the system soon afterwards). The result of target-setting is thus lying organized on an industrial scale, with the concomitant destruction or deformation of the human personality.

The solution adopted by one very famous hospital was ingenious, though very simple. Like patients who want to find reasons for not doing what the doctor suggests, bureaucrats who have never previously evinced any obvious signs of creativity can be induced by their situation to think very nimbly and very fast. The solution was this: that no patient brought to the hospital in an ambulance was to be allowed out of the vehicle into the hospital until such time as he could be guaranteed a bed within the four hours stipulated, should he need one.

The inconveniences of this manner of proceeding, from the point of view of the ostensible purposes of both hospitals and ambulances, may readily be imagined. Perhaps for the first time in the history of the world there was a traffic jam that consisted entirely and solely of ambulances. Since the supply of ambulances in the district was what economists call inelastic, the traffic jam led to delays further upstream in the flow of emergency patients to the hospital. But the target was met, and that was the important thing.

The managers of other hospitals adopted different tactics, proving that variety is still possible even in the most centralized of systems. Henceforth, hospital trolleys in corridors upon which patients were required to wait, sometimes for twenty-four hours or longer before a hospital bed became available to them, were redesignated hospital beds and the corridors as extensions to the wards. Thus was the target laid down by the central power met with triumphant ease, though without any improvement in the service from the worm's eyeview.

Of course, Britain is still a relatively free country, where comment and the exposure of problems are concerned, and publicity was soon given to the practices. The managers then found themselves in a situation in which the four-hour rule, as it was called, had to be obeyed in reality rather than virtually, at least if the target was to be met and the financial rewards obtained and the penalties avoided. The consequences were even worse.

For the first time managers appeared both in emergency rooms and in the wards, in the former to sniff out any patients who, in the technical argot that soon developed, were in danger of breaching the rule, and in the wards to seek out any patients who, in their opinion, might be fit for discharge, at least in the sense that they would not die immediately or embarrassingly soon after they were pushed out of the hospital. The job of the managers was to instill a sense of urgency, if not of outright panic, not according to any medical criteria, but purely to increase compliance with bureaucratic imperatives.

One anecdote is worth a thousand statistics, at least in a situation in which the statistics, for reasons that I have hinted at, are completely unreliable and corrupted. A junior doctor of my acquaintance was called to a ward to attend to a patient in need of the most urgent care; but while he was engaged upon saving his life, he was told by a nurse that he was needed in the emergency room because a patient there had been waiting for nearly four hours and was about to "breach the rule."

He decided that a human life was worth more than compliance with a rule, and continued his efforts at resuscitation. He received a second, more urgent message, in the form of an order from a manager, which he likewise ignored. When he had finished with the patient—who survived—he discovered that the manager had moved the patient into a ward on his own authority.

When the junior doctor went to that ward, he discovered that there had been no medical imperative for the patient to be admitted at all, and he discharged him. The manger, far from being abashed, was delighted by the outcome, and felt vindicated. For the patient's short stay in hospital would improve the statistics overall, and make the hospital look even more efficient in the eyes of the central power, which of course would have no knowledge of the cruel absurdity of at least one "successful" hospital episode.

I could continue almost indefinitely with illustrations drawn from my own experience. I will, however, give only one more. The government, claiming to wish to reassure the public about the level of competence of the medical profession—though in reality doing (if not intending to do) the precise opposite, namely raise doubts about its competence and fitness to practice because the profession, like all other professions, constitutes an alternative source of authority to the government's own—instituted a system of annual appraisals of senior doctors such as I. The annual appraisal consists of a visit by another senior doctor who is required to ask the appraisee certain pro forma questions. (There are now doctors in the NHS who derive a considerable income from performing such appraisals on family doctors: every regulation is an income opportunity.)

One of the questions to be asked is, "Are there any concerns about your probity?" The first time I was asked this question, I told my appraiser that I would answer it on condition that he would answer two questions beforehand. He asked what they were.

"The first is 'What kind of person would answer such a question?' And the second is, 'What kind of person would ask it?'"

The appraiser saw my point at once. We were both knowingly taking part in a process in whose virtue or necessity neither of us believed, but only because it had been mandated by authority as a condition of continued employment, and it was therefore easier to comply than to object. This was bad enough for our sense of our own integrity; but the actual question itself set about brilliantly to destroy the very quality that it was supposedly to enquire about, both of the person who asked and of the person who answered. I know of no doctor who did and does not feel demeaned by the whole time-consuming process, and who does not despise himself, at least a little, for having unresistingly co-operated in it. And professionals who despise themselves are easier to co-opt, coerce, and corrupt than those who retain a sturdy sense of their own independence and probity (though, of course, this too can be exaggerated).

I need hardly point out that the question arises whether my anecdotes are emblematic or representative of widespread processes, or are merely tales of absurdity and malfeasance such as could have been, and have been, told throughout the ages. There is, perhaps, a law of the conservation of absurdity, or at least of discontent, that means that complaint is the one permanent mode of thought about human affairs.

Nevertheless, precisely the kind of complaints I have just made are now made by virtually all the professions in all branches of the public service in Britain. No branch is exempt. Compliance with absurdity or worse is exacted as the price of preferment (which is often very lucrative); dissent or opposition is punished by career stagnation. This, of course, has a leveling effect and promotes groupthink, or at least group-speech, but it also creates the atmosphere of fear that is the natural consequence of a lack of freedom. Self-disgust renders participants ill-equipped to criticize, much less to refuse, orders. They are reduced to apparatchiks, however distinguished in their field they might otherwise be.

The prevalence of the malaise is illustrated by a recent survey of workers in the NHS in Scotland, 80 percent of whom said that they had been bullied at work, principally by their near and distant managers—who, of course, were themselves among the 80 percent who felt they had been bullied. Of course, the promotion and encouragement of fragility of feeling is one of the ways by which managers increase and maintain their power, and create what is for them a desirable and necessary atmosphere of conflict and anxiety, such that the people under their control are forever looking over their shoulder; for fragility of feeling leads to complaint, and complaint leads to the need for adjudication, and thus to power for the adjudicators.

For example, the definition of bullying adopted by many institutions requires no objective correlates: a person has been bullied if he thinks he has. This results in the creation of a Foucaultian world in which questions of fact are entirely replaced by questions of power and correlates of forces. Extensive and time-consuming investigations are carried out as if they were to establish matters of fact, investigations that not only divert resources from the ostensible but by now secondary purposes of the organization to those of management, but are used to undermine or destroy the authority of those who would once have been considered authoritative because of their intelligence, knowledge, and experience. In other words, a transfer of power has been effected, from a relatively stable and defined professional hierarchy to an unstable, amorphous, and shifting one, whose members themselves live in constant fear and are never allowed to grow institutional roots.

Pride in institutions is another target of managerial destruction: hospitals in the NHS, some of them with very long and distinguished pre-NHS histories, and to which people in the past dedicated their entire working lives, are now merged, de-merged, re-merged, changed in function, closed, and re-opened with what would appear insouciance, were it not that insouciance implies a certain lightheartedness, which is not a characteristic of managerialist culture (I use the term "culture" in its anthropological sense).

Here, for example, is a small straw in the wind: hospitals in the NHS once had their own logos or heraldic devices on their notepaper, but were instructed, by fiat of the Department of Health, to abandon them all and replace them with a generic symbol of the NHS. It is difficult to develop a loyalty to a giant and diffused organization, and in the new circumstances, no one would make the mistake of developing a powerful emotional attachment to his institution or fail to regard it other than as a mere, and perhaps temporary, source of employment. Such pride as still exists in institutions is a shrinking asset of cultural capital.

A Social Revolution

I come now to the question of the origins of what, in my opinion, is a social revolution. Since societies and their histories are seamless robes, it would be both fruitless and ridiculous to attempt to be too precise in this matter. James Burnham noted many of the changes sixty years ago in *The Managerial Revolution*, and his theory was not entirely original even then.[2] The fact is, however, that change has occurred in the British public administration at an accelerated rate in the last quarter century or thereabouts; and I will now speculate on the possible reasons for this, without the hope or expectation of being definitive.

There is the realm of ideas and the realm of interests; the relationship between the two realms is dialectical.

First I want to draw attention to what might be called the sociologization of thought (the fact that I can use such a locution is an indication of how far the process has gone). Human behavior has come less and less to be understood as the result of choice based upon conscious reflection, however fleeting, and more and more as the vector of forces acting upon people, forces of which they may be unaware, and which in any case they are powerless to alter or affect, much less control. Whether this attitude is justified or not, from the purely intellectual point of view it clearly confers upon supra-individual authority—in effect, government—increased responsibilities. The government has not merely the right but the duty to readjust the forces acting upon people so that they may behave in a better way. Thus is the stage set for the advance of managerialism.

At the same time, there has been a concerted intellectual attack on the very notion of public service. The charge is not merely that public service in practice often fails to serve the public; it is that the very idea is virtually meaningless, or logically incoherent, since every individual in the public service must act in his own interests. The so-called public interest, then, is but a smokescreen for private and sectional interest.

On this view, bureaucracies inevitably increase their own power and extent, the better to appropriate economic resources, because that is what individuals invariably do. As for professions, they are all what George Bernard Shaw called conspiracies against the laity.[3] The motive of the conspiracy, of course, is self-interest: driving up the price of the services provided, behind a smokescreen of concern for professional standards and so forth.

Unfortunately, for political and other reasons, there is an ineradicable need for a public service in modern societies: none is without one. Its size and scope of activities will vary according to the particular circumstances of each country, but no country can eliminate the state sector entirely. How, then, to ensure that the public service actually serves, that is to say, pursues the interest of the tax-paying public rather than its own interest? The question is more urgent the larger the public-service sector becomes.

The solution adopted in Britain—or perhaps I should say the pseudo-solution—is managerialism, that is to say, control by management. A cadre of managers armed with techniques that are applicable to all institutions whatsoever (management being an abstract science), had to be created. It would discipline the organizations that it managed, that had hitherto retained an amateurish independence that left them free to be inefficient and act in their own interests. The cadre of managers would be disciplined in turn by the setting of targets by what one might call the meta-managers, that is to say, the government.

There was one small problem with this scheme: there was no independent criterion by which the success or failure of the newly managed institutions could be measured, and that was not provided by the managers themselves. We have already seen how easily statistics could be manipulated in a centralized system. The only limit placed upon intellectual dishonesty was that of public unrest, more likely to be aroused by some bad services than by others. For example, there would soon be a public outcry if the emergency services of a hospital failed utterly to succor the ill and the injured, but leaving the children of the poor unable to read or write properly evokes no such protest, and therefore it was (and is) done. The illiteracy rate in Britain is approximately 25 percent, despite expenditures on education four times higher in real terms than in 1950.[4]

But this is not the end of the matter. Once in control of the budgets, the cadre of managers found themselves in a position to loot them without fear of legal reprisal. In effect, corruption was legalized, though it was corruption of a peculiarly insidious kind. This happened in both small ways and big. The managers were able to spend large, indeed vast, sums of money on contracting allegedly private and independent services, particularly in the field of consulting, allegedly in the pursuit of perfect or 100-percent efficiency.

Increased efficiency, of course, required increased quantities of information, and also information systems to process them. Without information, improvements in efficiency could not be measured. But since it was obviously necessary to make all parts of the system equally efficient, the gathering of information became not only a priority, but a task of Sisyphus. Indeed, you could never have enough information; and this had the happy consequence that the numbers of people employed in such administrative tasks had to grow. Another happy consequence was the provision of a rationale for the perpetual interference in the work of professions, whose diversion to non-professional tasks necessitated ever tighter or more stringent management. Let us return to the phenomenon of consultancy, a world where (in its dealing with government) nothing succeeds like failure. One day my secretary, a woman who had spent forty years as secretary to various doctors, and who was due to retire in three weeks' time, was told by her manager that she had to attend a day's course on how to answer the telephone. She was, in fact, both efficient and obliging; had she not been, it would have been a little late in the day to try to train her. Attendance was compulsory. What was the meaning of this curious, but in my view emblematic, little incident? In all probability, the organizers of the course were a consultancy firm contracted by the hospital. It—the firm—would be able to charge according to the number of people attending, so why take the risk of inflating the numbers when it was so easy to ensure real numbers? It was also highly likely that the owners of the allegedly private enterprise running the courses were actually former members of the public service known to the managers of the hospital. Certainly, something has become very common that only a few years previously would have been unthinkable: that the families of high-echelon bureaucrats had interests in consultancy firms whose sole business was consulting with the public service. All corrupt, but perfectly legal.

It must not be imagined that this is a minor phenomenon, or confined to a small scale. A book recently published, titled *Plundering the Public Sector*, suggests that in Britain scores of billions of dollars have been expended on useless consultancies in the last decade, without any obvious improvement (and obvious improvement is the only improvement worth speaking of, since subtle improvements are easily manufactured by statistical legerdemain) in what is provided to the public.[5]

Corporatist Society

The results are these. A very considerable number of people become directly dependent on managerialism in the public service for their comfortable livelihood. (The expansion of the managerial class also helps to absorb the ever-growing numbers of people with nonvocational degrees produced by our universities, who might otherwise, if unemployed, be a focus of serious and dangerous discontent.) This creates an extremely prosperous and nominally private subsector within the private sector, one that is actually utterly dependent on the favors of government and is in turn supportive of the government. In other words, society becomes increasingly corporatist.

Apart from the economic inefficiencies of the system, by far the worst effect is on the human personality. Intellectual and moral dishonesty becomes necessary for survival, and because most people are not by nature scoundrels, who do wrong with open eyes and a glad heart, their very souls undergo deformation. In addition, genuinely talented people suffer frustration and humiliation.

Several important questions are raised by my observations. First, are the processes I have indicated unique to the public service? Second, are they inherent to the enterprise of management itself? Third, if they are not, how are they to be controlled?

I have little doubt that the public service is peculiarly but not uniquely susceptible to the pathologies I have indicated, in large part because it is so difficult to measure success or failure objectively, and because in any case the mea-surement is largely in the hands of those whose success is being measured. The French Ministry of National Education, for example, which controls the highly centralized French education system, claims great success because more than 80 percent of children now pass the baccalaureate, whereas only 5 percent did so in 1910. But since the ministry itself sets the standards required to pass, and changes them constantly from year to year, the real meaning of this "success" is difficult to assess.[6] Procedurally, perhaps, it is a success, but socially and educationally it is a disaster.

The replacement of real goals by procedural goals is easier in the public service than in the private sector, since in the private sector, absent creative accounting, the balance sheet provides an objective measure of success or fail-ure. When commercial companies become too large, however, no doubt the relation between profit and the activity of large numbers of employees becomes more doubtful, and there is the temptation to replace real goals with procedural ones. Certainly, I find dealing with my bank just as frustrating, and for the same reasons, as dealing with Social Services on behalf of a patient.

When management becomes a skill and career in itself, unconnected to any other skill or body of specific knowledge, the pathologies will increase. It is essential in the public service that people with technical skills and knowledge should retain considerable powers over management, and not the other way around. Furthermore, there should be considerable oversight from unpaid vol-unteers in the running of public institutions. This for two main reasons: first, the great majority of professionals, precisely because they have to deal with practical problems faced by actual people, retain a preference for real rather than procedural results, and second, because volunteer overseers have no vested interest in increasing their own powers or the size of their staffs. Public institu-tions therefore need not professional, but amateur management (which is not the same as amateurish management, of course).

A public service that actually serves will not be produced by bureaucratic control. In the absence of electoral oversight, esprit de corps is the essential quality of such a service. This is not a quality found in giant, centralized orga-nizations, but only in smaller, partially independent ones. Only a degree of trust that most people left alone will try to do a good job is compatible with the independence of public organizations. Managerialism, however, is the firm enemy of esprit de corps. In the prison in which I worked, for example, I was able to encourage the wardens to go beyond their strict duty in assisting me precisely because I ignored completely a specific management directive not to give the wardens any medical advice or treatment. The power of managers in the public service depends upon the formalization of all procedures and relationships, and thus sees esprit de corps not as an asset but as a liability.

In dealing with managers who pass on orders from higher up the command chain, I have often asked them, "What is the instruction that you would refuse to obey on the grounds that it was unethical, or even just harmful to the service?" They have never been able to answer; and the history of the twentieth century is not encouraging in this regard. The dangers of unethical obedience to orders are less in decentralized organizations, and where there are fewer monopolies.

In Britain, at any rate, managerialism is triumphant. The great Hungarian writer Sandor Marai published a memoir which begins with the last bourgeois dinner party in Budapest before the arrival of the Red Army. There were 14 people around the table; there was not much to eat but a little to drink. One of the guests was an enthusiast of the Nazis, and he said that the Hungarians should support their allies to the bitter end. Marai, who was not a Nazi sympathizer, asked him why.

"It's all right for you," replied the Nazi enthusiast. "You have talent. But we, who have no talent, we need the Nazis." And as he left the dinner party, he turned to Marai and said, "Remember, the future belongs to the untalented."[7] Managerialism is the fulfillment of this prophecy.

Notes

1. John Willman, *A Better State of Health* (London: Profile Books, 1998), 54.

2. James Burnham, *The Managerial Revolution: What is Happening in the World* (New York: John Day, 1941).

3. George Bernard Shaw, *The Doctor's Dilemma* in *The Doctor's Dilemma, Getting Married, and the Shewing-Up of Blanco Posnet* (London: Constable, 1911).

4. Melanie Phillips, *All Must Have Prizes* (London: Little, Brown, 1997).

5. David Craig and Richard Brooks, *Plundering the Public Sector* (London: Constable and Robinson, 2006).

6. Jean-Robert Pitte, *Stop a l'arnaque du bac* (Paris: Editions Oh!, 2007).

7. Paraphrasing Sandor Marai, *Memoires de Hongrie* (Paris: Albin Michel, 2004).

Chapter Seven

A STRATEGIC HUMANIST: GEORGE KELLER, *ACADEMIC STRATEGY,* AND THE MANAGEMENT REVOLUTION IN AMERICAN HIGHER EDUCATION

Wilfred M. McClay

When the humanistic disciplines in particular are in massive disarray, and seem to have lost both their morale and their sense of purpose, perhaps the world of ideas needs a stiff dose of a reality principle that the experiences of business and organizational management can (in their better moments) administer. Of course, faculty in American higher education see the very concept of "management" as a synonym for manipulation and control, intrinsically inapplicable to the unique work of higher education, and often for good reason.

There is undeniably a certain blend of sentimentalism and self-interestedness lurking behind such suspicion, but there is also something genuine at stake. When the U.S. Department of Education clumsily intrudes itself in the work of higher education to demand standardization of educational "outputs," as it has recently in the infamous Spellings Report, it misunderstands the character of the very activity it is attempting to regulate and improve.[1] Management, rightly understood, is an activity tailored to the thing being managed and the objectives being sought. Improperly used, however, it is either an obfuscation, which uses high-flown, quasi-technical language to conceal the true nature of one's acts, or a form of reductionism, which mistakenly treats the activity of an educational institution as if it were that of an assembly line or a service industry. One must always use the tools appropriate to the task at hand, and one's objective must be the bringing forth of institutional fruit proper to its kind.

Energy in the Executive

David Riesman's 1968 book *The Academic Revolution,* co-authored with Christopher Jencks, identified the rise of the independent power of the faculty, particularly as embodied in the trans-institutional disciplines, as the single most notable change in the structure of modern academia.[2] But his identification of that change was far from being a celebration of it. Indeed, by the end of his career Riesman had become convinced that recovery of responsible executive power, and particularly of presidential power, was absolutely essential to the improvement of American higher education. Riesman is well-known as a thinker of extraordinarily wide-ranging interests, whose magnum opus, *The Lonely Crowd* (1950), with its celebrated account of the transformation of American social character in the twentieth century, remains one of the classic works of American sociology.[3] Less well-known is the fact that the bulk of his activities from the fifties onward revolved around the subject of American higher education, and more particularly, by the end of his career, around the college and university presidency, and in the search processes through which such executive positions are filled.[4] He was unusual in his understanding of, and sympathy with, the unique problems faced by university presidents, and his impatience with the shortsightedness and turf-defensiveness of faculties. But such sympathy flowed from a larger conviction about the institutional needs of the modern university. He believed that a more general recovery of energy and confidence in the executive office would be essential to the flourishing of academic institutions in the late twentieth century and beyond. And such recovery would surely entail a renewed respect, however grudging, for the peculiar skills and insights that go under the rubric of "management."

This was, and is, a hard sell. In all too many academic circles, where the permanent antagonism of faculty and administration is regarded as an essential and unchanging fact of life, as permanent as the law of universal gravitation, it is particularly verboten to speak in positive tones about "modern management" and the administrators who employ it. Consider this not unrepresentative statement from a 1970 article in the journal *Daedalus*: "Trustees, presidents, deans, registrars, secretaries, janitors, and the like are not, strictly speaking, part of the university at all. . . . They are ancillary to the real business of the university."[5] Few go as far as did Thorstein Veblen, who concluded his influential study, *The Higher Learning in America,* by declaring airily that "as seen from the point of view of the higher learning, the academic executive and all his works are anathema, and should be discontinued by the simple expedient of wiping him off the slate; and . . . the governing board, in so far as it presumes to exercise any other than vacantly perfunctory duties, has the same value and should with advantage be lost in the same shuffle."[6]

Such fantasized final solutions, however, reflect the self-delusions of people who never have to imagine how food appears on the table in front of them, or how a signed and non-bouncing check appears in their mailbox at the end of every month. Such people never give any serious thought either to the vast number of institutional supports that they need, simply to be able to do what they do, or to the vast amounts of work, contributed by people performing all kinds of different and non-scholarly tasks, that are required for the institution simply to exist. It is, frankly, the height of narcissism to imagine that the work one does oneself is the *only* work that matters. But the existence of such narcissism is a central peril, not only of academia, and not only of all large bureaucratic organizations, but it is a peril inherent in the division of labor itself, and forms the basis for one of the greatest of all challenges faced by any manager, particularly a good and conscientious and effective one.

This is bound to be true in any organization, no matter its size. In the most ideal settings, the good manager wants to find a way to educate the parts of the organization about one another, so that the organization can maximize the productive benefits of specialized labor without suffering from the impoverishing sense that the parts are permanently set against one another. Such management can no longer be an act of propagandistic mystification, undergirded by constant pep talks and false personalization. We are too suspicious for that, and rightly so. Instead, it needs to seek to expand the knowledge and imaginative apparatus of all workers, not least in helping them to understand and appreciate what other members of the organization are doing, and convincing them of the humanizing benefits of living and working in combination with one another—in short, of seeing one's work as an element in the larger life of a collective enterprise.

There will of course be many times when such imaginative expansion is simply not possible. Janitors cannot really comprehend the life-position and work of professors, and vice versa, and many employees simply have neither the desire nor the detachment to understand the other person's problems. Management's task is then one of containment and channeling and temporizing, finding humane ways to contain, deflect, and divert the frictions, resentments, conflicts, and mutual incomprehensions that inevitably arise in organizational life. In short, management must keep the peace and keep the machinery humming. Allowing for such realities, however, we may find it more useful here to think about more ideal situations, precisely because those offer the greatest promise of general reform, something higher education stands in need of. Institutions of higher education promote the human aspiration toward higher ideals, and we should be able to look to them hopefully as exemplars of those ideals and of the possibility of realizing those ideals more generally.

A Managerial Answer

How to restimulate thinking about organizational ideals is always a problem, but perhaps especially so in the field of higher education, where the processes of hiring and firing are so convoluted and problematic, the activities of employees are often so individualistic and tenuously related to the organizational whole, and where organizational objectives themselves are often obscure, even nonexistent. But there has to be a way in which sensible techniques of management can be introduced into such a field without vitiating its core values. The insightful work of educational analyst George Keller, whose death in February 2007 at a very youthful seventy-eight was a very great loss to the cause of educational reform, throws an uncommonly bright light on the subject, although the tasks he set for higher education remain largely unfinished, and even untried.

Keller was a true believer in the high democratic calling of education. Indeed, one could find few better examples of the transformative potential of American higher education than Keller himself, the son of a Latvian father and south-German mother, born in 1928 in working-class Union City, New Jersey, whose life would be changed forever by his encounter with Columbia University, and with the likes of Jacques Barzun and Lionel Trilling, first as a student and later as a colleague and assistant dean. That special milieu of mid-century Columbia, and the lofty vision of higher education it promoted, became his ladder to a wider and richer world, and he never ceased to be grateful for it.

He wanted the same ladders, and also many more various ones, to be available to the coming generations of Americans. Higher education was for him nothing less than an expression of the promise of America itself, in institutional form. Small wonder that he was regularly asked by the citizens of Dickeyville, the charming restored mill town in Maryland where he and his wife, Jane, made their home for the past three decades, to deliver the town's Patriotic Declamation presented on the Fourth of July, a task he gladly performed in 2006 for what he knew would be his last time. It was all of one piece for him. He loved working in higher education because he was an American patriot, and he loved his country because of the opportunities for self-transformation it affords.

Keller's curriculum vitae was lengthy and unusually diverse, including service as professor and chair of the program in higher education studies at the University of Pennsylvania's Graduate School of Education and as editor of *Planning*, the quarterly journal of the Society for College and University Planning, as well as a stint as a strategic-planning consultant at the Barton-Gillet Company in Baltimore. After retiring from Penn in 1994, he worked as a freelance consultant and writer in higher education, helping to create the journal *University Business* and producing several notable books, including his forthcoming *Higher Education and the New Society*, to be published by the Johns Hopkins University Press.

But his most lasting achievement was his influential 1983 book *Academic Strategy: The Management Revolution in Higher Education*, also published by Johns Hopkins. Crisp and luminous, *Academic Strategy* was the right book at the right time, and few involved in higher-education administration during the 1980s did not find their lives touched and their thinking affected by it. It sold out its first printing in ten weeks, has gone through six more printings, and was named, in a poll of college and university presidents, as the decade's most influential book of its kind. It remains in print, continues to sell steadily, and was even recently translated into Chinese—a clear indication that its value transcends the conditions it was written to address. It has become a canonical text of higher-education management.

Why did a book on such an unsexy subject strike such a chord? It is easy to forget, in these relatively flush times, when announcements of multimillion-dollar capital campaigns are as common as fireflies on a summer night, what a sense of impending doom was then hovering in the air in the late seventies and early eighties. "A spectre is haunting higher education," Keller declared, voicing the sentiments of many, "the spectre of decline and bankruptcy."[7] After many years in which its chief troubles had been those brought on by rampaging growth, American higher education was suddenly in the grip of an entirely different set of difficulties, the characteristic problems of contraction and limitation: declining enrollments, increased competition, ever-inflating costs, diminishing governmental support (with ever more plentiful strings attached to it), and shifting priorities among those who were increasingly being regarded as higher education's "customers." The very future of many traditional institutions, especially the venerable but chronically under-endowed American liberal arts colleges, was clearly in jeopardy. But the outlook for even the most well-heeled institutions was suddenly uncertain at best.

The only enduring solution to these problems, Keller argued, would lie in taking a more vigorous and focused approach to the management of academic institutions, using tactics and objectives that could only be developed on an individualized, institution-by-institution basis. His book attempted to explain what such an approach would mean in practice, and the difference it could make.

To begin with, it would mean acknowledging that one size did not fit all. It no longer made sense—if, indeed, it ever had—to treat all institutions of higher learning as if they were essentially the same, and were expected to accomplish the same things and meet the same standards in the same ways. Nor, it need hardly be said, did it make sense anymore to treat the large, expensive, complex, and heavily capitalized modern university as if it were a genteel and genially ramshackle operation, to be governed casually and inattentively, if at all.

Instead, the future flourishing of vulnerable higher-educational institutions would depend upon their ability to identify their particular areas of comparative advantage—the things they did best—and then to seek, in a highly conscious and methodical way, to recast their institutional life to emphasize such strengths, and thereby provide a fresh and more competitive profile for the institution. Such reorientation would inevitably mean making the institution more responsive to the academic marketplace, but Keller argued that, far from being a sellout of educational values, this is a very good thing, when done properly. Not only because it would help struggling institutions to survive, but because their survival would be a direct result of their ability to address the needs and hopes of the particular people they serve. Like Riesman, whom he resembled in many ways, he always insisted that the astonishing institutional diversity of American higher education was one of its greatest strengths, and should be preserved and enhanced at all costs.

Clearly colleges and universities could no longer afford to be grandly insouciant about their performance in the educational marketplace, but would such a reorientation undermine the intellectual life of the university? How could modern marketing strategies be introduced without diluting and cheapening the educational mission of colleges and universities, and turning higher education into just another commodity for sale?

Keller urged his faculty colleagues to acknowledge, however reluctantly, that the techniques of modern management would inevitably come to be employed in any economic activity as sprawling and complex and expensive and competitive as American higher education. The real question was the uses to which such techniques would be put. Who would dictate the ends toward which they would be directed? Would it be the accountants and budget officers and the other conquistadors of the spreadsheet or, perhaps worse, the politicians and bureaucrats, as we are now seeing in the misguided initiatives of the Department of Education to establish national outcomes standards, an undertaking that will only subvert the very institutional diversity that Riesman and Keller celebrated? Or, more hopefully, could the new management methods, used properly and judiciously, actually preserve the central role played by the activities of learning and inquiry—by the humanists, scientists, scholars, and students who have always formed the core of the university? Is it possible to understand strategic planning as the sustaining patron of the very best features of the modern college or university?

This may well seem impossible, or at least implausible. But for Keller, strategic planning provided a fresh way of addressing these new kinds of problems. What he proposed in *Academic Strategy* was a process that began with a brutally frank institutional self-assessment. That was absolutely essential. Institutions had to ask themselves where they were strongest, where they were weakest, and how their unique set of strengths and weaknesses positioned them with respect to the ever-shifting requirements of the educational marketplace. Such a view sought a middle ground between the idea of the university as a timeless repository, grandly indifferent to everything but its own internal imperatives, and the idea of the university as a crass, commercial operator, seeking above all else to increase its market share.

Neither approach would prove adequate to the new realities, because neither did justice to the complex mixture of the ideal and the practical inherent in American higher education. The university had to stand for something larger and greater than the values of the marketplace, else it ceased to be what it was. But it also had to employ its resources as skillfully and intelligently as possible, and find better ways to meet people where they are, or else it simply would not be able to survive at all.

Radical Ideas

Keller's ideas excited a generation of academic leaders struggling to find new ways forward, but it turned out they were more challenging, even radical, in their demands than they seemed at first glance. Properly understood, strategic planning meant an institution's finding the strength to say "No" to many things, even things that had formerly been a part of its settled identity. To adopt a "strategy" was not merely a question of determining what the institution would do, but deciding what it would *not* do, since others could do it better.

Moreover, even though Keller stressed the need for mutuality and constant institution-wide consultation in strategic planning, such processes had to lead to decisions, and then actions. It was not enough for strategic planning to be *participatory;* it also had to be *decisive*. And the decision-making buck would have to stop in some executive office, preferably the office of the president.

In other words, the effective implementation of any academic strategy would require vigorous presidential leadership, both in setting the institutional agenda and seeing to it that the agenda was enacted. And such presidential leadership has been increasingly hard to find, after many years in which the combination of external demands and internal intransigence has caused presidents' substantive on-campus leadership role to diminish steadily. Changing such a dynamic is easier said than done. The problem is not only that so many presidents do not try to lead boldly and imaginatively, but that so often they are not permitted to. One need only consider the fact that the best-known university presidents of our day are those who have been thwarted and rebuked by their own faculties. Small wonder that so many presidents choose to stay low and keep moving. But the notion that serious and sustained institution-wide reform could ever be led by the faculty is almost entirely fanciful. Serious academic reform will either be pushed forward by strong executive leaders, or it will not occur at all.

Keller roundly disagreed with those who charged that the use of strategic planning treated the college or university strictly as a business. No, he insisted, it treated the college or university as an *organization*. A crucial distinction, but also one that entailed a more radical assertion than it might seem. For it meant that a college faculty needed to be understood as something more than a collection of certified specialists representing the full range of accredited academic fields, housed under a single institutional roof. It meant that a college's academic offerings amounted to something more than a large vending machine for the dispensing of certified programs of study.

It meant that an ideally functioning college is better regarded as *an organic unity,* a knit-together organizational structure that is animated throughout by a sense of common purpose, a purpose that is qualitatively different from the aggregate ambitions of individuals and the imperatives of their professional disciplines. To be sure, a good college seeks to provide all its employees with the fullest possible range of opportunities for their own achievement and advancement. That is a given. In American higher education, self-realization and institutional service are seen as complementary, rather than opposing, forces. But it also requires something else: a strong sense of the college as a *collegium*, as the institution to which one's most primary professional loyalty is owed.

This loyalty cannot be a mere slogan or a one-way manipulative appeal. A strategic plan depends for its success on the existence of strong centripetal forces binding all individuals willingly, and happily, to the institution, including the institution's leaders. It cannot succeed in a place where institutional loyalty is not cultivated, and rewarded, and reinforced, and exemplified from the top down. It certainly cannot succeed in an atmosphere in which careerist executive leaders are no sooner hired into one job than they are laying the groundwork for their next jump. Keller's idea of academic strategy was actually a quite demanding one, demanding more of both faculty and leaders than, in many cases, they have been willing or able to give.

As this last sentence implies, despite the popularity of *Academic Strategy*, the lessons Keller sought to teach were not entirely learned. Many institutions survived the structural challenges of the eighties not by strategic concentration but by endless and often indiscriminate internal diversification, finding new constituencies of "nontraditional" students, inventing new programs to attract them, admitting vast numbers of foreign students, and thereby keeping their enrollments up. Such programmatic additions often included the development of jerry-rigged MBA programs taught by part-time faculty, or poorly conceived and undemanding MLA and other master's degree programs, designed for the certification needs of secondary-school teachers—programs that were fresh and plentiful sources of paying customers, but often had nothing to do with the existing programs of the institution, and that sometimes were, in effect, a corrupt bargain between vendor and customer, a fraud whose perpetration risked tainting the entire product line. Schools also reduced costs by relying more and more heavily on less expensive irregular or adjunct faculty to carry the load of teaching, or by multiplying faculty contact hours by using "distance learning" or other online instructional methods—a second "academic revolution" that, by eroding the prestige and authority of the regular tenured faculty, threatened to undo even what was good about its predecessor.

Such innovations sometimes may have reflected creative short-term managerial thinking, but in general these adaptations exacted a price, by eroding institutions' sense of their core academic mission, and making them more and more bottom-line oriented, more and more like diversified corporations of any other kind. In other words, they moved in precisely the opposite direction to that which George Keller was advocating.

Even among the many institutions that embraced strategic planning in theory, far too many merely went through the motions in practice, assembling a wide array of committees and study groups, and soliciting reports and projecting ambitious goals with much fanfare, but lacking the leadership required to make any hard choices. Unless an institution has intelligent and brave leaders willing to make hard choices and stick by them, "strategic planning" is just another word for endless committee meetings, paperwork, and gassy rhetoric, none of it to any good end.

Of this, I can speak with the sad wisdom of personal experience, as an active participant in a massive strategic-planning review conducted by the large, private research university with which I was then associated. Countless meetings were devoted to the setting of the most extravagant goals imaginable, all of which were completely disproportionate to the university's means, and were completely oblivious to the nature of our academic competition. In other words, Keller's first step, the frank, internal self-analysis, was never quite undertaken. The university's then-president made it clear that one of his top priorities for the university was that it would break into the ranks of the top twenty research universities. When asked which of the *current* top twenty his own badly under-endowed and tuition-dependent university would displace, he changed the subject. When asked which programs could be trimmed in order to streamline the institutional mission, he offered none. I came away from our meetings reminded of a brilliant Volvo television commercial of the late 1970s, in which a business executive, clearly patterned upon Lee Iacocca, stood up before a meeting of workers and shareholders and proposed to restore the company's fortunes by . . . chanting the word "Quality!" over and over again. This was not an exercise in true strategic planning; this was an exercise in self-hypnosis.

Still, some institutions followed the path Keller recommended, and have, as a consequence, experienced an exhilarating rebirth. One of them, Elon University, was the subject of Keller's fascinating recent book *Transforming a College*, which details the steps by which this once-imperiled North Carolina liberal arts college made itself over into a competitive and appealingly distinctive institution, with a bundle of comparative advantages.[8]

It may well be the case that Keller's understanding of strategic planning will work best at smaller institutions such as Elon, which are more flexible and more willing to make dramatic changes in order to keep the institution alive and functioning. Large state or private universities with the full plenitude of countervailing forces and "veto groups" firmly in place—faculties, students, graduate assistants, influential alumni, staff, athletic programs, prospective donors, and so on—may be far more resistant to dramatic change. And it may take severe crises, even near-death experiences, to concentrate an institution's mind, and make it willing to consider the big changes, and support the strong leaders, that can bring new life to a campus. Donors with a keen and genuine interest in the renewal of American higher education should bear in mind the "comparative advantage" of putting their funds into an institution where those funds have some chance of being genuinely transformative.

Indeed, the fact that Keller's prescriptions seem so much more likely to succeed in smaller institutions suggests in turn the need to disaggregate our thinking, and make stronger distinctions between colleges and universities, and indeed between the great majority of universities and the handful of major research universities, private and public, than we are generally accustomed to making.[9] As our wealthiest and more influential research universities become more and more deeply committed to being "producers of knowledge" and incubators for economic development and technological innovation operating in a global context, they seem less and less likely to be effectively answerable to the kind of governance that Keller describes. The task of managing vast institutions such as Harvard or Berkeley is a creature of an entirely different order from that of managing an Elon University.

Necessary Planning

In the end, however, Keller's analyses are more relevant today than ever before to the vast majority of institutions of higher education in the United States, and especially to those primarily devoted to the task of education. Strategic planning in higher education is just as sound an idea as it ever was, because it is, at bottom, about being purposeful, about achieving a deeper understanding of the proper ends toward which an institution's energies should be directed and dedicated. Harvard can afford, literally and figuratively, to operate without such organizational purposefulness. But the Elons of the country cannot.

Although the economic and demographic pressures on higher education have eased, or at least stabilized, the need for institutions to clarify the ends toward which their work is directed is, if anything, even greater, especially when tuitions are higher than anyone twenty years ago would have dreamed possible, and poised to go even higher. I often wonder if the sprawling industry of American higher education dwells inside a bubble of its own, and if the day will not come when the rising cost of higher education will finally have risen too far, and engendered a consumer revolt. Some rumblings to that effect can be heard. The social critic Barbara Ehrenreich argued recently that "the higher education industry is becoming a racket," one whose implicit come-on—"Buy our product or be condemned to life of penury, and our product can easily cost well over $100,000"—is being undermined by the steadily declining value of the credentials that such money buys.[10]

Such a view is still an outlier. But it should serve as a warning that the educational aims and benefits of higher education are not obvious to the greater public, and as long as colleges and universities defer the work of making them clearer, both to themselves and to their constituencies, they may find it even harder to make that case when times are not so flush. Such times will come, perhaps sooner than we think. And when they do, the Elons, not the Harvards, will be the more vulnerable, and will suffer the worse consequences.

Those who look for the means to address these problems effectively will hardly be able to do better than to return to the work of George Keller. Whatever the barbarities committed in the name of "strategic planning," he cannot be blamed for them. Instead, as any reader of *Academic Strategy* can see, and as some of us were privileged to know firsthand, he was a great defender of all that is best about American higher education, an old-fashioned Columbia humanist who managed to learn the language of management without being consumed by it, and had an openness to the possibility that its benefits might extend usefully, and beneficially, to the very realms that are generally inclined to disdain them. He was wise as a serpent, and beneficent as a dove. We do well to emulate him, and follow his advice.

Notes

1. U.S. Department of Education, *A Test of Leadership: Charting the Future of U.S. Higher Education*, by the Commission appointed by Secretary of Education Margaret Spellings (Washington, D.C., 2006), September 2006, http://www.ed.gov/about/bdscomm/list/hiedfuture/reports/final-report.pdf. The Spellings Report elicited many howls of displeasure from academics who dislike the notion of accountability itself, but for an exemplary response that raises the deeper issues in a memorable way, see the response by Christopher B. Nelson, President of St. John's College (Annapolis), "Remarks before the Cato Institute Forum on the Spellings Commission Report," St. John's College, remarks presented at the Cato Institute Policy Forum entitled "Ivory Tower Overload: How to Fix American Higher Ed," Washington, D.C., 27 September 2006, http://www.stjohnscollege.edu/about/resources/06cato.pdf.

2. Christopher Jencks and David Riesman, *The Academic Revolution* (Garden City, N.Y.: Doubleday, 1968).

3. David Riesman, Nathan Glazer, and Reuel Denney, *The Lonely Crowd: A Study of the Changing American Character* (New Haven, Conn.: Yale University Press, 1950). See Wilfred McClay, "Fifty Years of *The Lonely Crowd*," *Wilson Quarterly* 22 (Summer 1998): 34–42.

4. See David Riesman, *Constraint and Variety in American Education* (Lincoln, Nebr.: University of Nebraska Press, 1956) on educational diversity; on the presidency, see Judith Block McLaughlin and David Riesman, *Choosing a College President: Opportunities and Constraints* (Princeton, N.J.: Carnegie Foundation for the Advancement of Teaching, 1990), and Judith Block McLaughlin and David Riesman, "The President:

A Precarious Perch," in *Higher Learning in America, 1980–2000,* ed. Arthur Levine (Baltimore, Md.: Johns Hopkins University Press, 1993), 179–202.

5. Peter Caws, "Design for a University," *Daedelus* 99 (Winter 1970): 98.

6. Thorstein Veblen, *The Higher Learning in America: A Memorandum on the Conduct of Universities by Business Men* (New York: B. W. Huebsch, 1918), 286.

7. George Keller, *Academic Strategy: The Management Revolution in American Higher Education* (Baltimore, Md.: Johns Hopkins University Press, 1983), 3.

8. George Keller, *Transforming a College: The Story of a Little-Known College's Climb to Strategic Distinction* (Baltimore, Md.: Johns Hopkins University Press, 2004).

9. Hugh Davis Graham and Nancy Diamond, *The Rise of American Research Universities: Elites and Challengers in the Postwar Era* (Baltimore, Md.: Johns Hopkins University Press, 1997); Julie A. Reuben, *The Making of the Modern University: Intellectual Transformation and the Marginalization of Morality* (Chicago: University of Chicago Press, 1996).

10. Barbara Ehrenreich, "The Higher Education Scam," *The Nation,* 14 May 2007, http://www.thenation.com/doc/20070514/ehrenreich.

Chapter Eight

KEEPING WOMEN IN BUSINESS (AND FAMILY)

Robin Fretwell Wilson*

NEWLY MINTED young professionals in business, law, and medicine navigate taxing careers in which they have heavily invested at a time when people their age once formed families. For a growing segment of these professionals, work and family have become either-or propositions. Massive debt loads, staggering salaries, grinding work schedules, lengthening career tracks, and begrudging corporate cultures all set career and family on a collision course.

The media has chronicled extensively the growing "opt-out revolution," in which women professionals are exiting the workplace in droves. Less appreciated is the converse phenomenon: huge numbers of professionals who remain in the workplace but *opt out of family.* These men and women forego parenting and stable, long-term relationships in surprisingly high numbers, believing that they cannot have both. This depressed childbearing and family formation by those in whom society has invested the most should be of deep concern. It is bad for children, bad for business, bad for the women and men themselves, and bad for everybody.

In many ways, young professionals learn to treat work and family as either-or choices at the very beginning of their graduate professional educations. The intense time demands and pressures of graduate professional education teach students early on to place professional obligations over the personal. Consequently, graduate professional schools must change the perception that work and family cannot coexist. Until graduates leave prepared to advocate for and take advantage of family-friendly workplace policies, work and family will continue to be either-or propositions for many professionals.

Graduate programs can do much to change the calculus that young professionals engage in when deciding whether to combine family and work. They should not only tangibly support a student's choice to have children during school, but should also better equip him or her to insist on workplace changes that make it easier to have families while working. Educators can support family by modeling good behavior in their own institutions, decreasing the admission age for women, giving preference in admissions to applicants with children, providing financial support for student-parents in the form of scholarships and better loan terms, establishing alumni mentoring networks, and outlining for students the real costs of various practice settings for forming and maintaining families. Once armed with stronger expectations that they *can* have both, these young professionals will be important agents for transforming the workplace from the inside out.

This chapter does not make any normative judgments about the value of one path over another. Some people want to stay home with their children, others want never to have children. Graduate education that takes family seriously should make both paths easier to navigate, and ultimately more livable.

I. The Paths Young Professionals Take

Nearly a quarter of women with graduate degrees currently stay at home with their children, and a third of women with MBAs do not work full-time.[1] Women lawyers are also leaving law firms in overwhelming numbers. Although women now comprise half the entering class of new associates at law firms, less than one in five partners are women—a paltry increase over the percentage of women partners in 1993. Women in medicine are having no more success at remaining in demanding workplaces.

This movement out of the workplace and into the home represents one path that professionals can and do take. Among women over forty who are able to have children, 29% are "traditionalists" who have at least three children and are employed very little or not at all, while 18% are "postmodernists" who are completely devoted to their careers with no children. Between these extremes lie the "neo-traditionalists" (35%), who put their career second to family and have, on average, two children, and the "modernists" (17%), who have only one child and commit a considerable amount of their time to the workplace.

Even more than the general population, professional women are walking away from having children. A study published earlier this year found that four-fifths of senior male lawyers have children, while two-thirds of senior women do. A 1999 Boston Bar Association report declared, "We are in danger of seeing law firms evolve into institutions where only those who have no family responsibilities—or, worse, are willing to abandon those responsibilities—can thrive."[2]

This break from parenting mirrors a similar break from long-term committed relationships that has been largely overlooked.[3] The abdication by professionals of long-term adult relationships shows up in current marital status, as well as the percentage of professionals who have never married. When compared to all college graduates, fewer women in business and law are presently married (68.2% of female college graduates are married, compared to 62.2% of women JDs and 66.4% of women MBAs). This is not true of women in medicine, 72.3% of whom are married. (See Table 1 in the Appendix.) By contrast, more men in law, medicine, and business are married than male college graduates (79.8% of male lawyers, 85.9% of male MBAs, and 86.1% of male doctors are married, compared to 79.5% of male college graduates). (See Table 2 in the Appendix.) Even in medicine, where a greater percentage of women are married than college graduates, the number of unmarried women is still *twice* that of men (27.7% of female doctors, compared to 13.9% of male doctors). Likewise, the percentage of unmarried women with MBAs is more than double the percentage of men who have not tied the knot (33.6% versus 14.1%). These differences are statistically significant at a high level of significance, as Tables 1 and 2 in the Appendix show.

Even when professionals enter long-term adult relationships, these often take a beating. Women outstrip men in the number of failed or failing personal relationships. Women with MBAs are divorced or separated more often than college graduates (12.1% of women MBAs, compared to 11.3% of female college graduates), and twice as often as men with MBAs (5% of whom report being divorced or separated). (See Table 3 in the Appendix.) Even though women with JDs and MDs divorce or separate less often more often than college graduates, they still are more likely to divorce or separate than their male counterparts (10.1% of women JDs and 9% of women MDs versus 7% of men with JDs and 5.1% of men with MDs). As before, these differences are statistically significant at a high level of significance, as the Appendix shows.

The complete break from marriage tells an even starker story. A whopping 21% of women with JDs and 17% of women with MBAs have never married, compared to 14% of women college graduates. Women professionals abstain from marriage at double and sometimes nearly triple the rate of men. (See Table 4 in the Appendix.) By contrast, professional men are *less* likely never to marry than other college graduates. Again, these differences are statistically significant at a high level of significance, as the Appendix shows. Although women, more than men, are opting out of parenting and long-term relationships, a slice of professional men do so as well, as the Appendix illustrates. In this respect, the family opt-out is an equal-opportunity phenomenon.

A. Signal Importance for Women

While men and women both make trade-offs between work and family, the trade-offs do have signal importance for women. Among persons who graduated from college in 1992–93, mothers were far more likely to leave the workforce or work part-time than fathers. A decade after graduating, 23% of mothers had left the workforce, while another 17% worked part-time. Less than 2% of fathers did either. Mothers were also far more likely to leave the workforce than women without children.[4]

The departures by mothers rather than fathers are hardly surprising. While it is socially acceptable for women to stay at home, it is not for men. A 1998 *Washington Post* survey found that for many people "accepting a family's smaller income by having a husband stay home was not a socially acceptable option for them."[5] In addition, men receive less support from their employers for their parenting choices.

For instance, women receive longer leaves following the birth of a child. Thirty-one percent of large employers provided more than twelve weeks of maximum job-guaranteed leave for women after the birth of a child, while only 20% did so for men.[6]

Pay differentials may also play a role in the gendered nature of who stays at home. A study released this year found that a substantial pay gap opens between men and women one year after they graduate from college and widens over the ensuing decade—even when graduates are matched by field of study and similar jobs. A year out of college, men who work full-time earn 20% more than women, while ten years later they earn 31% more. This gap persists even after controlling for number of hours worked, occupation, and parenthood.[7]

Workplace departures by women underscore that women experience the tensions between work and family in a way that men largely do not. As Table 5 in the Appendix illustrates, professional men can have both work *and* family because they disproportionately have stay-at-home spouses. Among married professionals with one to three children, male lawyers were over six times more likely to have a stay-at-home spouse than female lawyers, while men in business and medicine had a stay-at-home spouse roughly four times more often than their female colleagues.[8] These differences are statistically significant at a high level of significance. As a group, men are not put to a choice between work and family in the same way that professional women often are.

The departures by women hardly come as a surprise. An overwhelming majority of women—67%—believe that commitment to family hurts their chances in the workplace, a view shared by 49% of men.[9] This belief is not misplaced. A monumental study by Sylvia Ann Hewlett and Carolyn Buck Luce revealed that a woman who takes one year off faces an average salary penalty of 11%, and one who takes three years off loses 37%.[10]

The effects of family commitment are also felt by those who continue to work. Men and women alike believe that they cannot take advantage of existing policies without hurting their chances at advancement. A 2000 survey by the Department of Labor revealed that, of those workers who needed to take the twelve weeks of unpaid, job-protected leave per year provided to certain employees under the Family Medical Leave Act (FMLA) but did not, 42.6% decided not to take leave because "job advancement would have been hurt," and another 27.8% said "they did not want to lose seniority."[11] Even in reportedly family-friendly work settings, such as in-house counsel offices, only one in ten women believe they can avail themselves of flexible schedules without hurting their careers.[12]

In this contest between work and family, it should come as no surprise that professionals are choosing one or the other. It is incredibly difficult to combine both, especially for women. These adults are stretched to capacity. As any working mother is acutely aware, "[w]orking mothers are sleep-deprived and time-crunched."[13] Women working outside the home "spend significantly more time on childcare and housework than do men."[14] Moreover, dual-earner couples worked a combined workweek of ninety-one hours in 2002, up from eighty-four hours ten years earlier. Most of this extra effort comes at the expense of downtime for women in the households. The 1.6 hours of downtime that working mothers had in 1977 shriveled to fifty-four minutes per day in 2001. Working fathers' downtime fell from 2.1 hours per day in 1977 to 1.3 hours per day.[15]

Perhaps because they shoulder the lion's share of family work, women act on the desire to achieve a better balance between work and family in ways that most men do not (yet). For example, 57% of women who moved to in-house counsel positions did so to find a better balance of work and life, although most were sorely disappointed.[16] Two-thirds of women attorneys select positions based on how livable and family-friendly the position is, double the number of men who do so.

B. Begrudging Corporate Cultures

Although employers have come a long way in offering flexibility to workers, it is not nearly far enough. Only a fraction of employers offer meaningful assistance to employees with childcare responsibilities. Employers that appear supportive of family on paper often reserve flexible work options for an elite few. And for nearly all employers, availability on paper and availability in practice are two different things.

Few employers offer concrete assistance to struggling parents, such as childcare on-site or back-up emergency childcare when a child is sick, although large employers provide more generous supports for family than small employers. For example, just 32% of employers offer paid family leave, and even fewer, 27%, offer more leave than the FMLA requires. More than three-quarters of employers still do not provide lactation programs or designated breastfeeding areas.[17]

Almost half of women who work have "lost pay or job promotions or had difficulty retaining jobs because of the need to care for sick children, compared to 28 percent of men." Seventy-six percent of parents of children with chronic conditions have lost pay, jobs, or promotions due to caring for their children, or have experienced other difficulties at work.[18]

Many companies reserve significant accommodations for an elite few. Fifty-three percent of employers let some employees move from full-time to part-time and back again while retaining the same status, but only one in five make this option—so essential to getting a new parent through a child's first year—available to *all* employees. For those elite employees who received this accommodation, it made all the difference in their choice between paths. Sixty percent of professional and managerial women who had the luxury of reduced hours said they would quit if their jobs lacked this flexibility.

Why are employers so begrudging of greater accommodations for family? Many see them as expensive and unmanageable. Some corporate leaders had to forsake family for work in order to get ahead, and think it only fair that others do as well.[19] Some partners, both male and female, see junior attorneys who want to leave at 4 PM to attend a child's soccer game as "ungrateful whiners" who are "not committed." More commonly, senior attorneys see "the younger generation's expectations of balanced lives [as] unrealistic and unreasonable."[20] These mismatched norms and expectations lead to a disconnect between policies on paper and policies in practice. As one supervising partner for a large Georgia-based law firm protested when approached by a pregnant associate about flextime, "But no one ever uses it."[21]

When work and family cannot be balanced, something has to give. For traditionalists, it is work; for post-modernists, it is family; for neo-traditionalists and modernists, it is time for themselves and perhaps their families or jobs. While the balance between work and family is one for the individual to make, society has a deep interest in preventing forced choices.

II. The Impact on Society

To serve society well, we must support both the choice to stay at home to care for children *and* the choice to work while caring for children. No one doubts that children fare better when one parent stays home, as an ample literature documents. For this reason, society needs to offer parents the flexibility to opt for family over work. Society loses, however, when the most accomplished and productive are forced to say no to work. When capable and skilled workers who could be employed choose not to be, it weakens the job market and, ultimately, our economic structure.[22] Less money is earned, and less is plowed back into the market.

Although hardly intuitive, "The more women are active on a country's labor market, the more children are born in that country." Witness Iceland, with the highest birth rate in Europe and the highest rate of workplace participation by women, 90%. As the Berlin Institute explains, "invest[ing] in an infrastructure that allows women to have children while continuing to pursue careers" will succeed in ensuring replacement-level fertility where monetary incentives would not.[23]

The expressive effects of workplace departures should not be discounted. Corporate cultures that compel parents to abandon the workplace reinforce the perception that parenting and professional work are either-or propositions. Mass departures leave fewer role models for young professionals—an occurrence that may explain in part why so little progress has been made by women in law firms.[24] The lack of role models has important downstream effects, too:

women continue to vacate much-sought-after jobs in favor of saner lives because so little has changed.

The effects of the paths not taken are real, even if difficult to quantify. Wising up to the clash between work and family, fewer women will enroll next year in the nation's top business schools. At nearly half of these schools, fewer women will graduate this year than did in 2003. This waning interest spills over to the workplace. While 13% of women in top-tier business programs in 2002 preferred Wall Street as a career, by 2006 only 6.9% did.[25] Clearly, graduate schools and workplaces lose an important element of diversity as women walk away.

Although children do well when one parent stays home, children can also benefit in tangible ways when their mothers can choose to work. Working parents encourage children to achieve more in school and to obtain higher educations.[26] Children of working parents are more likely to learn to juggle responsibility, manage time, solve problems, and develop high coping abilities.[27]

Just as society loses when professionals are forced to choose family over work, society also loses when the most accomplished and productive are forced to say no to family. Depressed child-bearing, if sustained over time, may hasten a "breakdown" of our pension and welfare systems.

Further, if professional women abdicate motherhood in large numbers, fewer children will have firsthand familiarity with successful women as role models. For some of these children, especially girls, perception of one's inability to have both work and family may morph into reality.

Depleted childbearing at the top of the economic ladder also alters the talent pool in subsequent generations. A smaller number of children will receive the benefit of highly educated, capable parents. An increasing number will come from families with less education, fewer resources, and consequently fewer life-chances. This demographic swing will place additional strains on the school system, social supports, and other safety nets.

In short, whether professionals opt out of work or opt out of family, society loses. As the next part explains, choices between work and family are influenced in very real ways by crushing debt, lengthening work weeks and paths to success, salaries that are so rich that no one can forego them, and the quickly retreating chances for conceiving naturally as professionals get their financial and personal lives in order.

III. Doing the Math

Why are so many young professionals saying no to family? Graduate students across the professions face a host of challenges that their predecessors largely escaped decades earlier. Faced with massive debt and the ability to earn staggering sums of money, more and more new professionals are delaying long-term committed relationships and family until they establish their careers. In the pressure-cooker of modern firms and business, many perceive that they can either have thriving careers or thriving families, but not both.

Last year, the average age of graduating law students climbed to twenty-eight,[28] of business students, to twenty-seven,[29] and of medical students, to twenty-eight.[30] For many students, this signifies evaporating opportunities to form relationships, and especially, families. Less than a third of the students in graduate programs are married or in committed relationships, and only a fraction already have children.[31] For the vast majority, marriage and family are things of the future.

Yet at a time when peers are marrying and starting families, young professionals face the challenges of beginning and cementing new careers. For most, this means working punishing schedules over ever-lengthening partnership tracks—fresh on the heels of the stresses of graduate school. MBA graduates report workweeks of fifty hours;[32] physicians, 53.2 hours.[33] In 2006, attorneys reported working an average of 2,065 hours annually, although some worked considerably more.[34] Residency hours for new physicians can be brutal, capped at eighty hours per week.[35]

Long hours disadvantage women, and parents, in important ways. In a battle of hours, those who shoulder less family responsibility will win over those who shoulder more (usually women), earning coveted promotions and raises. Moreover, when workers perceive that others are working long hours, they strive to work similar hours to compete. Lawyers especially view long hours as the key to partnership. Yet as one attorney who later went in-house explained, "This is no life."

Although few can keep up this pace for years, lengthening paths to success are the norm across professions. Consider MBAs. Almost all MBA programs require some amount of work experience (at least two years, and usually four to five) before they will accept an applicant. The applicant who is twenty-two when she finishes her undergraduate degree will be twenty-seven when she matriculates and twenty-nine when she graduates. If she spends two years establishing herself before having children, she will be in her early thirties before she can begin a family. Lawyers and doctors face similar challenges in finding a "good time" for children.

Waiting to parent until after reaching partnership or upper-level management is not a workable solution either. These positions no longer signify a well-earned reprieve from grueling hours. Instead, young partners and executives routinely outwork their senior counterparts.[36]

Grueling hours bring with them generous salaries that are difficult to walk away from. The average starting salary for an MBA in the class of 2006 was $71,593, with an average signing bonus of $13,106.[37] In 2006, salaries for first-year attorneys topped $100,000, with some brand-new attorneys earning over $160,000.[38] These rich starting salaries presage even greater sums in later years, when bonuses kick in. On average, eighth-year associates earn $153,895 before bonuses, and $160,948 when all compensation is counted. The median salary for physicians with one to four years of experience is $137,331.[39] After five years of experience, some specialties top $200,000 per year.[40]

Ironically, six-digit salaries do not ease the financial burden that many shoulder after graduation. Instead, a significant share of this income goes to loan repayments. The average MBA borrows $36,200, funding 38.3% of their education with debt.[41] The median debt for graduating law students reached $70,000 in 2007.[42] Physicians average $112,900 in debt, having funded 83.4% of their education with borrowed money.[43]

This debt figures prominently in the life choices new professionals make. As a recent graduate of Washington and Lee University School of Law explained, "My parents had me when my mother was twenty-two and my father was twenty-three. My fiancé is thirty and I'm twenty-eight, and we're still trying to get our act together. There's no way we're having children until we pay off our loans."

Racing the Biological Clock

Whether they realize it or not, these newly minted professionals are racing against time if they want to parent. For women over 30, the already relatively slim chances of pregnancy (30% begin to decline by 3.5% each year, ebbing to 12.5% by age 35 and 2% by age 40. By 45, it's nearly impossible for a woman to conceive using her own eggs. Men face shrinking odds of conceiving after 35 as well. While a quarter of men under the age of 25 are infertile, by the mid-30s that number balloons to half.[44] Assisted conception partly allays the urgency of conceiving naturally, but the chances of conceiving still drop off. Moreover, assisted conception poses risks of birth defects for the resulting children.[45]

IV. The Role of Educators in Making Family More Achievable

Young professionals learn to treat work and family as either-or choices during their graduate professional educations. The intense time demands and pressures of graduate school teach students to place professional obligations over the personal at every turn. Rather than viewing work-life balance as a problem for employers to address, professional schools *must* take an active role in calling for a transformed corporate culture. Graduate schools are in a unique position to change the perception that work and family cannot coexist.

It is difficult for schools, however, to urge corporate change when we neither model good behavior nor cultivate an expectation of it among our students. Most professional schools do not provide meaningful counseling about the balance of work and home life after graduation, nor do they assist students in navigating the collisions they experience *while* in school. Indeed, many fail to support their own faculty and staff in the decision to form families, sending a clear message to students about the chances of combining career and family.

Schools can change this culture and, consequently, the expectations of young professionals with a number of straightforward, concrete measures.

A. Modeling Good Behavior

First, graduate professional programs should model good behavior. They must support the family formation decisions of their own faculty and staff. Like other professionals, women faculty members are "significantly less likely to be married or partnered."[46] Academia is a world in which "at each step of the continuum from graduate student to full professor, women face small differences in treatment, and these small disadvantages accumulate to produce large disparities in status and opportunity." Work-family policies represent one "structural barrier to full participation."[47]

Some schools are taking steps to remedy the "chilly climate" that "sometimes discourages faculty from taking advantage of work-family policies."[48] They are acknowledging family-friendly practices that are already in place unofficially and disseminating information about formal policies to faculty. They are also developing new policies with active support from the administration. By attracting, supporting, and retaining faculty with family obligations, they demonstrate to students that balancing work and family really *is* possible.

Schools must also give tangible support to students who have family obligations. They can, for example, provide better on-ramps and off-ramps in and out of full-time programs. Recognizing that biological and career "clocks" often run concurrently, Stanford University took the innovative step in 2006 of developing a "Childbirth Accommodation Policy."[49] This new policy supplements Stanford's leave of absence for parents, which covers expecting mothers and new biological, adoptive, and foster fathers and mothers. Acknowledging that "a woman's prime childbearing years are the same years she is likely to be in graduate school, doing postdoctoral training, and establishing herself in a career," the policy allows expecting mothers to remain enrolled full-time but postpone course assignments, examinations, and other obligations. Students also remain eligible for healthcare benefits and student housing and may use Stanford's facilities. New and expecting student-parents who have teaching or research obligations are excused from their duties for six weeks, during which time they continue to receive financial support. The policy "establishes *minimum* standards for accommodation for a woman graduate student giving birth." It directs advisers, faculty, and staff to "work with sensitivity and imagination to provide more than this minimum . . . , according to the particular circumstances of the woman student." Taken together, these accommodations erase the forced choice between parenting while in school or taking a leave of absence, and convey to students that career and family can, in fact, coexist.

Other schools have pioneered innovative ways to support the adult relationships that students have when they enroll or form while in school. Taking seriously the MBA's reputation as the divorce degree, a handful of business schools have begun to tackle head on the wear and tear that graduate school places on relationships. For instance, Dartmouth's business school offers partner support groups. Life coaches also offer couples advice on weathering the strain, from tried-and-true strategies such as "date nights" to making a wish list of activities to do together.[50]

This support can extend to helping students' families during the graduate program. For instance, the University of Maryland School of Law holds a special orientation for students' spouses and children, with a mock class and primer on the Socratic Method. Unlike most schools, which largely subscribe to a sink or swim mentality, these schools recognize the strain that graduate school places on family, and address it head on.

B. Grooming New Professionals Earlier

Second, graduate programs can respond to anemic family formation by assisting professionals to get their careers in order while it is still possible to have families. Recognizing that timing is everything, some business schools, such as Wharton, now focus their recruiting on a younger class of women.[51] Younger graduates are more likely to gather the skills and credibility to demand work accommodations before it is too late to have families. With seniority and clout, flexible schedules can become a real option.

C. Giving Preference to Families

Third, schools can support the decision to have children by giving preference in admissions to applicants with children. Student-parents will not only enrich the diversity of everyone's education, but will also demonstrate vividly to students without children that balancing career and family is genuinely possible.

Moreover, because debt plays such a prominent role in the life-calculus that students make, schools share responsibility for the impending collision between career and family. Consequently, their support of parents should extend to the financial. The staggering debt amassed by graduation weighs heavily on professionals when deciding whether to combine work and family. One answer is to develop scholarship programs tailored to students who have families when they enroll, and to lobby for increased loan deferment and forgiveness options for graduates with families.

Many universities in the United States enjoy significant endowments. They should use their endowments to fund scholarships and fellowships tailored to meet the needs of student-parents. Scholarships for student-parents would directly reduce the financial burden on families. Because endowments underwrite a number of existing needs and may be "unavailable" for this purpose,[52] schools can, and should, solicit new donations for family-friendly scholarships.

D. Providing Networks of Alumni Mentors

Fourth, the lack of female role models who combine work and family represents a distinct deficit for professional women; professional men, by contrast, have an abundance of role models.[53] Graduate schools are uniquely situated to compensate for this "invisibility of white male privilege" by marshaling their extensive networks of women alumni to serve as the mentors so frequently absent in the workplace. Female students could be matched with alumnae mentors while in school and benefit from those relationships well into their professional careers.

E. Family-Friendly Career Advice

Fifth, career counseling offices can do a better job of outlining the real costs for families—and the possibility of forming families—when selecting one practice setting over another. As Table 6 in the Appendix illustrates, the size of one's employer matters to the likelihood that a young professional will be able to combine work and family. Although college graduates with one to three children are distributed roughly equally among employers of all sizes, for professionals it is a very different story. Female lawyers working in a small-firm setting are much more likely to have children living at home. Indeed more than 40% of women lawyers in firms with eleven to twenty-four employees have children under age thirteen at home, compared to less than a third in the largest employer settings (by contrast, male lawyers with children are more equally distributed among employers of all sizes). Fifty-four percent of women with MBAs who worked for companies with eleven to twenty-four employees had children living at home, compared to 24.6% of female MBAs at firms employing between 500 and 999 employees (again, male MBAs are more equally distributed among employers).

Of course, it is not clear in which direction the causal arrow runs. It may be that professionals committed to family are gravitating to these employers because they are better able to combine work and children in these settings, or it may be that these employers give greater support and encouragement to families. Whatever the explanation, however, size matters. Unfortunately, most placement offices never alert students to this crucial fact.

Now it is true that it is much easier for employers to advertise a big salary than family-friendly policies. Even young professionals racing the parenting clock are not as attracted by flexible work options as they are by salary. As one associate at a New York law firm billing twenty-three hundred hours per year quipped, "Incoming associates don't care as much about things like lifestyle initially; they only start to care more about this when their debt is paid off." This problem of moving targets makes it unlikely that firms will begin to compete for brand-new professionals on the basis of work-life balance. Schools, however, can do more to sensitize graduates to the trade-offs between time and money—and between money and family—before it is too late. Many of these professionals will quit in the first few years and seek new employment in the lateral market, where work-life balance can and does figure more prominently.

Schools should also tap the rich well of information that alumni can provide about the family-friendliness of individual employers, especially by highlighting any disconnects between policies on paper and policies in practice. While professionals seeking work that is more conducive to family can consult a number of surveys of employee happiness, these give very little concrete information about family-friendly policies and provide information only on an exclusive set of "top" corporations and firms.[54] Schools should push for Family Support Report Cards from employers interviewing on campus. They should also recognize and celebrate employers that accommodate work and family, much as Catalyst does with business firms.

F. A Voice for Change

Finally, in addition to this direct support of families, graduate professional schools should advocate for family-friendly policies. As one linchpin reform, schools should advocate for loan deferments that will promote and support a young professional's choice to form a family. This choice should not be burdened by the need to meet an enormous monthly loan payment. At present, students can defer loan repayment in only a tightly circumscribed set of circumstances. For instance, both the Income Contingent and Income Sensitive repayment plans have very low income-eligibility caps, largely shutting out two-professional and even one-professional families. Deferments extend to twelve months for working mothers and six months for other parents, but are available only to borrowers whose first Federal Family Education Loan was issued before 1993 *and* is still in repayment. Economic-hardship deferments do not fill the gap, since these require full-time employment; nor do unemployment deferments, which require the debtor to actively seek employment.[55]

The College Cost Reduction and Access Act of 2007 is a step in the right direction.[56] It allows for forgiveness of outstanding loan balances after twenty-five years of repayments, and adjusts repayment schedules for family size. This is only a partial solution, however, since forgiven loan balances are treated as taxable income and the repayment schemes extracts a "marriage penalty."[57]

Universities should use their not inconsiderable political muscle—including mobilizing alumni and professional associations—to advocate for loan repayment and deferment options tailored to meet the needs of professionals who choose to take a break from their careers in order to raise a family. For example, the existing Working Mother and Parental Leave deferments could be expanded by relaxing the austere financial and temporal eligibility requirements and lengthening the deferment period to a more meaningful three years.

V. Perceived Drawbacks

Some will see a renewed concern by graduate schools for family life as helping only women and not men, or helping neo-traditionalists and modernists who combine work and family but not traditionalists and post-modernists. But that is shortsighted. A culture shift in which employers cater to employees' workload and lifestyle concerns benefits everyone. Armed with a different set of expectations, students across the board will be better prepared to say no to a seventy- or eighty-hour workweek, whether they choose to be parents or not.

Many men also want to have families and to spend meaningful time with them. When cultures change, men gain the flexibility to spend more time with their families. But reduced time schedules and other family supports do not assist only those caring for children; they also assist professionals who support parents or spouses. In this way, men gain along with women, whether or not they have children.

These reforms most clearly benefit the neo-traditionalists and modernists, but they benefit the traditionalist as well. A woman who stops out of work to raise a family ultimately faces a number of opportunity costs, foremost among these how to cover massive loan repayments. Suspending loan repayment for three years would buy families time to adjust to new family demands and to find other ways to manage loan payments if the spouse who stopped out chose not to return to work.

These reforms also benefit post-modernists, albeit more indirectly. Clearly, very different choices may animate the decision to forego children. Some desire children but run out of time because they cannot attend to both work and family. One executive explains that "Looking back, I can't think why I allowed my career to obliterate my 30s. . . . I just didn't pay attention. I'm only just absorbing the consequences."[58] Opening a space for family and work may permit professional women to realize those desires. Others genuinely want to forego family. These proposals do not affect them in any direct sense. Yet these proposals may change the culture and the expectations of what it means to be a committed, full-time person, helping professionals who are uninterested in family—these professionals will, for example, be better positioned to demand time off to care for parents or even just to take meaningful vacations. Some may even welcome the opportunity to step up for a colleague on parental leave, to work the extra hours, shoulder the extra responsibility, and reap extra rewards.

Now, it is possible that family-friendly policies will short-change professionals without families, forcing them to take up the slack for parents on reduced schedules. It is not self-evident that this will occur, however. Not every accommodation leads to reduced effort by the beneficiary. With on-site daycare, parents can work *longer* hours. Moreover, reduced loads will not necessarily come at the expense of colleagues. Employers may hire another employee, instead of trying to cover the "shortfall" with the existing workforce.

VI. Conclusion

In the pressure cooker of big-money jobs, young professionals believe they face a stark choice: forego work or forego family. Nearly weekly media reports show record numbers of women leaving coveted, high-paying jobs. Less obvious, but arguably of greater concern, are the droves of women, and men, who are simply taking a pass on marriage and family. When family comes at the expense of work, society loses in tangible and intangible ways; these losses, however, may be a cost of having functioning, healthy families. But when family no longer makes sense to those in whom society has invested the most, society really loses. This abdication of family robs all of us of a vibrant, functioning community—weakening the economy, weakening families, weakening the professionals themselves.

The graduate professions have an opportunity to exercise leadership by modeling good behavior for our corporate counterparts and advocating for tangible family supports. Until educators transform the culture of graduate school and the expectations of young professionals, many professionals in business, law, and medicine will continue to struggle to balance demanding careers and family, often choosing one to the exclusion of the other. They should not be put to this choice.

Appendix

Table 1. Presently Married Women by Professional Association*

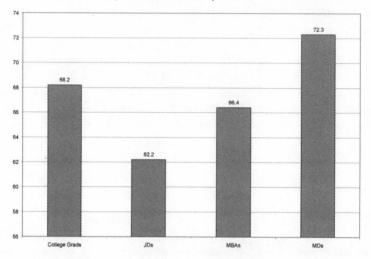

Table 2. Presently Married Professionals by Gender*

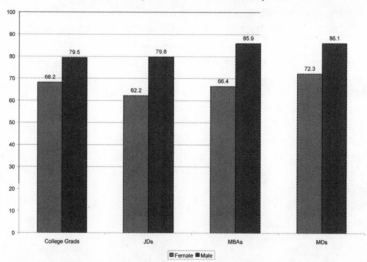

* P < .001 for each value

Table 3. Divorced or Separated Professionals by Gender*

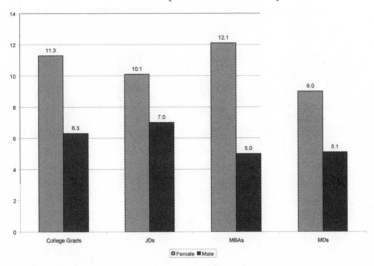

Table 4. Never Married Professionals by Gender*

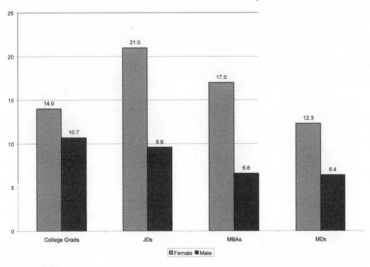

* P < .001 for each value

Table 5. Percentage of Professionals with Stay-at-Home Spouses by Gender*

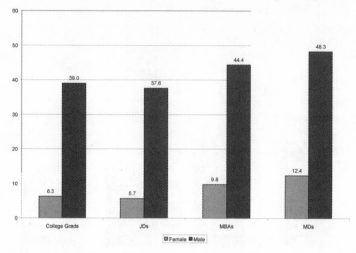

Table 6. Percentage of Professionals with Children by Employer Size**

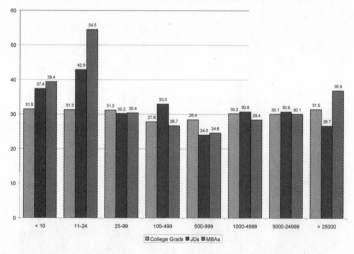

Original data on file with author.

* P < .001 for each value

** This table presents the raw data for professionals with children by employer size, using the coding in the original data set. When firm size is recoded into four categories (< 25, 25–99, 100–499, and > 500), differences in the percentage of professionals with children in various firm sizes were significant for doctors and all college graduates (p < or = .001), approached significance for lawyers (p = .06), and were not significant for MBAs.

Notes

* I am grateful to Erin Willoughby, Carolyn Hohn, and Garrett Ledgerwood for their painstaking research, to Sally Wieringa for her first-rate administrative assistance and technical expertise in creating the Appendix, and to John Keyser for assisting me with the data analysis presented in the Appendix.

1. The figures in this and the following paragraph are taken from Neil Gilbert, "What Do Women Really Want?" *The Public Interest*, January 2005, http://www.the publicinterest.com (also available at http://findarticles.com/p/articles/mi_m0377/ is_158/ai_n8680969); The National Association for Law Placement [NALP], "Partnership at Law Firms Elusive for Minority Women—Overall, Women and Minorities Make Small Gains," 8 November 2006, http://www.nalp.org/press/details.php?id=64; and Mona Harrington and Helen Hsi, "Women Lawyers and Obstacles to Leadership," Women's Bar Association of Massachusetts, April 2007, http://www.womensbar.org/ images/WBA/EC%20report%20summary.htm.

2. Sacha Pfeiffer, "Many Female Lawyers Dropping Off Path to Partnership," *Boston Globe*, 2 May 2007, third edition, p. 1A (discussing Harrington and Hsi, "Women Lawyers").

3. This and the other figures in this section are taken from an original data analysis of the 2003 National Survey of College Graduates (NSCG) (National Science Foundation, *2003 National Survey of College Graduates*, n.d., http://www.nsf.gov/statistics/ showsrvy.cfm?srvy_CatID=3&srvy_Seri=7), the findings of which are presented in the Appendix. The NSCG surveyed individuals born after September 30, 1927, who received a bachelor's degree or higher prior to April 1, 2000, and who were residing in the U.S. or its territories as of April 1, 2000. The analysis in the Appendix examines college graduates who went on to obtain an MBA, a JD, or an MD as their highest degree. It codes as JDs all individuals who were practicing as either lawyers or judges at the time of the survey (n=1894). It coded as MBAs all individuals whose highest degree was a master's degree that focused on business administration or management (n=3086), and coded as MDs all persons whose highest degree was a professional degree that was in the field of medicine (n=3928). This coding exempts, however, professionals who went on to get a higher degree—for instance, the MD who goes on to a PhD.

4. Judy Goldberg Dey and Catherine Hill, *Behind the Pay Gap* (Washington, D.C.: American Association of University Women Educational Foundation, 2007), 2.

5. Kirstin Downey Grimsley and R. H. Melton, "Full-Time Moms Earn Respect, Poll Says," *Washington Post*, 22 March 1998, final edition, sec. A, p. 16.

6. Catalyst, "Quick Takes: Work-Life Benefits," Catalyst Information Center, n.d., http://www.catalyst.org/files/quicktakes/Quick%20Takes%20-%20Work-Life.pdf; James T. Bond et al., *2005 National Study of Employers*, Families and Work Institute, n.d., http://familiesandwork.org/site/research/reports/2005nse.pdf. Despite disparities by gender, signs of improvement for men's benefits have emerged recently. Between 1998 and 2005, the maximum job-guaranteed leave for men after the birth of a child rose from 13.1 weeks to 14.5 weeks (Bond et al., *Study of Employers*, 10).

7. See Dey and Hill, *Behind the Pay Gap*, 17–18, (analyzing data from the U.S. Department of Education for over 9,000 students who graduated from college in 1992–1993; estimating that about a quarter of the pay gap can be attributed to gender alone;

and concluding that even "if a woman and a man make the same choices, . . . they [will not] receive the same pay").

8. Catalyst, "Work-Life Benefits"; Bond et al., *Study of Employers*. Original data, on file with author.

9. Catalyst, "Law Women Anticipate Leaving Their Employer Three Years Earlier Than Men," press release, 30 January 2001, http://www.catalyst.org/pressroom/press_releases/women_in_law.htm, citing Catalyst, *Women in Law: Making the Case* (New York: Catalyst, 2001).

10. Sylvia Ann Hewlett and Carolyn Buck Luce, "Off-Ramps and On-Ramps Keeping Talented Women on the Road to Success," *Harvard Business Review*, March 2005, 46.

11. U.S. Department of Labor, Office of the Assistant Secretary for Policy, *Balancing the Needs of Families and Employers: The Family and Medical Surveys 2000 Update*, by Westat (Washington, D.C.: Government Printing Office, 2001), 2.2.4, http://www.dol.gov/ESA/WHD/fmla/fmla.

12. Deborah L. Rhode, *Balanced Lives: Changing the Culture of Legal Practice* (Chicago: American Bar Association, Commission on Women in the Profession, 2001), n. 99.

13. Phyllis Moen and Stephen Sweet, "The New Workforce, the New Economy, and the Lock-Step Life Course: An American Dilemma," (working paper, no. 02-21, Cornell University, College of Human Ecology, 2002), 3; Juliet Schor, "Time Crunch among American Parents," in *Taking Parenting Public: The Case for a New Social Movement*, eds. Sylvia Ann Hewlett et al. (Lanham, Md.: Rowman and Littlefield, 2002), 83.

14. Linda R. Hirshman, "Homeward Bound," *The American Prospect*, December 2005, 20; Arlie Hochschild and Anne Machung, *The Second Shift: Working Parents and the Revolution at Home* (New York: Penguin, Viking Press, 1989), 271–79.

15. Catalyst, "Work-Life Benefits," 4; James T. Bond et al., *The National Study of the Changing Workforce* (New York: Families and Work Institute, 2003), 10.

16. See note 12 above.

17. Catalyst, "Work-Life Benefits," 3.

18. Harvard School of Public Health, "Globalization: Children and Working Parents Pay Too High a Price," press release, 27 February 2006, http://www.hsph.harvard.edu/news/press-releases/2006-releases/press02272006.html.

19. Jody Miller and Matt Miller, "Get A Life!" *Fortune*, 28 November 2005, 109–24.

20. Rhode, *Balanced Lives*, 15.

21. Sidney Evans, personal communication at Women's Retreat, Washington and Lee University School of Law, Lexington, Va., n.d.

22. Martin Carnoy, *Sustaining the New Economy: Work, Family, and Community in the Information Age* (Cambridge, Mass.: Harvard University Press, 2000), 111 (observing that the women's movement preceded the "new economy"); Mona L. Hymel, "Consumerism, Advertising, and the Role of Tax Policy," *Virginia Tax Review* 20 (Fall 2000): 347, 380–90.

23. Andrea Brandt et al., "Women Face an Unfair Choice: Career or Children," *Spiegel Online*, 5 May 2006, http://www.spiegel.de/international/spiegel/0,1518,41 4451,00.html.

24. The National Association for Law Placement [NALP], "Women and Attorneys of Color Continue to Make Small Gains at Large Law Firms," press release, 17 November 2005, http://www.nalp.org/press/details.php?id=57; Harrington and Hsi, "Women Lawyers," (discovering in a study of nearly 1,000 attorneys in Massachusetts firms over a five-year period "an extremely low number of women among equity partners—the present ratio being 17% women, 83% men,").

25. Jenny Anderson, "The Fork in the Road," *New York Times*, 6 August 2006, late edition: final, Money and Business section, p. 1, col. 2.

26. Ibid.

27. S. Jody Heymann and Alison Earle, "The Work-Family Balance: What Hurdles Are Parents Leaving Welfare Likely to Confront?" *Journal of Policy Analysis and Management* 17 (Spring 1998): 313, 314.

28. Joe G. Baker, "The Influx of Women into Legal Professions: An Economic Analysis," *Monthly Laboratory Review* 125 (August 2002): 14–24.

29. Kerry Miller, "Can Your Relationship Survive B-School?" *BusinessWeek.com*, 13 February 2007, http://www.businessweek.com/bschools/content/feb2007/bs2007 0213_189035.htm.

30. See Association of American Medical Colleges, "Table 15: Applicant Age at Anticipated Matriculation, 2003–2006," *FACTS—Applicants, Matriculants, and Graduates*, 27 October 2006, http://www.aamc.org/data/facts/2006/2006age.htm.

31. Miller, "Can Your Relationship Survive?"

32. Graduate Management Admission Council, *MBA Alumni Perspectives Survey: April 2006 Comprehensive Data Report* (MacLean, Va.: Graduate Management Admission Council, 2006), 1-2, http://www.gmac.com/NR/rdonlyres/CD1B44D6-9DB9 -4589-9A86-7A7CFC1379BB/0/MBAAlumni_April06_DataReport.pdf.

33. Ha T. Tu and Paul B. Ginsburg, "Losing Ground: Physician Income 1995–2003: Tracking Report No. 15," Center for Studying Health System Change, June 2006, under Table 2: Average Hours per Week Spent on Medically Related Activities, 1995– 2003, http://www.hschange.org/CONTENT/851/#table2.

34. The National Association for Law Placement [NALP], *2006–2007 NALP Directory of Legal Employers* (Washington, D.C.: National Association for Law Placement, 2006).

35. Accreditation Council for Graduate Medical Education, "ACGME Duty Hours Standards Fact Sheet," n.d., http://www.acgme.org/acWebsite/newsRoom/newsRm_ dutyHours.asp.

36. Hewlett and Luce, "Off-Ramps," 64.

37. Graduate Management Admission Council, *MBA Alumni Perspectives Survey: September 2006 Comprehensive Data Report* (MacLean, Va.: Graduate Management Admission Council, 2006), 12, http://www.gmac.com/NR/rdonlyres/875284A0 -99CF-4E9C-9211-9A6244367174/0/MBAAlumniDataReportSept06.pdf (accessed 6 August 2007).

38. The National Association for Law Placement [NALP], *2006 Associate Salary Survey* (Washington, D.C.: National Association for Law Placement, 2006), 11.

39. PayScale, "Salary Survey Report for People with Jobs as Physicians/Doctors," n.d., http://www.payscale.com/research/US/People_with_Jobs_as_Physicians_%2f_ Doctors/Salary/by_Years_Experience (accessed 7 August 2007).

40. See PayScale, "Salary Survey Report for Job: Cardiac Surgeon," n.d., http://www.payscale.com/research/US/Job=Cardiac_Surgeon/Salary/show_all (accessed 7 August 2007), listing the average salary for a cardiac surgeon with five to seven years' experience.

41. U.S. Department of Education, National Center for Education Statistics, *Student Financing of Graduate and First-Professional Education: 2003–2004 Profiles of Students in Selected Degree Programs and Part-Time Students,* by Susan P. Choy and Emily Forrest-Cataldi, statistical analysis report, NCES 2006185 (Washington, D.C.: National Center for Education Statistics, 2006), 61, 67, http://nces.ed.gov/pubs2006/2006185.pdf (accessed 7 August 2007). Swelling salaries also act as "golden handcuffs," consumed by expensive, high-maintenance lifestyles that require a lot of "bank" to support.

42. Gita Z. Wilder, "Law School Debt among New Lawyers," *After the JD* (Overland Park, Kans.: NALP Foundation for Law Career Research and Education; Washington, D.C.: National Association for Law Placement, 2007), 11.

43. Ibid., pp. 62, 69.

44. Pregnancy-info.net, "How Age Affects Fertility," n.d., http://www.pregnancy-info.net/age_and_fertility.html; Allison Van Dusen, "Men's and Women's Fertility Facts—Explained," *Forbes.com,* 11 April 2007, http://www.forbes.com/2007/04/10/fertility-men-women-forbeslife-cx_avd_0411fertility.html.

45. Robin Fretwell Wilson, "Uncovering the Rationale for Requiring Infertility in Surrogacy Arrangements," *American Journal of Law and Medicine* 29, no. 2 and 3 (2003): 337–62.

46. Hewlett and Luce, "Off-Ramps," 285.

47. Susan Sturm, "The Architecture of Inclusion: Advancing Workplace Equity in Higher Education," *Harvard Journal of Law and Gender* 29 (Summer 2006): 256.

48. Beth Sullivan, Carol Hollenshead, and Gilia Smith, "Developing and Implementing Work-Family Policies for Faculty," *Academe* 90 (November-December 2004), http://www.aaup.org/AAUP/pubsres/academe/2004/ND/FEAT/04ndsulli.htm (accessed 21 September 2007).

49. Leland Stanford Jr. University Board of Trustees, "Childbirth Accommodation Policy for Women Graduate Students at Stanford University," *Stanford Graduate Student Handbook,* under Section 3: Important University Policies: Other Policies, n.d., http://www.stanford.edu/dept/DoR/GSH/childbirth_policy.pdf (accessed 26 November 2007).

50. Miller, "Can Your Relationship Survive?"

51. Anderson, "Fork in the Road."

52. Proceeds from the investing of endowment funds are often used to fund construction projects and new teaching positions, as well as financial aid for students. See Adrian Campo-Flores, "So Nicely Endowed," *Newsweek,* 1 August 2004, http://www.newsweek.com/id/54660 (accessed 10 September 2007).

53. See Hewlett and Luce, "Off-Ramps," 16.

54. See, e.g., Vault's Top 110 Law Firms survey (Vault.com, "Top 100 Law Firms: 2007 Rankings," n.d., http://www.vault.com/nr/lawrankings.jsp?law2007=1&ch_id=242); the *Working Mother* 100 Best Companies survey (Working Mother Media, "Methodology: What Makes a Winner," Working Mother, n.d., http://www.workingmother.com/web?service=vpage/85); *The American Lawyer*'s Annual Midlevel

Associates Survey (Tom Brouksou, "Midlevel Associates Methodology," *The American Lawyer,* 1 August 2007, http://www.law.com/jsp/law/LawArticleFriendly.jsp?id= 1185820706978); and the Avery Index (AveryIndex, "2007 Family 25: The Top Family Friendly Firms," n.d., http://www.averyindex.com/2007_family_friendly.php).

55. See U.S. Department of Education, "Federal Family Education Loan (FFEL) Program: Deferment," 34 CFR [Code of Federal Regulations] §682.210 (Washington, D.C.: Government Printing Office, n.d.).

56. Senate, *Higher Education Access Act of 2007,* 110th Cong., 1st sess., S.R. 1762.

57. FinAid Page, LLC, "Income Based Repayment," FinAid!: The SmartStudent Guide to Financial Aid, n.d., http://www.finaid.org/loans/ibr.phtml (accessed 10 September 2007).

58. Silvia Ann Hewlett, "Executive Women and the Myth of Having It All," *Harvard Business Review,* April 2002, 71.

Chapter Nine

LEADING WITH ETHICS:
THE COOPERATIVE MODEL AND THE
EXAMPLE OF WORKPLACE SAFETY

Sean Kelsey and
Thomas R. Krause

Making businesses ethical means changing behavior, which in a corporate setting means changing culture. This is the work of leadership, and like all leadership is a matter of turning a vision into a reality. As such, it requires *having* a vision, and being able to communicate that vision effectively.

In a business setting, communicating an ethical vision can be tricky. People who care about ethics have their own personal reasons for doing so, and it is not always easy to articulate them in a vocabulary that will be compelling to an organization composed of individuals with diverse values and points of view. For this reason it is tempting to fall back on the law, justifying a professional concern about ethics by appeal to recent legislation and regulations. After all, the law is an impersonal objective feature of the business and social landscape, visible to everyone. The trouble is that a legalistic approach stands at odds with the vision that business leaders who care about ethics want to communicate. Quite apart from the fact that not everything unethical is illegal, the emphasis on "law" and "compliance" fosters the attitude that ethical rules lie outside the mainstream of business conduct and impose arbitrary, artificial, external constraints that make little sense from a business point of view; that although we abide by them when we must, in order to stay out of trouble, they are otherwise annoyances and obstacles to be gotten around.

Another approach, familiar from the academic literature, speaks in terms of a "theory" on which ethics is part and parcel of business. Think for example of stakeholder theory and Corporate Social Responsibility[1] (or CSR) and neo-Aristotelian approaches and their appeals to "virtue."[2] The trouble with these approaches, we believe, is that the theories of business with which they operate are unrealistic and as a result often give rise to cynicism. Reasonable people find it difficult to believe that all the talk about "community" or "environment" or "virtue" is for real, and conclude that it is not for real but about a way to project a certain image. The predictable effect on organizational culture is not a renewed commitment to high ideals, but rather the sinking feeling of finding oneself complicit in a sham.

The challenge then is to find an idiom with which business leaders can articulate their ethical ideals effectively, in a way that appeals to a pluralistic audience and without being false to the nature of the business enterprise. The resources necessary to meet this challenge can be found close to home in reflection upon the origins of business. In brief, our argument is as follows: First, business is a fundamentally cooperative undertaking: an arrangement for the exchange of goods and services, freely chosen, for the mutual benefit of the parties involved. Second, it is not necessary to pretend that business has other, noncommercial, humanitarian objectives—that the aim of business is something other than making a profit. Businesses can articulate and defend their intolerance for bribery, embezzlement, nepotism, extortion, and the like by bringing out how such behavior transforms cooperative relationships into relationships of mistrust, antagonism, and exploitation. Third, we assert, based on strong evidence from empirical research in organizational behavior, that we know how to identify and change the elements of an organizational culture that predictably occasion unethical behavior. This problem has been encountered before, and dealt with effectively, in the form of the challenge to turn the workplace into a safe venue. It is not a pious hope to think that business leaders can make their ethical vision a reality in their own organizations. It is rather a practical expectation based on thirty years of positive experience in shaping organizational culture to foster workplace safety and sustainability.

I

We begin with two stories about the origins of cities, taken from Plato's *Republic*. Cities are the pre-eminent form of human association in Plato; they are the locus not only of politics and law but also of commerce. As such they provide a useful model for thinking about business.

The first story is ostensibly about the nature and origins of justice, but it also tells of the origins of law and of political communities more generally. The speaker, Glaucon, is playing devil's advocate, and his cynical account runs as follows:

> By nature doing wrong is good, and being wronged bad, but the bad that comes of being wronged exceeds the good that comes of doing it. Thus when people do wrong to, and are wronged by, one another, and have a taste of both, those who are not powerful enough to do the one and avoid the other think it will profit them to make a deal with one another not to do or suffer injustice. This is the beginning of legislation and contracts;

what the law enjoins we call "lawful" and "just" and this is the nature and origin of justice—an intermediate between the best, which is to do injustice without paying the penalty, and the worst, which is to suffer injustice while being powerless to avenge oneself. We value justice, which is in-between these, not as something good, but as something to be honored because we are not strong enough to do injustice. No one capable of doing injustice, no real man, would make a deal neither to do nor to suffer injustice—that would be insanity.[3]

Regarding Glaucon's speech, we note three things. First, on this telling, human associations arise out of conflict and strife; the pre-existing dynamic between the parties involved is essentially antagonistic and violent. In this respect the passage presages Hobbes's *Leviathan* and his warning that, absent such associations, human life will be "solitary, poor, nasty, brutish, and short."[4]

Second, the purpose of these associations is to put a halt to the increasing disintegration of the parties' collective fortunes, which results from the fact that none of them is alone powerful enough to win a decisive victory. In other words, the "contract" by which the association is constituted is essentially a truce—a compromise between "the best, which is to do injustice without paying the penalty, and the worst, which is to suffer injustice while powerless to avenge oneself."

Third, once the association is established, the underlying dynamic remains antagonistic. The "peace" born of this association is only superficial; it is better than the alternatives lying within reach, but not better than the alternatives we can imagine (and sometimes, sporadically, taste).

This is a fair statement of how a jaded and cynical public nowadays thinks about business. We want to contrast it with a second story, also taken from the *Republic*, but differing markedly in tone from the first. The speaker this time is Socrates, and he is brief and to the point:

The origin of cities lies in the fact that none of us is self-sufficient, but we all need many things. Thus we ally ourselves, with one person for one need, with another for another; and since the things we need are many, many of us gather into one dwelling as partners and helpers. We call this common dwelling a city, and people give things, and (when they do) receive things in exchange, each thinking this better for himself.[5]

Although both stories locate the origins of cities in a kind of agreement or contract, the differences between them are significant. First, Socrates argues that human associations arise in a situation not of conflict and strife but of need. There is no pre-existing dynamic between the parties—they start out in a condition of comparative isolation. Second, the purpose of these associations is not to halt a decline, but positively to improve the collective fortunes of the parties involved, by means of the creation and exchange of goods for mutual benefit. Third, from the outset, the underlying dynamic in these associations is essentially voluntary and cooperative. Violence, antagonism, and exploitation are completely foreign to the spirit of the original enterprise.

We believe this second story provides manifestly the better model for thinking about the nature and origin of business. "Better" means not just more salutary, but also more realistic: a truer representation of the spirit of the commercial enterprise. Entrepreneurs do not typically begin their joint undertakings by calling a truce. Nor do the relationships within developing organizations, and those between them and their suppliers, clients, and customers, typically begin in a spirit of mutual antagonism. The underlying original dynamic of the enterprise is not one of mutual violence and exploitation, but one of cooperation for mutual benefit.

Although this is a modest point, it is important. It provides a useful and workable framework for talking about ethics in business.

II

We are all familiar with the tired assertion that the very idea of "business ethics" is an oxymoron: that talk of "ethics" and "morality" is not realistic because ethical norms are at best irrelevant, and at worst inimical to the pragmatic values that organize business practice. It is true that there are pragmatic reasons for businesses to care about ethics. Recent legislation mandates the implementation of ethics programs; recent studies indicate the value of a reputation for fairness, integrity, and trustworthiness to long-term sustainability; the rapid growth of information technology makes keeping malfeasance secret increasingly difficult.[6] However, it is not hard to see that legislation provides reasons for compliance, but not for genuine ethical reform, and that while the value of reputation and the growth of information technology give businesses a reason to polish their reputations, reputation is often but indirectly related to underlying realities. Thus it is no surprise to find that businesses use most of the resources they spend on ethics on ensuring compliance and projecting a public image. This seems to confirm the tired line that in business the only motive that matters is the profit-motive.

The standard reply to this skepticism is to enlarge our conception of business—to urge that the business of business is not primarily or exclusively making money. After all, it is said, businesses do not exist in a vacuum; they are situated in a larger social environment, an environment that is deliberately structured in ways that permit them to arise and help them to flourish, and along with this favor comes responsibility. It is also said that although many people enter business to make money, many find their professional work fulfilling in other ways as well. It provides them an arena in which they can exercise their talents and realize their values, and for them work becomes not just a way of *earning* a living, but part and parcel of life itself. In this way the values people prize in private life, among them ethical values, become integral to the business enterprise as they conceive of it. The standard reply is, in short, that business and ethics seem related at best indirectly because we are operating with a small-minded and impoverished conception of business—business is not exclusively about making a profit.

We believe this reply at best secondary. Most people enter business and stay in it primarily to make a living, and although societies do take measures to encourage business, they do so primarily because business creates wealth, not because it can save the environment or accomplish other humanitarian ends.[7] Many people *do* flourish in the workplace and find personal fulfillment in their professional avocations,[8] and businesses can and do accomplish things not easily or efficiently done by individuals or government. Nevertheless, it is important to recognize these valuable side-benefits for what they are: side-benefits.[9] To say that the company's first commitment is to "social responsibility" or "virtue and personal fulfillment" is to risk being regarded by serious people as a fanatic, a fool, a fraud, or all three. It is not an effective way to communicate an ethical vision.

We take it as axiomatic, then, that businesses are partnerships primarily for making money—that is their point and purpose. But this does not mean that businesses are somehow intrinsically amoral or immoral. *Making* money is not the same thing as *taking* it by force or deception. That's the difference between business and organized crime. Though both are partnerships for getting money, one simply *seizes* its profits, by theft, extortion, or violence, by hook or by crook, while the other *earns* its profits in exchange for goods and services, on terms that have been mutually and voluntarily agreed upon in advance. Crime is by nature violent and antagonistic: the parties from which it seizes its profits are victims. Business, by contrast, is essentially peaceful and cooperative: the parties from which it earns its profits are willing partners in an exchange for mutual benefit. The fundamental dynamic is not exploitative but cooperative.

In short, to explain why ethics matters in business, it is not necessary to pretend that businesses are something they are not: high-minded, altruistic, social do-gooders or Aristotelian city-states bent on fostering virtue in their citizens. It is enough (and a lot) to insist that although business is all about profits, it is about *earning* profits in exchange for goods and services, on terms agreed upon willingly in a spirit of cooperation and not about *seizing* profits in a spirit of hostility, antagonism, exploitation, deception, and violence.[10] (We do not deny that some forms of global enterprise do violence to the people and resources of developing countries.) We may condemn bribery, fraud, deceit, embezzlement, nepotism, extortion, and so on, not just because they are immoral, or illegal, or embarrassing, or short-sighted, but because they are also bad business. They corrode the nature and spirit of the business enterprise by transforming cooperative exchange into antagonism and exploitation; they turn what began as alliances and partnerships—with clients, suppliers, stockholders, supervisors, colleagues, support staff, what have you—into unlawful relationships with accomplices or victims. This result follows even if business is conceived narrowly as a partnership for making money.

In a phrase, the reason ethics matters in business is that ethical norms and values, far from being arbitrary and artificial constraints on cooperation, are its prerequisites. To put the point another way: *ethics is native to business,* not by virtue of its secondary, noncommercial aims, but by virtue of its cooperative form.

III

Most people in business, even those in it principally for the money, will identify with this conception of their enterprise. (Those who don't are criminals, or at least would-be criminals.) That is, they can be brought to see that ethical values are intrinsic to the enterprise *as they themselves conceive of it.*

Some will object (Glaucon-like) that this conception of business as a fundamentally cooperative undertaking is idealistic, not true to life, that it is no more realistic than the familiar academic approaches that focus on "virtue" or "social responsibility." What distinguishes businesses from syndicates of organized crime, the objection runs, is that businesses operate within the confines of the law. When businesses *can* legally seize profits by deceit or coercion, they do so; indeed, even when they can't do so legally, they often do so anyway, when they think they can get away with it undetected, or when they think they can bribe or intimidate potential whistle-blowers. Let's stop pretending, it might be urged, and lift the veil: in both business and crime the controlling dynamic is essentially predatory and exploitive; the only difference is that the one is lawful, the other lawless. But this difference is arbitrary and inessential—both activities are about essentially the same game.

So, the objection concludes, ethics is *not* native to business, not when business is viewed in the clear, realistic light of day. On the contrary, ethics is just what it appears to be: a source of externally imposed *constraints* on business, justified from a point of view business must regard as at best alien and at worst hostile. When businesses operate within these constraints, they do so out of a sense of necessity and compromise; were circumstances more favorable, had they the power to act otherwise with impunity, they would.

We reply that although this is a fair caricature, with few exceptions it is no more than that. The vast majority of businessmen and women are not would-be criminals. This is revealed by the values they prize and cherish, by their understanding of the kind of people they wish to be, and the kinds of lives they want to live. Most people in business are not the sort who would stoop at anything, if only they could get away with it. Their ethical values and ideals are not well-characterized by the vocabulary of "necessity" and "compromise." On the contrary: this vocabulary best describes their attitude toward injustice and wrongdoing.[11] Glaucon's cynical story has it exactly backwards.

IV

Of course this approach does not solve every problem. Business brings us into contact with many people with whom we are not, properly speaking, doing business. It would be strange to suppose that a just appreciation of our rights and responsibilities in relation to these people will fall out of reflection upon the nature of the business enterprise. The ethical norms governing our non-commercial relationships are grounded in other, noncommercial facts, e.g., that the persons in question are family, or neighbors, or fellow citizens, or human beings. (Our responsibilities as stewards of the environment are likewise rooted in broader considerations.)

How can we talk about these issues credibly in a business setting? It's a mistake to fall back on legalistic, compliance-driven ways of thinking. Even where there is an effective legal system, an emphasis on "compliance" sends the wrong message: that ethical rules are to be compromised wherever needed and possible. Likewise it is a mistake to pretend that the aims of business are altruistic, humanitarian, and grandiose. If we try to anchor our responsibilities not to coerce or exploit or mistreat other people in some make-believe, altruistic, grandiose, humanitarian objectives, the effect will be to make the former seem as unreal as are (usually) the latter.

Our responsibilities are rooted in (at the very least) in our common humanity. We do not exploit children, because that is inhumane and monstrous.[12] We do not bribe public officials, or murder political leaders, or enslave populations, or prostitute our children, because such actions are vile and corrupt; our humanity cries out against them. Even bribery, though ubiquitous, is done in secret, or under cover of euphemism.

The best way to talk effectively about these issues in a business setting is to take the high road by making a frank appeal to common decency, mostly just by drawing attention to the pertinent facts, not whitewashed and sugarcoated, but told as they are. They must also deal with the institutional structures that make their people feel compelled to look away from the plain facts, or to suppress or contravene their sense of decency.

Perhaps some will object that this is too idealistic—that, for example, a policy of not paying bribes is in effect a policy not to do business in developing countries. No doubt this is in some cases true, though perhaps not as often as is thought. If paying a bribe is always the easy way out, it is not always the only way out—companies often have more leverage and clout than they exercise.

However, even where paying a bribe *is* the only way out, does it follow that we must just roll over and pay the bribe? Everyone draws a line somewhere; virtually no one would prostitute his or her own children as the unavoidable cost, the *sine qua non* of doing business in a culture that required it.

And if we must draw a line somewhere, what is to stop us from drawing it where it belongs: at offering no affront to human dignity? If we are willing to cross that line, not out of fear and compulsion but from deliberate calculation, we prove ourselves willing to cross any line. And if we cross that line because we turn our eye from the plain facts—if we "just don't go there"—the effect is just the same.

V

Enough about how to articulate and justify ethical norms and values in a business setting. The practical objective is to make that vision a reality. Is this at all feasible? After all, venality and corruption are permanent fixtures of the human landscape, and they often find fertile soil in the business world. How can the attempt to make businesses more ethical not seem hopelessly quixotic? Though the scandals we hear about with depressing regularity provide little encouragement, the practical problem of reducing or eliminating incidents of corporate ethical malfeasance is a problem we already know how to solve.

Accidents happen and people get hurt. They happen in quarries, they happen in factories, they happen in hospitals. Fatigue, inattention, carelessness, badly designed systems and processes, bad luck are endemic to the human condition. The idea that we could reform our quarries, our factories, our hospitals, so as to virtually eliminate the incidence of life-altering accidents, in a word, to make them *safe*—the prospects of this are about as likely as the prospects of making businesses ethical.

So thought many business leaders thirty years ago, and so think many even today. And yet the fact remains that this pessimism about safety is simply misplaced. In a given industrial setting, we know the types of accident that are most typical and costly in human and financial terms; we know how to isolate and identify the antecedent behaviors that give rise to them; we know how to isolate and identify the specific behavioral elements of the culture that permit these behaviors and even give them incentives; and we know how to implement in a systematic way the changes necessary in order to eliminate these behaviors almost completely. This claim has been demonstrated empirically.[13]

Some perhaps will worry that ethics is different. In the wake of recent scandals, businesses have been trying to reform their practices, to make them more ethical, and recent legislation mandating various schemes for reform are being implemented, at considerable cost—with limited success. Often such schemes are met with diffidence or hostility on the part of employees and their supervisors, and so far they do not appear to have been terribly effective.

The reply to this concern is straightforward: the difference between business ethics and industrial safety lies in the *methods* applied in the two arenas. The great progress made in industrial safety is the result of organizational change strategies that aim at leadership, culture, and behavior change; in ethics nothing comparable has even been tried. Yet the analogy between ethics and safety is broad and deep. Ethical scandals are the exact analog of industrial accidents. Both are strongly related to cultural influence, which in turn is related to leadership capability. Both have behavioral antecedents; like all behaviors, these antecedents can be observed and are intelligible in light of their perceived consequences. These perceptions in turn can be discovered and measured, and what is more they can be changed, via concrete and specific changes made to the systems and behaviors to which they are the sensible and intelligent reaction. The implementation of such changes can be monitored, as can the perceptions and behaviors they are designed to produce or avoid; interventions can be modified and fine-tuned in an ongoing process until they succeed in their intended effects. The time is ripe—companies now have incentives—to begin applying these methods in the area of ethics.

It might be objected that ethics is not likely to be amenable to such techniques, because ethical conduct is not easily quantified. To us this objection seems uninformed. Ethical conduct narrowly conceived—for example, abstention from petty theft, false accounting, or bribery—is no less amenable to definition and measurement than other, broader forms of pro-social organizational behavior, manifesting such qualities as sportsmanship, organizational loyalty, and civic virtue. Yet these and other such behaviors are even now the subject of a flourishing body of empirical research.[14] For this reason we persevere in our confidence that the methods that have proved so successful in improving organizational safety can be similarly successful in improving corporate ethics. If there's a will, there's a way.

VI

If changing an organization's behavior means changing its culture, the way to change culture is, first and foremost, to change the behavior of leadership. Culture involves attitudes and values, not just behavior, but it is behavior that we can directly and objectively define, measure, and change, and it is the behavior of leadership in particular that most determines the shape of an organization's attitudes and values. Thus the way to make organizations more ethical is to cultivate in their leadership the behaviors that strengthen and support an ethical culture.

Though this may seem like a truism, it adumbrates a practical strategy whose effectiveness has been demonstrated empirically.[15] Recent research has identified the factors of organizational behavior that most affect organizational culture and improve safety.[16] These factors include procedural justice (whether matters are resolved fairly), leader-member exchange (the quality and character of upward and downward communication), management credibility (the consistency of what is *said* with what is *done*), teamwork (the effectiveness of work-teams), work-group relations (the harmony of team working relationships), and upward communication (the ease of speaking to superiors on difficult matters). These factors have been measured, managed, and coached in many organizations, both domestic and overseas, moving unsafe organizations into a sustainable state of worker safety, and moving generally safe organizations from good to superior conditions of worker safety. Witness Alcoa under the leadership of Paul O'Neill during the period 1987–2002.[17]

These same dimensions of organizational behavior just spell out concretely what it means in a commercial setting to say that the form of the enterprise is fundamentally cooperative. For this reason they give board members—directors and trustees alike—a way to fulfill their responsibilities to establish and monitor the ethical culture of the companies they serve. They can do so by insisting on the establishment of ongoing mechanisms for measuring, reporting, and coaching specific behaviors, so that they become normal practice and receive consistent, reinforcing feedback from the culture shaped by the organization's leadership. With interventions of the quality, depth, and duration that have improved industrial safety, we can also expect to see material and sustainable improvements in commercial ethics as well.

Notes

1. See, for example, Michael Porter and Mark Kramer, "Strategy and Society: The Link between Competitive Advantage and Corporate Social Responsibility," *Harvard Business Review*, December 2006, 78–92.

2. See, for example, Robert C. Solomon, *A Better Way to Think about Business: How Personal Integrity Leads to Corporate Success* (New York: Oxford University Press, 1999), xxiii.

3. Plato *Republic* 358E–359A (our translation).

4. Thomas Hobbes, *Leviathan*, ed. Edwin Curley (Indianapolis, Ind.: Hackett Publishing, 1994), 76.

5. Plato *Republic* 369B–C (our translation).

6. See Thomas L. Friedman, "The Whole World Is Watching," *New York Times*, 27 June 2007, final edition, Editorial Desk section, p. 23.

7. See Milton Friedman, "A Friedman Doctrine: The Social Responsibility of Business Is to Increase Its Profits," *The New York Times Magazine*, 13 September 1970,

17ff., where Friedman argues that individual businessmen lack a mandate to pursue such ends.

8. Nor do we deny that this is a good thing. Given the time most of us spend working, and given that much of our "free time" is spent recuperating so that we can return to the fray, it would be a shame if work were nothing but labor and toil; we would be left with virtually no time to spend *living* the living we had worked so hard to earn.

9. Indeed, the fulfillment many of us find at work is bound up inextricably with the narrowly defined objectives we come together at work to pursue in the first place. We enjoy cultivating and deploying our professional expertise, overcoming obstacles, working with others we admire and respect for their creativity, intelligence, efficiency, energy, and perseverance; we derive a sense of satisfaction in being part of something bigger than we are, on a scale beyond the capacities of any one man or woman; we take pride in a spirit of professionalism and a job well-done; and so on. These side benefits come with being part of a well-run organization, and we risk *losing* precisely these benefits if we take our eye off the task at hand in order to focus on our own personal fulfillment.

10. See, for example, the work of Sebastião Salgado at Sebastião Salgado, n.d., http://www.terra.com.br/sebastiaosalgado/.

11. See, for example, Barbara Ley Toffler, ed., *Tough Choices: Managers Talk Ethics* (New York: John Wiley and Sons, 1986).

12. Acknowledging that it took at least one hundred years of legislation and regulation (roughly 1832–1938) to bring about the effective control of child labor in the U.S.; for a succinct history of child labor laws, see The University of Iowa Labor Center, "Child Labor in U.S. History," Child Labor Public Education Project, n.d., http://www.continuetolearn.uiowa.edu/laborctr/child_labor/about/us_history.html.

13. See T. R. Krause, K. J. Seymour, and K. C. M. Sloat, "Long-Term Evaluation of a Behavior-Based Method for Improving Safety Performance: A Meta-Analysis of 73 Interrupted Time-Series Replications," *Safety Science* 32 (April 1999): 1–18.

14. For recent reviews, see Philip M. Podsakoff et al., "Organizational Citizenship Behaviors: A Critical Review of the Theoretical and Empirical Literature and Suggestions for Future Research," *Journal of Management* 26, no. 3 (2000): 513–63; Brian J. Hoffman et al., "Expanding the Criterion Domain? A Quantitative Review of the OCB Literature," *Journal of Applied Psychology* 92 (March 2007): 555–66.

15. See Thomas R. Krause, *Leading with Safety* (Hoboken, N.J.: John Wiley and Sons, Wiley Interscience, 2005).

16. See, for example, M. Dodsworth et al., "Organizational Climate Metrics as Safety, Health, and Environment Performance Indicators and an Aid to Relative Risk Ranking within Industry," *Process Safety and Environmental Protection: Transactions of the Institution of Chemical Engineers Part B* 85 (January 2007): 59–69; Edgar H. Schein, *Organizational Culture and Leadership* (San Francisco: Jossey-Bass Publishers, 1985); David A. Hoffmann and Frederick P. Morgeson, "Safety-Related Behavior as a Social Exchange: The Role of Perceived Organizational Support and Leader-Member Exchange," *Journal of Applied Psychology* 84 (April 1999): 286–96.

17. See Sandy Smith, "America's Safest Companies: 17 Award Winners Share Best Practices," *Occupational Hazards,* October 2002, 47–62; see also Michael Arendt, "How O'Neill Got Alcoa Shining," *Business Week,* 5 February 2001, 39.

PART THREE

Teaching Ethics in Business School

Chapter Ten

BUSINESS AS A HUMAN ENTERPRISE: IMPLICATIONS FOR EDUCATION[1]

R. Edward Freeman and David Newkirk

THE CHALLENGES facing business education grow out of a fundamental misunderstanding of the nature of business itself: business is a thoroughly human institution, but business schools and business scholars rarely recognize this. Much current research and teaching treats business as a deterministic phenomenon, and management as a science. By embracing business as a human institution and management as a creative act, we can correct many of the problems identified in the modern critiques of management scholarship and education.

We begin with a brief, stylized history of the business academy, primarily in the United States, where it finds its most dominant form and, historically, its largest audience. We juxtapose this history with the tremendous changes that have occurred in business over the last forty to fifty years, and suggest that the time is ripe for change. Next we demonstrate that recent critiques rest on a faulty and outmoded view of business. Using stakeholder theory, we argue that we need a new approach, most easily characterized as "business as a human activity." We suggest two central questions and four problems business education must place front and center. We then discuss how we might draw on all of the disciplines of the academy for a more robust and useful view of business, and more powerful research and educational tools.

I. A Brief History of Business Schools in the United States[2]

Management education is a recent, relatively unexamined, phenomenon. One can identify at least four distinct periods in the United States leading up to the current state of chaos.

The Formative Period. While there is a great deal of debate about the original purpose of business schools, we argue that their original purpose was grounded in the idea of moral education. According to L. C. Marshall, one of the earliest proposals for a collegiate business school was made by Robert E. Lee, the first president of what is today Washington and Lee University.[3] (The proposal was not put into action.) Lee's idea was not confined to the business details of bookkeeping and the like "but [aimed] to teach the principles of commerce, economy, trade, and mercantile law." At its very beginning the American collegiate business school sought to articulate and teach the basic principles of commerce and economics, as well as their counterparts in the law.

The Wharton School of the University of Pennsylvania was founded in 1881 with funds from the steel magnate Joseph Wharton and the number of business schools rapidly increased in the next forty years in both the United States and Europe. Francis Ruml argued that the existence of business courses in secondary schools and so-called commercial colleges made it easy and natural for the university and collegiate schools of business to focus their attention more on professional and social ends; to place an emphasis upon dealing with the complicated social organization in which the businessman does his work; and to accept as its objective the training of persons with a social point of view for executive and professional positions in business.[4]

Business schools produced several results, such as (1) replacing the apprenticeship system, largely dismantled by the industrial revolution; (2) training businesspeople in the fundamentals of scientific management; (3) addressing the growing need for financial as opposed to industrial administration; and (4) training an elite capable of managing more complex social organizations.[5]

Ruml summarized Joseph Wharton's initial stated purpose as being "to establish means for imparting a liberal education in all matters concerning Finance and Economy."[6] In his address to the trustees of the newly formed Wharton School, Wharton remarked: "It is reasonable to expect that adequate education in the principles underlying successful business management would greatly aid in producing a class of men likely to become pillars of the state, whether in private or public life." And on this original theme of imparting "moral education" to managers, Ruml approvingly quotes E. P. Cubberly's *History of Education*:

> As the industrial life of the nation has become more diversified, its parts narrower, and its processes more concealed, new and more extended training has been called for to prepare young people to meet the intricacies and interdependencies of political and industrial and social groups and to point out to them the importance of each one's part in the national and industrial organization.[7]

The American Assembly of Collegiate Schools of Business (AACSB), founded in 1916, reinforced this idea of a liberal education for business people by requiring accredited schools to require students to take at least 40 percent of their credit hours in subjects other than economics and commerce. In speaking to their 1927 conference, Alfred North Whitehead echoed the view that management was ready for professional education, if we only knew what it was:

Universities have trained clergy, medical men, lawyers, engineers. Business is now a highly intellectualized vocation, so it well fits into the series. There is, however, this novelty: the curriculum suitable for a business school, and the various modes of activity of such a school, are still in the experimental stage.[8]

To reinforce the argument that that original purpose of business schools was grounded in the idea of moral education, consider Joseph Wharton's original plan. Wharton proposed and implemented a program to take humanities faculty, trained in the liberal arts, and put them in the classroom to teach business subjects. This experiment, tried in 1882, failed miserably, according to Ruml, because the liberal arts professors were resentful and did not necessarily believe that knowledge should be practical. (This attempt to found a business school on the capabilities and resources of a liberal arts institution has been repeated more recently at Yale and Oxford, both of whom recapitulated the history, ultimately replacing professors from the parent institution with dedicated business academics.) By 1883 the Wharton School had hired instructors versed in business, leaving the ensuing one hundred–plus years barren of meaningful interchange between business and the humanities.

The early history of business schools is rife with arguments about the same controversies that dominate today's discourse. Should faculty be trained in economics? Were graduate economics departments sources of ignorance about business? Could business people be used as adjunct professors, and if so, how many? What was the proper balance between research and consulting? Should the study of business be scientific, or largely storytelling? Was business to be a profession with established ethical norms, or were schools of business merely to socialize students into the practices of business and prepare them for the world of work?

Unspoken are the questions of what is the nature of business itself, and therefore of management and leadership, an essential foundation for addressing the challenge of how best to develop people for these roles. Is management, as Whitehead's comments might imply, a profession, with a body of knowledge to be mastered? Or is it a craft, with skills to be learned?

While these questions are still relevant, the second period in the history of the American business school makes answering them all the more difficult.

The Scientific-Modern Period. Two well-known reports published in the late 1950s gave voice to a crisis of legitimacy in the business school. The Carnegie Report and the Ford Foundation study by R. A. Gordon and J. E. Howell both claimed that business schools needed academic legitimacy, and essentially proposed the adoption of a social sciences approach to the subject matter of business.

According to Thomas Mulligan, writing in an important 1987 retrospective in no less than *The Academy of Management Review*, these reports represented a turning point, where the culture of business schools became overtly scientific and, we would argue, adopted the positivism that underlay much of the scientific thinking of the period:

> The often unsubstantiated descriptive content of earlier business school curricula and research has been replaced by quantitative description based on rigorous data collection, computer-assisted mathematical modeling, and the foundational concepts of science—testable hypotheses (or, at least, testable networks of hypotheses), correlated observations, and causal explanation.[9]

The state of business schools, he argued, suggests a desperate need for something like the humanities, but the culture of science that emerged in the business schools has only recently begun to be challenged by the introduction of humanities-based ethics courses.

While Mulligan is correct that the culture of science dominates business schools, there is an alternative to his view that the two cultures of arts and sciences are incompatible. He rightly points out the emergence of "practitioner" books critical of the scientific approach, but there is more at issue here than practical criticism of academic abstractions.

The Porter-Peters Era. Two seemingly unrelated phenomena from 1980 through the 1990s catapulted business and business thinkers into the center of society and provided a countervailing force to the increasing scientism and irrelevance of business school research. The result was the emergence of another branch of business education, largely through bestsellers, consultants, corporate universities, learning centers, and the like.

The practical leadership in development of management techniques had moved outside the universities. DuPont had pioneered capital budgeting and return on investment calculations in 1903. The Navy created critical path management during World War II. In the fifties and sixties, GE established small business units and the processes for managing them. By the sixties, Bruce Henderson and BCG were offering services built around experience curves and growth-share matrices. All of these managerial innovations were rooted in an analytical view of business.[10]

In the 1970s, economist Michael Porter published his groundbreaking book *Competitive Strategy* on the economic basis of business strategy.[11] From this book, offering his theory of "the five forces of industry analysis," it was easy to reestablish the dialogue between social scientists such as Porter and businesspeople. He had a coherent narrative with real-life implications for executives and how they thought about their business.

During roughly the same period, Tom Peters and his colleagues at the consulting firm McKinsey and Company embarked on a study of why some organizations seemed to be successful year after year.[12] The report they produced formed the basis for Peters's and Robert Waterman's bestselling *In Search of Excellence*. Its power was, like that of Porter's theory, its systematic, albeit unscientific, narrative about what real companies and real leaders did and did not do to achieve success. *Search* was grounded in the real world and was coherent as a narrative, enhancing its believability.

Our argument is not that the scientific period is over in business schools. The existence of so-called scholarly journals, and the endless arguments in tenure committees about whether a particular journal is an "A, B, or C" journal, ensures an appetite for trivia in excess of either its production or its value. Porter and Peters show us the power of narrative, of telling a good story about how we can create and manage our organizations. Their financial success also shows the appetite for compelling business narrative. In short, they give us a basis for reintroducing the humanities in business education. The humanities contain powerful narratives and meta-narratives about human societies and cultures. These narratives are more or less coherent and more or less normative, as well as descriptive. Equally important, they are compelling to leaders and aspiring leaders.

The ensuing twenty-five–plus years have led to an explosion of the business bestseller, and the seminars and consulting firms telling these narratives. We have been treated to "business reengineering and process redesign," "customer intimacy and operational excellence," "being built to last" and "going from good to great," "managing stakeholders and stakeholder engagement," "supply chain management," "strategic alliances," and a host of other, oftentimes good and useful, ideas. During this time, the leader himself (or occasionally herself) has become the subject of inquiry, with their successful traits first described then, increasingly, prescribed. Companies have begun their own "corporate universities," both to teach business skills and to develop leadership, sometimes in conjunction with leading business schools, while the schools themselves have made commitments to executive education as a source of lucrative funding.

Recent Changes to Business and Business Schools. As business schools have evolved to become more self-contained and "scientific," alienated from both practice and from the rest of the university, the real world of business has changed greatly.[13]

Every industry has become more global. The coherence of business strategy is influenced by far-flung and disparate events in many corners of the globe. The purely analytical approach to strategy (such as the one advocated by Porter) has become less and less relevant. The issues of outsourcing jobs, government policy, supply chain management, value chain responsibility, environmentalism, and the rise of power of NGOs, are all now central to thinking about strategy. India and China have emerged as serious global players in business, with Russia and Brazil not too far behind. Every aspect of business, from brand values and communications to employee relations, operates in a changing cultural context.

The explosion of the Internet and the emergence of the dot-com companies laid waste to traditional ideas about how to start a business. Thousands of young people began to develop business plans for companies that were targeted to change people's behavior around ideas such as information, shopping, healthcare, and other basic facts of life. YAHOO!, Google, eBay, LendingTree, *Web*MD, are just a few among thousands of companies started either outside the traditional model of business, often by business school students who were pursuing very different aims from traditional businesses and their narrow "economics only" paradigm. And many of these start-ups were successful. IPOs were offered often before there was any revenue at all, and this flaunted the traditional way of thinking about a business.

Underneath the bubbling of the dot-com economy, business itself was changing. Information-age institutions looked fundamentally different from their industrial-age counterparts. Businesses seemed to be creating, rather than meeting, consumer needs. Financial resources were less critical than ideas and customers. Products were "co-created" with customers, and "extended enterprises" began competing in "eco-systems." The "physics" of business began to change. Companies lost mass through outsourcing. Geography began to disappear, and boundaries between markets became more permeable. And Internet time seemed to move faster than normal time. We seemed to be living in a world of creativity and unpredictability, rather than the predictable, repeatable phenomena of the past.

During roughly the same time period, we saw the fall of communist and socialist regimes all around the world. Bill Clinton's mantra, "It's the economy, stupid," became the watchword for developing capitalist economies, and business took on a renewed importance as a central institution for human interaction.

Concurrently, we have had several waves of scandal, from the Wall Street trading scandals of the late 1980s to the Enron genre of scandals in the late 1990s and early part of this century. Paralleling these scandals have been renewed interest in "corporate responsibility," "environmental sustainability," and issues such as "the public trust of business."

At the same time, there has been an explosion in the need for quasi-managerial white-collar labor familiar with the vocabulary and techniques of business and finance. There has been an equally rapid growth in the population of business schools to meet this need. As the armies of managers have grown, the MBA has become a qualification for both the officers and the foot soldiers, with little differentiation between the two.

The response of business schools has been to highlight how their MBA programs have been made "global," largely through exchange programs with students and faculty, "field trips," or a week or two in China or India. The schools also have made a token attempt to put ethics into the curriculum, although, repeating Joseph Wharton's experiment on a different scale, often taught by business school faculty untrained in ethics, or philosophy faculty untrained and uninterested in business. Some schools have adopted some new technology for "distance learning" to help meet growing demand at lower cost. The responses have, for the most part, been traditional disciplinary answers.

At the same time, we have the phenomena of "ratings" of business school and the adoption of techniques of corporate branding. To attract students paying higher prices in this more competitive market, schools have begun to worry about their "brand," their "image," and the means of differentiating. Business has changed on a massive scale during the last twenty-five years, and we believe that it is fair to say that business schools have simply "moved the deck." Consequently there is a malaise, whose true cause is difficult to pin down.

II. Recent Critiques of Business Education

The dominant narrative of business schools, rooted in the Scientific-Modern Period, has a real grip on the hearts and minds of business school professors and administrators, who transmit it to students, so that it becomes self-perpetuating. However, there is some light. A number of recent critiques have begun the process of self-examination.

Jeffrey Pfeffer and Christina Fong.[14] Pfeffer and Fong argue that the MBA is neither necessary nor sufficient for business success, and that a student's grades are not correlated with a flourishing career. Much of what MBAs learn is of limited usefulness, business school research is of limited influence, and true "evidence-based" management is rare.

Many of the bestsellers making an impact on business are based on what Pfeffer would call "nonevidential approaches." It is difficult to discern when one reads the entirety of his work whether he believes that the problem is simply a lack of "good science" in business school research or a more fundamental issue of how research problems are framed at business schools.

In short, Pfeffer and Fong suggest that most business school researchers get "good science" wrong, and that the resulting MBA is not useful and doesn't much matter.

Henry Mintzberg.[15] In a recent blistering critique of business education, *Managers Not MBAs*, management theorist Henry Mintzberg suggests that for the most part MBA programs have the wrong students, that students in their mid-to-late twenties are simply neither ready nor capable of learning management. He sees management differently from Pfeffer and Fong, as a craft rather than a science. Hence, studying management is a waste of time. One needs to be engaged in the "doing" rather than the "talking about doing." There is simply too much emphasis on the disciplines of business in the business schools, and too much emphasis on the traditional modes of teaching and learning. Consequently, MBAs have become exploiters rather than explorers and innovators. In addition, the managerial class, defined by MBAs, is responsible for a lot of economic misery in society.

Mintzberg rightly traces much of the problem back to the Scientific-Modern Period and the emergence of a "cult of methodology," whereby the worthiness of a particular piece of research is based not on how it allows us to live, but on the "validity" of the methodology by which it has been executed. However, it is perhaps disingenuous of him to make such a strong claim about the scientism in business school research, as he is routinely lauded for taking empiricism to its logical ends. His early studies of managerial work influenced a generation of students and managers, and have been defended by many as telling us what managers actually do, rather than what they should do to become good managers. His own eschewing of the normative aspects of business research seems to fit squarely into the cross hairs of his critique.

In short, Mintzberg suggests that we get "management" wrong, and the resulting MBAs do real and lasting damage in the world.

Sumantra Ghoshal. In an influential article titled "Bad Management Theories Are Destroying Good Management Practices," the late Sumantra Ghoshal argued that the dominant narratives that have taken hold in business schools are the real culprits.[16] He singles out the ideologues who, concentrating on the economic and financial aspects of business, propose that the only legitimate purpose of a business is to maximize shareholder value, and those who understand business as a complex agency problem where managers are seen as agents of shareholders. He invokes Hayek's idea of the pretense of knowledge to suggest that we misunderstand the nature of social science. Social science theories become known, "ideas in good currency" as Donald Schon would say, and students and business people begin to act as if these ideas were true. They enact the dominant narrative. And, in doing so, they create agency problems and corporations who are immune to any criteria other than shareholder value. He writes:

> In courses on corporate governance grounded in agency theory, we have taught our students that managers cannot be trusted to do their jobs— which, of course, is to maximize shareholder value. . . . In courses on organization design, grounded in transaction-cost economics, we have preached the need for tight monitoring and control of people to prevent "opportunistic behavior." In strategy courses, we have presented the "five forces" framework to suggest that companies must compete not only with their competitors but also with their suppliers, customers, employees, and regulators.[17]

Business school researchers have simply misused the scientific methods by pretending that business is like the physical sciences, with fixed rules and repeatable phenomena. The result is not the useless and uninfluential theory of

Pfeffer and Fong, but the highly destructive theory that Mintzberg's MBAs are inflicting on the world. In an incredibly enlightening passage, Ghoshal suggests that the answer might lie in a closer connection between the great thinkers of the sciences and the humanities, adopting a "scholarship of common sense." He writes:

> In describing himself and his work, Sigmund Freud wrote: "[Y]ou often estimate me too highly. I am not really a man of science, not an experimenter, and not a thinker. I am nothing but by temperament a conquistador—an adventurer, if you want to translate the term—with the curiosity, the boldness, and the tenacity that belong to that type of being. . ."
>
> Freud's inductive and iterative approach to sense-making, often criticized for being ad hoc and unscientific, was scholarship of common sense. So indeed was Darwin's, who, too, practiced a model of research as the work of a detective, not of an experimenter, who was driven by the passions of an adventurer, not those of a mathematician. Scholarship of common sense is the epistemology of disciplined imagination, as advocated by Karl Weick, . . . and not the epistemology of formalized falsification that was the doctrine of Karl Popper. . . .
>
> To protect the pretense of knowledge, we have created conditions under which this kind of scholarship can no longer flourish in our community. This is true of all social science disciplines, but curiously perhaps it is most intensely true in business schools where, in our desire for respect from scholars in other fields, we have become even more intolerant of the scholarship of common sense than those whose respect we seek. . . .[18]

In short, Ghoshal suggests that we get theory wrong, management wrong, and social science wrong, and we shouldn't be surprised at the resulting moral decline of business.

So What? The common theme to these critiques is that much malaise in and about business schools is a result of a misguided positivism or scientism, ultimately stemming from what we have called the Scientific-Modern Period of business school history. While there is much truth in this critique, it is difficult to see how such a tightly knit social system is going to change. Indeed, the authors' calls for reform are quite different and do not measure up to the level of passion in their critiques. This helps uncover a deeper issue.

III. Business as a Human Institution

Rejecting the Dominant Narratives of Business. What business schools get wrong is business itself. They may get science, theory, and management wrong as well. But the problem starts with the very idea of business. Intriguingly, little of the management literature and few of the critiques offer a view of what business *is*. And absent a view of business, they are equally unclear on management and leadership.

Implicit in much of the management discussion is a mechanical, deterministic, positivistic view of business—a financial engine controlled by the machinery of scientific management—with managers making judgments about them. (This is most evident in the analytical professions, including consulting and investment banking, which now hire over half the graduating classes of the leading business schools. A consultant's job is often to diagnose and describe a business problem, and an investor's is to predict which stocks will move in which direction. Both require rigorous analysis, and both tempt the practitioner to treat the business observed as an independent, determined phenomenon.)

A brief tour of the business school curriculum will find that the basic units of analysis are cash flows, products and services, processes, brands, and other stylized ideas that have acquired a metaphysical reality of their own. As Ghoshal and others suggest, our narrow ideas about value as only economic value to shareholders, our ideas about agency, about the purpose of the firm, and others are all part of the dominant narrative in business schools. They are also all artifacts of human interactions.

Like earlier mechanistic views, the scientific view of management makes it difficult to incorporate the human spirit. It leaves little room for ethics, or for other fundamentally human considerations such as creativity, trust, initiative, and will.

In very few places in business education do we begin with the basic human interactions that make business a profoundly human institution. Business, in its most essential form, is a way that we create value for each other by cooperating and specializing our labor. Business is fundamentally about value-creation and trade. Business simply does not work outside of some interpersonal-social-cultural-ethical context, yet most theories of business separate business decisions from this human matrix.

We have only recently separated management as a unique activity and begun treating business as distinct from other social phenomena. "The identification of management with business management began only with the Great Depression, which bred hostility to business and contempt for business executives. In order not to be tarred with the business brush, management in the public sector was rechristened public administration and proclaimed a separate discipline," as Peter Drucker points out.[19] "It is only the emergence of management since World War II, what I call the 'Management Revolution,' that has allowed us to see that the organization is discrete and distinct from society's other institutions."[20]

An Example: Challenging Separation from Ethics. This separation of business from more general human activity can be seen most clearly in the popular joke about "business ethics as an oxymoron." We might define the "Separation Fallacy" this way:

It is useful, first, to believe that sentences such as, "x is a business decision" have no ethical content or any implicit ethical point of view. And, it is useful, second, to believe that sentences such as "x is an ethical decision, the best thing to do, all things considered" have no content or implicit view about value-creation and trade (business).

This fallacy underlies much of the dominant story about business, and it is reinforced by the approach to research that the critics of business school have decried. Yet almost any business decision has some ethical content. To see that this true, we offer the "Open Question Argument." One need only ask whether the following questions make sense for virtually any business decision (the Separation Fallacy would have us believe that these questions aren't relevant for making business decisions, or that they could never be answered):

1. If this decision is made, for whom is value created, and for whom is value destroyed?
2. Who is harmed and/or benefited by this decision?
3. Whose rights are enabled, and whose values are realized by this decision (and whose are not)?
4. What kind of person will I (we) become if we make this decision?

These questions are always open for most business decisions, and therefore we need a theory about business that answers them. One such answer would be "Only value to shareholders counts," but such an answer would have to be enmeshed in the language of ethics as well as business. (Milton Friedman, unlike most of his expositors, actually gives such a morally rich answer.) However, to develop that answer meaningfully, we need an ethics capable of engaging the language and issues of business.

In short, we need a theory that has as its basis what we might call the "Integration Thesis":

Most business decisions, or sentences about business, have some ethical content or implicit ethical view. Most ethical decisions, or sentences about ethics, have some business content or implicit view about business.

Human Enterprise as a New Narrative. One of the most pressing challenges facing business scholars is to tell compelling narratives that have the Integration Thesis at their heart. Seeing business as a fundamentally human institution means that we can bring to bear on business the full panoply of ideas, disciplines, models, theories, and understandings from literature, the fine arts, history, anthropology, cultural studies, language studies, law, philosophy, the sciences, and other parts of the academy. It involves Sartre's idea that ethics begins with authenticity and the need to justify one's life to oneself and to others. This is no different in today's small businesses and global corporations than it was in post–World War II Paris.

Seeing business as a fundamentally human enterprise means accepting something like the "Responsibility Principle," which is implicit in most reasonably comprehensive views. It states:

Most people, most of the time, want to, actually do, and should accept responsibility for the effects of their actions on others.

Without something like the Responsibility Principle it is difficult to see how ethics gets off the ground. "Responsibility" may well be a difficult and multifaceted idea. There are surely many different ways to understand it. But if we are not willing to accept responsibility for our own actions (as limited as that may be due to complicated issues of causality and the like), then ethics, understood as how we reason together so we can all flourish, is likely an exercise in bad faith.

If we want to adopt the Integration Thesis, if the Open Question Argument makes sense, and if something like the Responsibility Thesis is necessary, we need a new narrative about business. This new story must be able to explain how value-creation at once encompasses both economics and ethics, and how it takes account of all the effects of business action on others.

Such a model exists, and has been developed over the last thirty years by management researchers and ethics scholars called "stakeholder theorists." They have challenged much work that is done in the name of "value-free economics and science." Indeed, they have adopted a critical stance toward much of what the critiques suggest is wrong in terms of the nature of management and its appropriate modes of analysis. But they have also invoked the second sense of the Separation Fallacy to challenge work done by philosophers who have little knowledge of either business or the business disciplines. (Sadly, recognition of their work is missing in most of the critiques of business schools, reinforcing our claim that these critiques are grounded in the dominant narrative.)

We are not going to review the particulars of stakeholder theory. This has been done many times over by many people.[21] We want stakeholder theory to serve as an example of the kind of work that could be done if we truly began to see business as a human enterprise. There is new work to be done to bring the richness of our colleagues' exploration of human activity and intellectual creativity to bear in the domain of management. There are many theories and research programs that could be developed. Getting the "metaphysics of business" (if you like) right opens up many possibilities. We believe these possibilities offer the only hope for rescuing our business schools.

A Valuable Corollary. If business were seen as a human enterprise, business people could again be seen as human beings. (The prevailing view, that business people are a different species, can be seen in our experience teaching ethics to high school seniors. Presented with the ethical decision of whether to read a folder left behind in a negotiation, the students split evenly on whether to read it. But 100 percent thought that businesspeople would read it.) We could encourage students and businesspeople to bring their human sensibilities and judgment into the business setting. Rather than teaching "business ethics" as a special discipline, whose very existence needed to be defended, we could teach ethics and their application in the business environment.

IV. Rescuing Business Education

If we put the humanity of business into the center of the way we think about it, we must deal with two fundamental questions and four problems of management and leadership in business, even if only by redirecting them. Once these have been addressed, there will remain one big challenge. We appeal to our "common sense" about business for the legitimacy of what we offer.

Two Fundamental Questions. We simply cannot understand business as a human enterprise without putting these two questions at the center of our inquiry:

1. What does it mean to be a fully complex human being?
2. How do complex human beings create value and trade with each other, and what is the meaning of such activity?

We are not arguing for a particular answer to these questions. There can be many. However, we must ask them if we are to understand the real world of business, where there are actual people engaging in relationships and transactions with one other. They cannot be reduced to questions of cash flows, markets, hierarchies, products, role-related behaviors such as consumer behavior, and other sometimes useful but nonfoundational ideas.

Four Problems. Having raised these two questions, we must address four problems of management and leadership.

First is the "Problem of Authority." How are we to understand the authority relationships that exist in business, and make sense of them in human terms? Is there a conflict between these relationships and our autonomy as moral agents? How can the work of thinkers such as Philip Zimbardo, Stanley Milgram, Hannah Arendt, Nietzsche, and others be brought to bear on the authority relationships in business? As globalization extends Western models into new cultures, are there other thinkers and models which we must address?

Second is the "Problem of the Self." How are we to understand the role of the self in business? Is the self to be understood as an autonomous agent acting "for itself," or is it to be understood as a complex, interacting set of relationships? What is the role of the history of a "self"? In particular, what is the connection between the development of self, its engagement in an enterprise, and the relationship of authority? How do race, gender, sexuality, and other "variables" connect to our ideas about the self? And, how does the concept of the self connect to how we create value and trade with each other?

The third problem is the "Problem of Ethics." Is the history of our ethics a history devoid of the effects of value-creation and trade? If human beings have been "value-creators and traders" for a very long time, how could this idea have been absent for most of our discussion of ethics? Would a better first question for political theory be "How are value-creation and trade sustainable over time?" rather than, "How is the state justified?"

And the fourth problem is the "Problem of Human Nature." Is there any such thing as "human nature"? What do traditional and new narratives about business assume about human nature? Can we have an idea of "humanity" that transcends individuals, without an idea of human nature? What is the role of institutions such as business in shaping our ideas about, or even the facts of, how humans can live? Conversely, should our views about human nature shape what we view to be acceptable, or even possible, business institutions and practices?

Each of these problems is large, and for the most part, all are ignored in the current business school curriculum. The dominant narrative must ignore them. They also must be ignored if Ghoshal and others are correct about the scientism that has taken hold in business schools. These problems simply cannot be addressed solely with traditional "scientific" or "social scientific" methods and concepts.

One Big Challenge. These questions and problems open a rich discussion about the nature of business, management, and leadership. However, they only lay the groundwork for the big challenge:

> What should business schools do—how, when, and for whom—to educate leaders and managers of these human enterprises?

The expanding scholarship of teaching and learning, especially in the liberal arts colleges, rightly draws the distinction between the "what" of education and the "how." Conservatories and creative writing institutes have long understood the differences between criticism and performance, as well as the role of the former in helping to develop the latter. We in the business schools need to understand the balance of our own activities between developing scholars of business and developing practitioners of business, and therefore understand the best means of achieving this. Here science may offer a better solution, since the laboratory environment develops scientists through apprenticeship rather than lecture.

The foundational questions raised here should give us a better sense of the phenomena of business and possibly of how to study those phenomena. They may also give us a deeper understanding of the nature of management. This only prepares us to ask the questions about the educational task ahead.

V. An Agenda for Change

If we put these questions and problems at the center of the educational processes for businesspeople, business schools may, over time, come to look very different. We want to suggest five items in an agenda for change. There are many others.

Lead a Conversation on the Connection Between Business and the Humanities. Scholars in the humanities need to become more literate in the real world of business, so that they can offer different lenses through which to understand value-creation and trade. PhD programs in business disciplines need to be broadened to use a wider range of texts and to become more interdisciplinary. Business educators need to look to the humanities for new ways of teaching, especially for developing students' judgment and creativity. Above all we need a set of Dewey-like experiments to create new modes of conceptualization.

Rethink the Business Disciplines. We can take each of the disciplines of business and identify concepts that we might call, after Michael Walzer, "morally thick." Our goal would not be to drive out the value implications from traditional conceptual schemes, but to welcome them as different lenses.

For instance, suppose that we understood business as a human enterprise and took the two fundamental questions and four problems to heart in marketing. We might ask whether a company's relationship with a consumer is a promise, like the promises that parents make to children, and if the value of its brand is rooted in trust. We might ask whether we should understand customers as ends in themselves, whose projects are important precisely because they are their projects, rather than means to our own ends. We might define our "value proposition" in terms of our contribution to consumers' own values. We might ask about the moral significance of brands and the effects of brands on civic space, on civil society, or on our understanding of the environment, possibly accepting that the consumer as well as the producer has rights regarding the brand.[22]

In finance, we might see markets as having moral relevance and cash flow as a utilitarian measurement of how well a company is creating value for its stakeholders. The challenge raised by Sharia finance might become real, i.e., how does a lender truly participate in the activities funded? Across all of these, we might explore where diverse global cultures should give rise to distinct, locally relevant answers.

Rethink the Disciplinary Matrix of Business Schools. We also need to rethink the disciplinary mix. The world has changed so much that the traditional, functionally defined subjects (defined, ironically, by stakeholder group) may no longer be appropriate. Most schools offer courses in marketing (customers), finance (shareholders or financiers), operations (suppliers and production), human resources or organizational behavior/theory or management (employees), and public relations, ethics, or business/government (community).

Where do students learn how to deal with consumers who are employees and shareholders as well? Where do they learn how to create value with NGOs who are critics, often very well-informed critics? Where do they learn how to deal with employees who are community leaders? What standing do traditional disciplines offer to the organizations whose symbiotic products and services are critical to a business's success? What are the thick moral ideas in the new "disciplines"?

Rethink Research. Here the critics, especially Ghoshal, are surely correct. Researchers need to take responsibility for their theories and for the effects of their actions. Theory needs most often to look more like narrative and only sometimes like "science." We need new narratives and new questions that better enable us to engage in value-creation and trade, and they should not duck explicitly human, and especially ethical, vocabulary. At a minimum, we must rethink the rampant positivism that Ghoshal has identified and debate what constitutes research appropriate to the issues studied. We need to understand how our colleagues in the humanities explore (and contribute to) performance and creativity. We need to redesign the core processes that shape our research, like publication, refereeing, tenure and promotion, and even the ratings game itself—or offer alternatives—in order to support more appropriate methodologies.

Rethink Teaching. Teaching needs to be very different. We need to design high-engagement experiences that allow the student to develop meaningful, theory-informed practices. Management is an art and learning by doing is important, but it is easier to learn with the knowledge of the theory, as music is learned by both practice and knowledge of scales and chords.

MBA programs need their equivalent of études, to teach traditional skills in the traditional disciplines as well as to open up these disciplines to insights from the humanities in the morally thick manner that we have suggested. But like all performers, business students need to have large experiential and practice components to their education, with the teacher as guide and coach, rather than source and judge. Students need to be exposed to at least some of the best thinking and thinkers from across the university, and one would hope these thinkers would also energize their own disciplines with the idea that the business school is more than a morally suspect relative who just won't leave.

VI. Conclusion

Schools that adopt this agenda for reform have a chance to distinguish themselves, but it will not be easy. Business schools are part of universities, which are essentially medieval institutions with high resistance to change: faculty have high needs for autonomy, among other psychological quirks; students are driven by their perceptions of what will work in the marketplace; employers need to fill immediate needs for analysts; and companies and business leaders hire graduates based on particular skill needs in the short term. Deans rarely have the courage to tackle such a project.

To adopt this agenda successfully, a school would have to be aligned around its purpose and have a live conversation about whether that purpose can be realized in the world described by Ghoshal, Mintzberg, and others. Unless schools adopt it, however, they will likely be but a long and uninteresting footnote to Joseph Wharton's failed experiment.

Notes

1. We wish to thank our many colleagues at the Darden School and elsewhere for helpful conversations about these issues. Versions of this paper have been delivered at the Schulich School, York University, and at Copenhagen Business School.

2. This section is based on R. Edward Freeman, "Epilogue," in *Business as a Humanity*, eds. Thomas Donaldson and R. Edward Freeman (New York: Oxford University Press, 1994). We are grateful to the editors and publisher for permission to recast some of that material here.

3. Leon C. Marshall, "The American Collegiate School of Business," in *The Collegiate School of Business: Its Status at the Close of the First Quarter of the Twentieth Century*, ed. Leon C. Marshall (Chicago: University of Chicago Press, 1928), 3.

4. Frances Ruml, "The Formative Period of Higher Commercial Education in American Universities," in *Collegiate School of Business*, ed. Marshall, 47.

5. Drew E. VandeCreek, "Power and Order: The Ideology of Professional Business Training at Wharton and Harvard, 1881–1933," (master's thesis, University of Virginia, 1994).

6. Ruml, "Higher Commercial Education," 54–55.

7. Ibid., 53.

8. Alfred North Whitehead, "Universities and Their Function," in *The Aims of Education and Other Essays* (1929; reprint, New York: Macmillan, 1966), 92.

9. Thomas M. Mulligan, "The Two Cultures in Business Education," *Academy of Management Review* 12 (October 1987): 593–99.

10. Gary Hamel, "The How, Why, and What of Management Innovation," *Harvard Business Review*, February 2006, 72–84.

11. Michael Porter, *Competitive Strategy: Techniques for Analyzing Industries and Competitors* (New York: Free Press, 1980).

12. Thomas Peters and Robert Waterman, *In Search of Excellence: Lessons from America's Best-Run Companies* (New York: Harper and Row, 1982).

13. These are laid out in more detail in R. Edward Freeman, Jeffrey Harrison, and Andrew Wicks, *Managing for Stakeholders: Survival, Reputation, and Success* (New Haven, Conn.: Yale University Press, 2007).

14. VandeCreek, "Power and Order."

15. Henry Mintzberg, *Managers Not MBAs: A Hard Look at the Soft Practice of Managing and Management Development* (San Francisco: Berrett-Koehler, 2004).

16. Sumantra Ghoshal, "Bad Management Theories Are Destroying Good Management Practices," *Academy of Management Learning and Education* 4 (March 2005): 75–91.

17. Ibid., 75.

18. Ibid., 81–82.

19. Peter Drucker, "Management's New Paradigms," *Forbes,* 5 October 1998, 156.

20. Peter Drucker, "The New Society of Organizations," *Harvard Business Review,* September-October 1992, 100.

21. A recent statement that reflects our view is Freeman et al., *Managing for Stakeholders.*

22. For an analysis of brands as social texts, see Mary Jo Hatch and James Rubin, "The Hermeneutics of Branding," *Journal of Brand Management* 14 (September 2006): 40–59.

Chapter Eleven

A NEW MINDSET FOR BUSINESS EDUCATION:

CULTIVATING REPUTATIONAL CAPITAL

KEVIN T. JACKSON

WHAT DOES IT MEAN to speak of a morally educated businessperson? It means a person armed with core ethical principles, ethical awareness, and ethical reasoning skills, capable of responding to a changing legal and compliance environment as well as complex, conflicting, and sometimes highly problematic interests and opportunities, and moreover prepared to assume the duties and rewards of stewardship, including taking into account multiple stakeholders' concerns before rendering decisions and wielding power responsibly.

A confluence of factors, ranging from the raft of recent corporate scandals to the growth of socially responsible investing, the escalating influence of corporations, a rise in legal and regulatory standards, and mounting forces of globalization, are bringing about an ethics-oriented paradigm for business.[1] Some business schools are ratcheting up their efforts—a few of them joining forces with corporate executives[2]—to blend ethics initiatives into their management curricula.[3] Modifications to the Association to Advance Collegiate Schools of Business (AACSB) guidelines are prompting business schools to emphasize moral reasoning and personal reflection.[4]

I. Re-Examining Assumptions

As one scholar has observed, "[m]any business schools educate managers to focus almost exclusively on profits and to base their professional careers largely on monetary achievements."[5] Business education must challenge the conventional assumptions underlying this phenomenon. One fundamental assumption is that there is a major opposition between economics and ethics. What new viewpoint can supply fresh assumptions about the nature of this relationship? In what ways might business education foster morally educated businesspersons and help them flourish as leaders in today's business environment?

The concept of reputational capital establishes a foundation for a new mindset about business education and business management. This enlightened outlook: (1) harmonizes financial and social imperatives; (2) deters business misconduct without adopting a compliance-compulsive orientation; (3) infuses moral awareness across disciplines; and (4) mediates cross-cultural worldviews to stimulate competitiveness and foster positive social integration. It establishes a connection between the cultivation of virtuous managers through business education, and the cultivation of virtuous companies through management guided by the moral and economic benefits of reputational capital.

Comparing Shareholder and Stakeholder Conceptions

The idea of reputational capital assimilates both shareholder and stakeholder conceptions, incorporating the best interest of shareholders by harmonizing both ethical and economic mandates. The received view of business is embodied in the shareholder conception advanced by Milton Friedman for promoting a free-market economy. "In such an economy, there is one and only one social responsibility of business—to use its resources and engage in activities designed to increase its profits so long as it stays within the rules of the game, which is to say, engages in open and free competition, without deception or fraud."[6]

According to this view, what matters most is beating the competition and maximizing the bottom line; business ethics is an oxymoron. Such a mindset, what R. E. Freeman terms the "separation thesis,"[7] rejects the idea that economic value is grounded in corporate social responsibility. Economics and ethics constitute polarized forms of discourse for managerial decision-making and business practices. "Social responsibility" betrays a fundamental misconception about the character and nature of a free economy; makes the interests of all groups other than shareholders impose constraints, rather than goals, on corporate activities; and leaves the proof of payoffs from investing in social initiatives unsubstantiated. The only plausible case to be made for obeying legal and ethical standards, under this position, is to avoid the monetary cost of noncompliance.

The standard alternative view, stakeholder theory, argues that maximizing profits for shareholders is not the sole purpose of a business; but also that it serves the larger society, including an array of other constituents: employees, customers, suppliers, and the communities in which the firm operates.[8] The scope of corporate social responsibility is wider than meeting the bottom line for shareholders, and business firms' ethical and discretionary responsibilities go beyond their purely economic and legal responsibilities.[9]

The Pros and Cons

What advantages do these approaches provide? Shareholder theory correctly assumes that corporations are structured to make money—they operate under an imperative to meet the bottom line to survive, not to serve as social-welfare agencies. Stakeholder theory, on the other hand, correctly assumes that corporations must deploy the power they wield in a socially responsible way—corporations should be governed so as to benefit all parties having a stake in the firm's activities.[10]

What are their limitations? Shareholder theory neglects the fact that a watchful public, the media, and government will not permit corporations to work exclusively to maximize profit in the service of shareholders while ignoring the ensuing blowback to other constituencies. Stakeholder theory (1) does not give sufficiently rigorous criteria for settling disputes about who or what counts as a qualified stakeholder; (2) lends inadequate guidance as to just how a firm's leaders should balance the competing interests of various purported stakeholders, especially when such interests are conflicting and mutually exclusive (e.g., allocating money to improve workers' wages diverts a firm's resources from giving consumers the same quality product at a lower price); and (3) does not provide an answer to the question of the extent to which individual firms can be held responsible for a certain outcome when success requires common effort on the part of a sufficiently large number of individual firms (e.g., ensuring cooperation of individual corporations in an anti-corruption policy).

Acquiring New Perspective: The Notion of Reputational Capital

Re-orienting business education demands a fresh concept that dismantles the wall between the shareholder and stakeholder theories and links integrity and fair dealing to the bottom line. This new polestar for business education is reputational capital. Reputational capital is a synthetic notion for three key functions of the stakeholder model: the descriptive, instrumental, and normative.[11] The firm's reputation is the stakeholders' *description* of the corporation from the standpoint of their respective roles. Pursuing reputational capital requires that corporate executives care about their shareholders, employees, customers, suppliers, and other affected parties. So the concept of promoting reputational capital *instrumentally* serves as a tool for managers to construct strategic stakeholder relations to generate profit. At the same time, it implicitly reflects a *normative* account of how corporations ought to treat their various stakeholders. A return on reputational capital realizes the "intrinsic value" of satisfying the interests of all stakeholders. The more reputational capital a firm builds, the greater the return to shareholders and other stakeholders.

Considering the Value of Intangibles

In the interest of grasping how reputational capital incorporates the best interest of shareholders by harmonizing both ethical and economic mandates, it will be helpful first to examine a conventional assumption about how to determine the firm's economic value. A prevailing view in the finance discipline deems that a company's economic value is measured by its equity (shareholder wealth), in book value (accounting) or in market value (stock price). This measure is somewhat illusory, however, since there is a range of ways to determine the economic value of firms. The task involves choosing whether the interests of just the shareholders, or of all constituents of the firm, or of all groups affected by the firm's activities, matter most, and whether short-term or long-term interests are taken to be paramount. Business decisions that generate short-term profits benefit well-diversified shareholders with a strong risk tolerance and a short-term outlook.[12] But those that cultivate long-term prospects of the firm—building up the firm's reputational capital, for example—advance the long-range interests of risk-averse shareholders as well as various constituencies having a stake in the firm.

If the value of a firm is assumed to be its value as an ongoing enterprise able to create wealth for society indefinitely into the future, managers should not focus on the interests of individual shareholders and on current stock price. Instead, they should weigh and balance the interests of all of the groups that make up the firm and focus on long-term performance. Hence, the real value of a firm lies much deeper than just its financial state. Along with the normal assets and liabilities, firms' balance sheets need to be extended, by adding intangibles running to and from various constituencies (employees, customers, suppliers, strategic partners, investors) and the costs incurred by the firm from damage to these intangibles. The intangibles encompass elements such as credibility, corporate culture, pride, trust, integrity, perception of fair dealing, and dignity.

The chiefly inchoate measurement scale for such intangibles ranges from reputational assets to reputational liabilities. Calculating the difference between these intangibles yields the net reputational capital of the firm. Drawing ethical considerations into the equation has the salutary result of spotlighting a dimension of wealth not captured by conventional financial accounting methodologies. Such a broadened conception paves the way for reckoning a firm's economic value beyond its financial state. Consequently, the economic value of business ethics is realized by an enterprise's strategic, financial, and operational success in establishing reputational assets. Accordingly, here is a practical idea for modern business management anchored to the ancient wisdom of Solomon: "A good reputation and respect are worth much more than silver and gold."[13]

Motivation Matters

Someone might be inclined to ask: if a firm is motivated to do things to improve its reputation purely by the wish to make a profit, can it ultimately be successful in growing reputational capital? In other words, does the profit motivation in business always taint any purported moral motivation that tries to accompany it? Addressing this important question requires some reflection upon two fundamental points.

First, the enterprise of profit-making, when placed in proper perspective—as a process of wealth-creation—is itself a source of doing good. There is no necessary contradiction between a company doing good and doing well.

Second, getting reputational rewards from good deeds does require a genuine desire to do good. One-hundred-percent purity is probably not necessary. People know that the typical for-profit company is not Mother Teresa, Inc. However, they deplore corporate marketing and PR campaigns masquerading as citizenship and social responsibility initiatives, especially when used to divert attention from a firm's own misconduct. Rolling out ethics training as litigation-proofing for senior management or the board dampens any positive outcomes that would otherwise be produced.

In other words, reputational capital is generated from moral action backed by sincere motivation. A company will find it difficult to realize the full financial benefits flowing from integrity and fair play unless it has an explicitly stated commitment to doing right. Attitude matters. Companies that too aggressively promote an instrumental "it pays to be ethical" attitude undermine their efforts. Taken from a completely financial perspective, one might say that it pays to appreciate the intrinsic value of good business conduct, and that it is most prudent to guide one's actions by this premise.

Admittedly it is often hard to know what is really fueling a company's apparent good conduct. Some act insincerely. Intel lost goodwill by refusing to replace defective Pentium microchips. Intel said that typical users might get a wrong answer once every twenty-seven thousand years, but people simply did not wish to be receiving defective microchips. Initially hit by a wave of negative publicity, Intel eventually agreed to replace the chips at no cost and apologized both for problems caused by flawed chips and its own lack of concern for its customers. But how noble was its motivation? Intel's actions were apparently more a strategic exercise in *ex post facto* crisis management than as a virtuous expression of day-to-day integrity.

Although some corporations act insincerely, not all do. Paradoxically, the companies that genuinely appreciate the intrinsic value of ethical conduct—as opposed to focusing exclusively on its instrumental value in increasing profits or deflecting attention from misdeeds—are most likely to be rewarded financially as people discern that they have a sound reputation rooted, at least in part, in sincere motives.

Indeed, the criticism that many corporations act insincerely assumes that it is possible to distinguish disingenuous public-relations ploys and pursuit-of-whatever-is-fashionable motives from sincere moral commitments. That is, the skeptic's argument assumes what it wants to deny: that corporations are behaving *wrongly* when they use ethics as an attention-deflecting or fashion-following strategy instead of honoring it for its own sake. If it were true that *all* corporations *always* acted insincerely, if it were not possible for them to act on a higher moral plane, what would be the point of drawing our attention to and condemning such behavior?

The Importance of Trust

Trust is a necessary precondition of legitimate successful business activity. Simply put, if there is no trust, it is exceedingly difficult to secure a deal in the first place, and even more so to preserve lasting, profitable commercial relationships. The world of business simply would not function if each part of every financial transaction needed to be spelled out expressly in writing or delineated in a contract. Furthermore, parties prefer to do business with people who are not out to cheat them. And sticking with trustworthy people cuts down on transaction costs, such as those for attorneys, auditors, and inspectors. There is no substitute for trust in making deals run smoothly.

Thus, because reputation is so firmly grounded in trust and because the proper functioning of business transactions requires trust, reputation is a primary attribute of commercial relationships. Building trustworthy relationships with stakeholders accumulates the intangible assets of reputational capital.[14] The value of shareholders' investment increases commensurately.[15]

It is critical to distinguish a morally educated businessperson from ethical opportunists—those bent on tweaking the firm's short-term attributes, such as corporate image and identity. Moreover, although it is common to use the terms "corporate identity," "corporate image," and "corporate reputation" interchangeably, these concepts are not the same. A firm's identity and image relate to elements of its "personality," such as corporate name, logo, advertising slogans, and brand image, which are targeted primarily at consumers. The reputation of the firm, by contrast, pertains to deeper attributes of the firm's character and integrity. Thus, unlike image and identity, yet somewhat akin to individual virtue, corporate reputation requires consistent moral behavior to develop over a period of time. Furthermore, reputation is associated with all aspects of a company, cutting across all of its departments and divisions.

A morally educated businessperson is deeply aware of how reputation is cultivated, earned over the long term by attention to integrity, respect, authenticity, and fair dealing. She grasps its potential for bringing specific strategic advantages. She knows there is no column on the balance sheet that assigns a monetary value to a firm's reputation, and no item on the income statement that gives a financial return for reputational capital. Yet equally she knows that having a strong reputation magnifies the worth of a business enterprise beyond the book value of "goodwill" contemplated by accounting rules.

II. Rethinking Goals

What are we to take the legitimate goals of business education to be? During a presentation on ethics education I gave at an AACSB conference a few years ago in New Orleans, one side of the audience believed that business schools should be motivated to invigorate ethics instruction to keep future MBAs out of jail. An opposing side stressed the importance of enlightening business-people to attain excellence and promote socially responsible and sustainable business. It seemed to me that the divisiveness with which the discussion played out betrayed an unbalanced conception within institutions of higher learning and corporate ethics offices alike of what it is to be a morally educated businessperson.

Pitting Practical Against Abstract

Business practitioners normally take the perspective of business law and specific ethical rules to be paramount. They take a hard-nosed, practical approach to management education. Inculcating crisp directives for right conduct into future business leaders will clean up the moral landscape of corporate America. The emerging mandate referred to in the Introduction, that business schools expand the teaching of ethics in their programs of study as a response to widespread business scandals, is one manifestation of this approach.

Others hold that, strictly speaking, there is no "*business* ethics" per se.[16] Ethics and morality are almost exclusively a matter of following the most fundamental, abstract, and universal principles. Such a mindset is reflected in the following passage from a well-respected textbook on business ethics:

> Business ethics is not a separate ethics that constrains business in a way that other human and social endeavors are not constrained. Nor does it permit business to do what one is not allowed to do in other areas of life. It is part of the general field of ethics and only within that wider sphere can it be properly understood.[17]

The first perspective consists of following specific norms. For example, the rules imposed by the Sarbanes-Oxley legislation and rules governing "yield burning" and "pay-to-play" in the mutual-bond industry. It forms a moral code of convention or customary practice. The standards are spelled out in corporate ethics programs such as voluntary codes of conduct and legal compliance regimes.[18] The second perspective consists of more abstract principles and goals by reference to which critical thinking about the first level takes place. Goals and principles are used to understand and evaluate specific rules. Examples include the goal of maximizing the total net utility in society and the principle that corporations should maximize wealth for shareholders.

In debates about the goals of business ethics education, almost always either the practical approach (focused on laws and rules) or the abstract approach (focused on reasoning-with-principles) is relegated to an inferior, or at least unimportant, position.

What Does Reality Dictate?

Effective management in the real business world requires coordinating the two levels on which moral thinking and ethical judgment take place. This reality should drive business education to achieve the right balance between both. The morally educated businessperson knows and obeys "the letter of rules"— specific norms. A legal, rule-oriented approach equips the student with knowledge of norms and facilitates her taking prudent actions in specific contexts. At the same time, she also complies with "the spirit of rules"—going beyond specific norms by garnering reasoning skill and ethical awareness based on her own self-accepted core moral standards.

Goals, Conventions, and Duties

Let us take it as given that some universally valid abstract principles and goals exist—for example, everyone has a right to equal respect—and net-total utility ought to be maximized. In many cases, such principles and goals by themselves fail to establish concrete rules. They require coordinated action on the part of many people if they are going to fly. Furthermore, two or more mutually incompatible plans of action may each advance the same principle or goal.

Here is an illustration. Suppose it is a fundamental goal that employees get financial support in retirement. What concrete duties can be derived from this goal? Does each company have a duty simply to support its own employees with pensions and no one else? Or does each individual (or corporation) have the duty to make a contribution to a social fund (Social Security), which will then be used to support retirees? Is every person obligated to contribute to his or her personal retirement account? A determinate answer could only be derived through a social convention coordinating everyone's actions.

If it is generally understood that everyone will contribute to a social fund, the goal will be adequately advanced if a sufficient number make their contributions, but it might also be adequately advanced if every business supported its own employees. At the same time, if one follows a rule different from the prevailing convention, the result might be to make no contribution or an excessive contribution to advancing the goal. To act in accordance with two or more of the rules might be to make sacrifices beyond what could reasonably be expected of any individual person or firm. In short, we often need to know what actions we can expect of others if we are to know what effect our individual actions will have.[19]

Having some convention or custom at hand can lend assistance to this inter-action problem by providing people with mutual expectations about each other's conduct. The existence of a convention also makes publicly known what we can reasonably expect of one another and when our actions or failures to act make us the proper object of external sanctions, such as criticism, blame, or internal sanctions of conscience. In other words, the presence of convention provides conditions for the existence of specific duties.

A degree of arbitrariness lingers in business ethics in the sense that there are different and incompatible codes around which business conduct can be coordinated to advance fundamental, universal ends. Which codes happen to get drawn up by various companies is largely arbitrary. That is, the codes are more arbitrary than the fundamental ends. Whatever may be the best way for arriving at valid universal principles, there remains the need for a code of fairly specific (though not necessarily formally promulgated) rules for implementing those principles.

Fitting Specific Rules Within Broad Principles

Laying stress on the letter of rules clearly has not stemmed the tide of corporate scandals. Neglecting to improve confidence in business integrity while crank-ing out more laws is counterproductive. Over-regulated firms channel tremen-dous energy toward compliance—meaning loophole-hunting—while gliding over the spirit of the rules.[20]

Today's business is dynamic and calls for forward-looking leadership. A "reasoning-with-principles" approach helps to guide the student into taking a moral position.

Looking to a broad principle or theory can give coherence and unity to specific rules and helps in correctly applying the rules. Consider this rule, a version of which is found in most banks: "Don't process your own personal bank transactions, and don't have relatives or close friends process them either." Just what is a "close friend"? Precisely how distant does a relative have to be? The rule is trying to avoid a conflict of interest, because conflicts of interest can interfere with one's legitimate contractual role at the bank and put stake-holders at inappropriate risk. We need to know the point of the rule to apply it intelligently. Taking a moral position means being willing to be bound by a principle acceptable to all other affected parties, give good reasons when that principle is challenged, and make a good-faith effort to reach a mutually ac-ceptable position and to stick to it without making ad hoc or opportunistic exceptions just to advance one's own interests or ideals. This is not to say that all of what is involved in being a morally educated businessperson is exhausted by being disposed to adopt and act on principle. As proponents of an "ethic of care" are keen to point out,[21] the moral person sees and identifies with the feelings and interests of others.

Recapitulation

Looking back at this section by way of summary, we see two sets of arguments. The first applies to those advocating a rule-oriented approach to ethics initiatives. Although recent scandals have prompted a turn to specific rules to increase corporate accountability, many business situations are too complex for a straightforward application of specific rules. One needs judgment and discernment to apply them. But judgment and discernment in turn depend upon an understanding of the goals and purposes of the rules. Ultimately these derive from the principle level. Therefore, a morally educated businessperson needs an appreciation of the abstract realm of principle.

The second set of arguments speaks to proponents of broader, principle-oriented ethics initiatives, such as courses in applied moral reasoning. The weakness of such an approach becomes apparent when one realizes that, at the end of the day, business education aims more at teaching business leaders how to work successfully in the real world than, say, at illuminating aspiring philosophers on the value of knowledge for its own sake. Plus, the depth of corporate scandals and the attendant stepped-up legal standards require detailed, legally compliant responses.

Some Practical Recommendations

Educators need to develop both kinds of skills and be familiar with both areas. Business professors might want to consider taking courses to keep them current in the more detailed rule-dominated regions. Teach-the-educator courses could be developed along the lines of continuing legal education courses, covering specific fields such as securities regulation, employment discrimination, information technology, and so on.

Business education should arouse a motivation not only to obey the law but also to go beyond that to obey the spirit of law. This is so for two good reasons. First, business leaders will not grasp the point of going beyond bare minimum legal requirements (into ethics) unless they first know what the law is. Second, maintaining and building a good reputation demands following both the letter and the spirit of law.

A path needs to be charted that avoids potential perils from two extremes. On the one hand, a business curriculum should not let, say, philosophy or theology courses mischaracterize business ethics issues by removing those issues too far from their essential business habitat (e.g., ignoring concerns for meeting the bottom line and maintaining a competitive edge). On the other hand, a curriculum should not let business law courses portray business ethics merely as a matter of legal compliance.

III. Reconstituting Disciplines

The challenge of bringing ethics education into business schools is often framed as a choice between having a separate business ethics course and using an "infusion" approach, with instructors from each discipline expected to raise students' awareness of ethical issues as they pertain to each of these disciplines. (A school can pursue both approaches simultaneously.[22])

There are several shortcomings with using traditional academic business fields as vehicles for teaching business ethics. Just directing a marketing or a finance professor to "raise ethics issues" that come up in the course does not ensure that any systematic examination of the issues takes place, even if the instructor has the best intentions of doing so. Such an approach does not necessarily lead to deep and lasting solutions to the ethical challenges of the new paradigm.

Even worse, it can become a pretext for not doing anything. Faculty may lack expertise in the finely detailed nuances in rules, or in linking the rules to broader matters of principles. They may feel they have a hard enough time getting the essentials of their own material across without taking a time-consuming detour through ethics. On the other hand, keeping business ethics restricted to a separate course has its own shortcomings, especially if the course is taught outside the business school, say, in the philosophy department. That arrangement can keep business ethics isolated from real world challenges.

By itself the deployment of abstract moral reasoning fails to provide satisfactory resolutions of many practical ethical dilemmas in business.[23] A regimen of moral reasoning may also fail to cultivate moral imagination, which can be defined as follows:[24] "the ability to perceive that a web of competing economic relationships is, at the same time, a web of moral relationships . . . searching out places where people are likely to be hurt by decision-making or behavior of managers;"[25] the "awareness of various dimensions of a particular context as well as its operative framework and narratives[;] . . . [t]he ability to understand that context or set of activities from a number of different perspectives, the actualizing of new possibilities that are not context-dependent[;] and the instigation of the process of evaluating those possibilities from a moral point of view."[26]

Moreover, it does not necessarily help students to leverage a firm's limited cash flow in order to achieve the moral ends they have come to appreciate so profoundly. Faced with specific problems in the real world, such a student finds that those problems do not come neatly packaged as the "ethics dilemmas" framed in his coursebook of case studies.

So how should business education cultivate a student's ability to respond to the dynamic business scenarios one confronts in the real world? How can business ethics courses be made more practical and down-to-earth? How can students be motivated to continue lifelong learning about the ethical dimension? How can what's going on in abstract case studies be linked to what students are going to be facing in the real world?

Working Across Disciplines

One way is to develop interdisciplinary business ethics courses. For instance, a course could use risk-control methodologies from the finance area to explore methods of controlling ethical risk. Or it might compare the conventional metrics of a company's financial success, such as earnings-per-share or revenue growth, with the various nonfinancial criteria that figure into the equation of corporate success (corporate citizenship, quality management, ethical leadership, responsible governance, fair marketing, brand equity). When integrated into business performance, these nonfinancial facets can be leveraged to build long-term reputational capital for the firm. Such intangible assets make up a substantial part of a company's net value.

Another possibility to consider is a course that merges ethics with marketing and communications to stimulate students' thinking about stakeholder relationships. Students could be challenged to enlighten marketplace participants about the significance of nonfinancial factors such as integrity and fair dealing in creating value for business organizations. A significant ethical challenge for public relations and advertising is to move beyond just "relationship building" to meeting the demands of conducting honest, open, fair, and compassionate business. Another is to find the proper degree of proactivity in getting the word out about what a firm is doing in terms of its commitments to the fundamentals of running an ethical enterprise.

Finally, business courses can be affiliated with psychology. Such a course might explore the questions raised by research exploring how cognitive limitations and personal biases influence ethical decision-making:[27] How is a person's perception of and judgment about ethical dilemmas influenced by workplace pressures (e.g., time and money) and demands (e.g., an overbearing boss)? Does having an interest in transactions tend to make people rationalize unethical behavior? Are there unforeseen consequences of being too stringent and diligent in enforcing legal and ethical compliance, such as causing people to act irrationally, from an excessive fear of sanctions?

It is interesting to note a similarity between the compartmentalization issue as it arises in business schools and its appearance within the business firm itself. Parallel to the debate about where ethics should be placed in the curriculum is a debate about whether there should be a separate ethics officer, a separate chief reputation officer (CRO), or whether such functions should be infused throughout the organization.

Some companies opt to appoint a CRO or a CRA (chief reputation adviser), whose task is to protect the company's intangible reputational assets. The

CRO's responsibilities entail oversight of advertising; corporate contributions; employee, customer, and media relations; quality; legal compliance; investor relations; and public affairs. The CRO usually works with specialists from each field, helping them to acknowledge the consequences of decisions for the company's reputation. Should a firm use a CRO, or have all of its responsibilities handled by the CEO? Setting up a distinct CRO function can put up walls when what is really needed is to integrate the firm's character into its actions. Smaller firms normally do not need to establish a CRO position, but whether a firm opts for a CRO or not, it should make everyone in each department of the firm a guardian of the company's reputation.

The board of directors has legal and fiduciary duties toward shareholders. Since reputational capital is a significant form of wealth from a stock-growth perspective, the board should also shoulder responsibility for fostering conduct that builds and protects this valuable asset of the business enterprise.

IV. Redefining Context

In our globalized business world, increased contact between different cultures escalates conflict and the need for intercultural and interregional cooperation. Differences of moral conviction notoriously give rise to a special kind of conflict of interests. Whether or not some practice affects their own liberty or economic prospects, or their interests in some narrow sense, people do, as a matter of fact, often take an intense interest in the convictions and behavior of corporations.

The expansion of multinational corporations, booms in emerging markets, and culturally diverse workplaces raise a question for business education: Is it better for future businesspeople to be more tolerant, or less so, in dealing with the moral conflicts posed by a multicultural world?[28]

Business educators should be mindful of their purposes in teaching ethics in the multicultural context. I submit that some central, legitimate purposes are: enhancing students' business skills for different cultural environments, not separating people but seeking to integrate them; improving corporate competitiveness; finding creative solutions to the pervasive "when in Rome" versus "righteous American" dilemmas;[29] and arousing students' awareness about the rationality (or irrationality, as the case may be) of their own and others' moral preferences and aversions.

Challenges of Pluralism

Today's pluralistic world embodies major differences in preferences and aversions together with ever-shifting expectations about corporate social responsibility. Generally speaking, Wal-Mart is viewed positively in Asia yet negatively in Germany.[30] Starbucks is widely adored in Asia but despised in some parts of Europe, in particular, France.[31] Consequently, such companies confront obstacles to entering countries skeptical of the social value that those companies may bring.

People's moral preferences and aversions are embedded in global capital, consumer, and labor markets—what Thomas Dunfee calls "marketplace morality."[32] Moral desires are reflected in capital markets, with mutual funds engaged in socially responsible investing and people screening their personal investments (say, eschewing gambling or tobacco stocks). They are reflected in consumer markets when consumers support their preferences for a clean environment by paying more for pollution-reducing fuel even though the law does not force them to buy it. Canned tuna sales increased for companies that switched to suppliers that protected dolphins even though the switch elevated prices. Consumers voice disapproval of a company's practices by joining boycotts. Moral preferences are reflected in labor markets when job seekers choose jobs according to their perceptions of ethical work environments.

People from one culture may have a strong opposition to what they perceive as another culture's denial of equal rights for women, deprivation of freedom of speech and political and religious expression, use of child labor or forced prison labor of political dissidents, or liberty-restricting family policies. They may link their disapproval to the idea that companies have a legitimate interest in addressing such behavior, whether by internal governance systems, lobbying efforts, criticism, economic boycotts, employee indoctrination, or proper moral development.

To express moral anger or resentment is to take the position of speaking, not just for oneself, but for one's organization or for society in defense of some legitimate collective or individual interest. (By "legitimate collective or individual interest" I mean that some behaviors may hurt many people, but not significantly hurt any one person, as insider trading hurts investors but not an individual investor. In suppressing such behavior, society would be protecting no significant individual interest but a collective one.) This is one reason why moral thought and language in transnational business contexts strikes many as imperialistic. If business students are encouraged to "moralize" in the sense of thinking of virtually all of their preferences and aversions as the legitimate objects of corporate involvement and/or society's protection, the resulting conflict may be inconsistent with building the foundations of cooperation and mutually shared principles needed in a pluralistic business world.

Virtually any activity that multinational enterprises undertake, even if the firm intends to do good, raises someone's ire it seems. H. B. Fuller Company, known as a good corporate citizen in Minnesota, was chastised for not doing more to prevent street kids in Central American countries from sniffing its product, Resistol glue, as an intoxicant, and seriously injuring themselves.[33]

Rational Scrutiny of Preferences and Aversions

What qualities are needed of morally educated businesspersons if they are to advance the productivity, stability, and enlightenment of a pluralistic world? The morally educated businessperson will have the developed capacity to sort out those preferences and aversions that, although intensely felt, can be dismissed as irrational or unimportant, and those of rational and of fundamental importance.[34] Some aversions are simply grounded in ignorance, or percolate up from early, submerged experiences that vanish if brought to light. Others, though neither irrational nor capable of being eradicated, are not sufficiently important to be the basis for moralizing about the behavior of business organizations. It can be instructive to reflect upon Jesus' admonition, "Judge not, that you may not be judged,"[35] and remember that it takes a good moral character to know when to raise the moral issue.[36]

It is important that the morally educated businessperson reflect on whether her moral judgments represent interests so fundamental, rational, and indispensable as to justify attacking the reputations of, or laying a significant claim on (without outright depriving) the liberty of people and businesses in other cultures.

The Idea of Reputational Sanctions

What are the sources of reputational liability in the new paradigm? Here a legal analogue is helpful. Whereas courts of law enforce sanctions for legal rules, reputational sanctions are created both by what we may term the "court of key constituencies" (the stakeholders: the employees, suppliers, business partners, clients, investors, and so on) and by the "court of public opinion." Unlike the judgments of legal tribunals, reputational judgments carry no right to an appeal. Companies have no due-process rights, no rights to confront witnesses, no presumption of innocence. In today's Internet and CNN world, a firm's conduct—whether exemplary or unscrupulous—is instantaneously broadcast to everyone, everywhere. If the groups comprising the court of key constituencies form negative judgments about a firm's comportment, they will simply withdraw support and give it to competitors to whom they ascribe a more favorable reputation. The Rainforest Action Network called for an international boycott of Burger King, alleging that the chain used cattle that grazed on pastures formed by denuding South American tropical forests. The company initially ignored the charges. Yet within two years Whopper sales had dropped nearly 17 percent. While it is not possible to know exactly how much of that decline was attributable directly to the boycott, the company eventually abandoned the practices in question.

Just because expectations of ethical conduct, social responsibility, and good citizenship for firms are rising, it does not follow that *all* of the expectations are legitimate. Some basic questions to consider are:

- Is the supposed moral standard universal, or is it only relative to a particular culture (or subculture)?
- Under what kinds of financial constraints and pressures is a firm operating? Do such factors excuse or justify its conduct?
- Is an alleged moral violation of a firm significant or trivial?
- Is the firm violating only a pointless norm, one without a rational basis or useful social purpose?

Regarding the first question, people in one culture may believe that fundamental human rights are abstract, universal moral principles; but people from another culture may see human rights as culture-specific rules. Moreover, cultures differ as to the degree to which legal norms figure into a shared understanding of what is right and what is wrong. For instance, in highly legalistic cultures, the law is often leaned on to dictate how companies ought to behave, whereas nonlegalistic cultures frequently depend upon more diffuse forms of social pressure to guide business conduct. Appreciating distinctions between theory and practice—between ideals and reality—matters. Should a firm abandon its operations using child labor in Bangladesh on the ground that this is violating human rights? What if closing the factory will catapult many families into complete poverty because their children's wages are their only income? It is hard to address such questions in the abstract. We need to know what the conventional business practices in a given culture or country are, what the local law is, whether the law is enforced, and how the country's people expect each other and U.S.-based businesses to behave.

An illustration of how the second question gets engaged is seen in debates about corporate inversions. Some companies reincorporate in Bermuda and similar offshore locations to cut their worldwide tax bills. Although some arrangements are outright illegal, critics allege that even the technically legal moves amount to unpatriotic, tax-dodging tactics. On the other side, some argue that firms are justified in pursuing offshore reincorporations as a response to overly burdensome U.S. tax laws.

The third and fourth questions harken back to the legal analogue of sanctions. Just as the law makes distinctions among degrees of offenses in meting out punishments, the court of public opinion and the court of key constituents assign reputational rewards and penalties to business behavior according to both its general level of significance and its bearing on the character of the enterprise in question. Areas of corporate behavior most advantageously governed by public, collective moral rules—violations of which would reasonably justify the imposition of substantial reputational penalties—are areas in which: (1) firms and the people working in them are tempted by interests that conflict with not only an impersonal good, but with the rights of other firms and individuals; (2) a single public criterion applying to all is needed to ensure efficiency and to forestall self-serving rationalizations; (3) judgments must be raised to the level of public discussion, pressure, and collective sanctions, the appropriateness of which can be efficiently decided in public moral debate (paradigm cases include the use and holding of other people's property, injury of other persons, and gaining unfair advantage); and (4) the efficacy of some rules, such as those imposing environmental controls and insider trading regulations, requires that all firms obey them.

In devising and implementing competitive strategies for building a company's reputational capital, a morally educated businessperson will seek innovative ways to advance such moral norms, particularly those carrying high relevance to the core identity of the firm. Consider initiatives undertaken by Interface Carpets. In 1994 its CEO, Ray Anderson, resolved to turn all of the firm's factories on four continents into environmentally sustainable operations. It set out to recycle wherever possible, reduce pollution, and cease dumping in landfills. The firm had been using over five hundred million pounds of raw material annually. It released about nine hundred tons of air pollutants, six hundred million gallons of wastewater, and ten thousand tons of garbage each year. Within two years the company obtained 23 percent more efficiency from recycling, and trimmed forty million dollars in costs. The savings aided Interface in capturing the winning low bid in 1997 to carpet the Gap's new headquarters. The Gap was prompted to solicit Interface's bid due to the latter's bold environmental initiatives.

Human Rights Obligations of Corporations

What about international human rights and reputational capital? For several decades, attention to the responsibilities of business for human rights has been growing. Following Shell's experience in Nigeria, and Levi Strauss and Co.'s deliberations about outsourcing in China, the United Nations (UN) instituted a Global Compact for Business in 2000, which enlists corporations to uphold human rights. More recently, the UN has launched other human rights initiatives, including a code of ethics for transnational corporations. On another front, at a meeting in Switzerland, the Caux Round Table—a body of business leaders from firms in Europe, Japan, and the U.S.—subscribed to an international code of ethics, providing a global framework for conduct and ethical standards.

On the positive side, numerous opportunities for building reputational capital present themselves for multinational companies willing to advance human rights and fundamental freedoms. A company might opt to sponsor a park beautification initiative in a foreign country, earning political support and public trust while thwarting requests for bribes from government officials. A firm might also commit to eliminating child labor from its production chain. In cases where unemployed children and their families would be hurt by this, a company could set up benefits programs that provide medical care and education for child laborers. Levi Strauss took a creative step by paying children's school tuition, providing uniforms and books, and offering each child a job at age 14. Other companies, such as Adidas, are requiring suppliers that hire children to agree not just to keep them in school, but also to pay the children normal wages while attending school.

On the negative side, significant reputational liability exists as investors, customers, employees, and human rights advocates press companies about their direct and indirect dealings with governments that systematically violate human rights.

For example, the government of Sudan is funding an Islamic militia in Darfur that is committing genocide against non-Islamic people. An estimated four hundred thousand people have died, and four million have been displaced. United States Trade Sanctions imposed under the Clinton Administration in November 1997 banned direct business operations in Sudan. Harvard University divested its stock in the Chinese oil companies PetroChina and Sinopec after a committee of faculty, alumni, and students examined the issues: the genocide itself, the importance of oil to the Sudanese government, the effect of PetroChina (wholly owned by the Chinese government), one of the largest companies operating in Sudan, which generates massive revenue for the Sudanese government. Yale, Stanford, and dozens of other universities followed Harvard's lead. California and other states' legislatures approved a divestment plan. Barclay's Global and Northern Trust are marketing Sudan-free investment funds. Canadian oil firm Talisman Energy pulled out of the country in 2003, and Siemens and ABB, Ltd., left in 2007.

The divestment campaign is now targeting Fidelity, the biggest investor in PetroChina. Fidelity responded by delivering passing-the-buck statements such as the following:

> We believe the resolution of complex social and political issues must be left to the appropriate authorities of the world that have the responsibility, and capability, to address important matters of this type. And we would sincerely hope that they would do so wisely on behalf of all of the citizens of the globe.[37]

The company is giving two excuses for keeping clear of human rights. First, the firm deflects responsibility away from itself to "appropriate authorities." This stance reflects the traditional "accountability argument," which holds that, since firms are private institutions, they are subject to a lower level of accountability than are public institutions. Without clear guidelines and accountability, the argument goes, even well-intentioned corporate pursuits of socially responsible activities might distort the governance process. However, whereas the accountability argument claims that it is dangerous to unleash the power of corporations from the discipline of the market, the new mindset for business brings in the counterargument that *not* using corporate power for social betterment itself poses a moral issue. So corporations act unethically by choosing not to get involved in matters where they could have a positive impact.

Second, Fidelity alleges that it lacks the capability to address human rights. That assertion embodies the traditional "expertise argument," holding that corporations should mind their own business, focusing on profit-making instead of social agendas. After all, companies enjoying expertise with their product or service lines do not necessarily have expertise in identifying and analyzing moral issues or in promoting socially beneficial activities. Corporations attain success in the market by identifying and satisfying customer needs, but that ability does not necessarily carry over into nonbusiness areas. However, that argument is also out-of-sync with the new paradigm for business. While a company certainly may lack the expertise to solve every social ill, it has an obligation at least to confront social problems that (as here): relate to the company's conduct, affect significant numbers of people, and can be addressed with the corporation's resources. Moreover, many government agencies (especially those in less-developed countries) themselves lack the expertise to effectively cure social problems. So corporations are able to pursue joint-action with nongovernmental organizations and other businesses in launching corporate citizenship projects. The Danone Group sponsors employees in Spain to work with a local organization, SOS Children's Villages Network, to support homeless or orphaned youth. Enlisting the assistance of UNICEF, Proctor and Gamble developed products aimed at alleviating malnutrition in poor countries.

The upshot is that Fidelity faces potential reputational sanction by not following the patterns of corporate conduct established in previous disinvestment initiatives—such as in South Africa—and patterns being established by its competitors with respect to the Darfur region. Dodging responsibility for human rights adversely affects a company's reputation and ultimately its reputational capital, the most valuable intangible asset it has. Today it is expected that companies will take a leadership role in promoting human rights. Meeting the demands of that role requires that business schools cultivate morally educated businesspeople with the very competencies and sense of accountability that Fidelity says it lacks.

Conclusion

This chapter examined how business education can foster morally educated businesspersons who can: (1) embrace a new paradigm in which businesses must follow social mandates as well as financial imperatives; (2) comply with an increasingly legalistic, compliance-focused approach to ethics triggered by major business scandals while venturing beyond compliance; (3) integrate ethics into all areas of business; and (4) mediate the conflicting forces of tolerance and intolerance occasioned by multiculturalism.

Section I urged that, since a company's reputational capital directly affects the bottom line, business education should present a broader conception of economic value than has traditionally been offered—one that accords legitimacy to intangible assets as well as tangible ones—and integrate the ethical dimension into the teaching of business strategy. Students should be encouraged, when studying cases, to explore opportunities for firms facing ethical dilemmas to cultivate reputational capital through integrity and fair play.

Section II demonstrated that business ethics education should preserve the essential rule-principle duality of moral thinking and judgment in the business world. Neither the rule nor the principle side should dominate. A morally educated businessperson will understand that to achieve lasting success, firms need not only to maintain reputation by legal compliance, but also to magnify reputation through deeper commitments to the spirit of law, informed by the realm of principles. Business schools should not lean on law courses as an exclusive vehicle for advancing business ethics education, while those teaching ethics must be fluent in both the practical-conventional and the abstract-philosophical domains and teach students to move adroitly between the two levels. Using case studies combined with ethical theory and critical thinking is a good way to do this.

Section III gave suggestions for designing interdisciplinary ethics courses that will help the morally educated businessperson function in the real world.

Finally, Section IV showed that the morally educated businessperson must know how to discern standards of global marketplace morality by examining their appearance in capital, consumer, and labor markets. Just as important, a morally educated businessperson will seek the wisdom to distinguish values that are of fundamental social importance (such that they should be advanced, protected, and honored) from those values that are not.

Notes

1. Lynn Paine, *Value Shift: Why Companies Must Merge Social and Financial Imperatives to Achieve Superior Performance* (New York: McGraw-Hill Companies, McGraw-Hill, 2003); Linda Treviño and Katherine Nelson, *Managing Business Ethics: Straight Talk about How to Do It Right* (Hoboken, N.J.: John Wiley and Sons, 2004).

2. Katherine Mangan, "Business Schools and Company CEOs to Create Ethics Center," *The Chronicle of Higher Education*, 30 January 2004.

3. James Flanigan, "Instilling Boardroom Ethics, Starting in the Classroom," *Los Angeles Times*, 10 September 2003, sec. C, p. 1; Sarah Murray, "Values Should Go beyond Rules and Regulations: Amid New Financial Regulations, Business Schools Are Putting Greater Emphasis on Professional Ethical Conduct," *Financial Times*,

23 June 2003, 2; Robert Weisman, "Harvard Raises Its Hand on Ethics: 1st-Year MBA Students Must Take New Course," *Boston Globe,* 30 December 2003, sec. C, p. 1.

4. AACSB International—The Association to Advance Collegiate Schools of Business, *Eligibility Procedures and Accreditation Standards for Business Accreditation,* 31 January 2007 revision (Tampa, Fla.: AACSB International, 2007). The standards provide, in relevant part: "The institution or the business programs of the institution must *establish expectations for ethical behavior* by administrators, faculty, and students," (Section 1[E]). "Normally the curriculum management process will result in an undergraduate degree program that includes learning experiences in such general knowledge and skill areas as . . . *Ethical understanding and reasoning abilities . . . Multicultural and diversity understanding . . . Reflective thinking skills.* . . . Normally the curriculum management process will result in undergraduate and master's level general management degree programs that will include learning experiences in such management-specific knowledge and skills areas as: *Ethical and legal responsibilities in organizations and society,"* (Section 2[15], italics added).

5. Ian Mitroff, "An Open Letter to the Deans and Faculties of American Business Schools," *Journal of Business Ethics* 54 (October 2004): 185–89.

6. Milton Friedman, *Capitalism and Freedom* (Chicago: University of Chicago Press, 1962), 133.

7. R. Edward Freeman, "The Politics of Stakeholder Theory: Some Future Directions," *Business Ethics Quarterly* 4 (October 1994): 409–22.

8. R. Edward Freeman, *Strategic Management: A Stakeholder Approach* (Boston: Pitman, 1984); Kenneth Goodpaster, "Business Ethics and Stakeholder Analysis," *Business Ethics Quarterly* 1 (January 1991): 553; Morey McDaniel, "Stockholders and Shareholders," *Stetson Law Review* 21 (Fall 1991): 121.

9. Archie Carroll, "A Three-Dimensional Conceptual Model of Corporate Performance," *Academy of Management Review* 4 (October 1979): 497–505.

10. John Boatright, *Ethics and the Conduct of Business* (Upper Saddle River, N.J.: Pearson, Prentice Hall, 2003), 390.

11. Thomas Donaldson and Lee Preston, "The Stakeholder Theory of the Corporation: Concepts, Evidence, and Implications," *Academy of Management Review* 20 (January 1995): 65–91.

12. John Boatright, *Ethics in Finance* (Oxford: Blackwell, 1999).

13. Prov. 22:1.

14. Kevin Jackson, *Building Reputational Capital: Strategies for Integrity and Fair Play That Improve the Bottom Line* (New York: Oxford University Press, 2004).

15. Ronald Roman, Sefa Hayibor, and Bradley Agle, "The Relationship Between Financial and Social Performance: Repainting a Portrait," *Business and Society* 38 (March 1999): 109–25; Curtis Verschoor, "A Study of the Link between a Corporation's Financial Performance and Its Commitment to Ethics," *Journal of Business Ethics* 17 (October 1998): 1509–16; Sandra Waddock and Samuel Graves, "The Corporate Social Performance–Financial Performance Link," *Strategic Management Journal* 18 (April 1997): 303–19.

16. John Maxwell, *There's No Such Thing as "Business" Ethics: There's Only One Rule for Making Decisions* (New York: Warner Books, 2003).

17. Richard De George, *Business Ethics* (Upper Saddle River, N.J.: Pearson, Prentice Hall, 1999), 19.

18. Susan Aaronson, "Oh, Behave! Voluntary Codes Can Make Corporations Model Citizens," *The International Economy* 15 (March-April 2001): 40–47; Thomas Donaldson, "Adding Corporate Ethics to the Bottom Line," *Financial Times*, 13 November 2000, 6.

19. I am indebted to the late Prof. Conrad Johnson for this idea as well as for the example that illustrates it.

20. Marianne Jennings, "A Primer on Enron: Lessons from a Perfect Storm of Financial Reporting, Corporate Governance, and Ethical Culture Failures," *California Western Law Review* 39 (Spring 2003): 163.

21. Nel Noddings, *Caring: A Feminine Approach to Ethics and Moral Education* (Berkeley, Calif.: University of California Press, 1984); Nel Noddings, *Starting at Home: Caring and Social Policy* (Berkeley, Calif.: University of California Press, 2002); Joan Tronto, *Moral Boundaries: A Political Argument for an Ethic of Care* (New York: Routledge, Chapman, and Hall, 1993).

22. Linda Treviño and Gary Weaver, "Business ETHICS/BUSINESS Ethics: One Field or Two?" *Business Ethics Quarterly* 4 (April 1994): 113–29.

23. Joseph Badaracco, *Defining Moments: When Managers Must Choose Between Right and Right* (Boston: Harvard Business School Press, 1997).

24. Mark Johnson, *Moral Imagination: Implications of Cognitive Science for Ethics* (Chicago: University of Chicago Press, 1993).

25. Archie Carroll, "In Search of the Moral Manager," *Business Horizons* 30 (March-April 1987): 13.

26. Patricia Werhane, *Moral Imagination and Management Decision-Making* (New York: Oxford University Press, 1999), 5.

27. Alice Gaudine and Linda Thorne, "Emotion and Ethical Decision Making in Organizations," *Journal of Business Ethics* 31 (May 2001): 175–87; Linda Treviño and Stuart Youngblood, "Bad Apples in Bad Barrels: A Causal Analysis of Ethical Decision-Making Behavior," *Journal of Applied Psychology* 75 (August 1990): 378–85; Elizabeth Midlarski and Manus Midlarski, "Some Determinants of Aiding under Experimentally Induced Stress," *Journal of Personality* 41 (June 1973): 305–27; George Lowenstein, "Behavioral Decision Theory and Business Ethics: Skewed Trade-Offs between Self and Others," in *Codes of Conduct: Behavioral Research into Business Ethics*, eds. David Messick and Ann Tenbrunsel (New York: Russell Sage Foundation, 1996); Robin Derry, "Moral Reasoning in Work-Related Conflicts," *Research in Corporate Social Performance and Policy*, vol. 9 (Greenwich, Conn.: JAI Press, 1987), 25–50.

28. Meryl Davids, "Global Standards, Local Problems," *Journal of Business Strategy* 20 (January-February 1999): 38–43; Thomas Donaldson, "Values in Tension: Ethics Away from Home," *Harvard Business Review*, September-October 1996, 48–62.

29. Richard De George, *Competing with Integrity in International Business* (New York: Oxford University Press, 1993).

30. Stephanie Armour, "Wal-Mart Takes Hits on Worker Treatment," *USA Today*, 10 February 2003, sec. B, p. 1.

31. Caroline Wyatt, "Starbucks Invades Parisian Café Culture," *BBC News*, 15 January 2004, http://newsvote.bbc.co.uk/mpapps/pagetools/print/news.bbc.co.uk/2/hi/europe/3401637.stm.

32. Thomas Dunfee, "Corporate Governance in a Market with Morality," *Law and Contemporary Problems* 62 (Summer 1999): 143.

33. Norman Bowie and Stefanie Ann Lenway, "H.B. Fuller in Honduras: Street Children and Substance Abuse," in *Ethical Issues in Business: A Philosophical Approach,* eds. Thomas Donaldson and Patricia Werhane (Upper Saddle River, N.J.: Pearson, Prentice Hall, 2008).

34. Richard Brandt, *A Theory of the Good and the Right* (Oxford: Oxford University Press, Clarendon Press, 1979).

35. Matt. 7:1.

36. John Dewey, *Democracy and Education* (1917; reprint, New York: Free Press, 1944), 354; John Dewey and James H. Tufts, *Ethics* (New York: Henry Holt, 1908), 254–58.

37. John Wasik, "Buffett Can Follow Harvard, ABB Lead on Sudan," *Bloomberg .com,* 29 January 2007, http://www.bloomberg.com/apps/news?pid=20601039&refer=columnist_wasik&sid=aDBiT.cG_7Rw.

Chapter Twelve

TEACHING BUSINESS ETHICS WITH ARISTOTLE

Edwin M. Hartman

CAN WE who teach ethics make our students more ethical? If not, what good are we? Is it really the job of those who teach business ethics to make their students ethical? Isn't it enough if we show them how to be ethical if they want to be? After all, accounting professors teach their students how to be accountants if they want to be; no professor is required to make students want to be accountants.

We have a complex challenge. We are supposed to teach our students ethics, and we are supposed to convince them that they have reason to learn ethics and to be ethical. But to begin with, we do not agree on ethical principles: we cannot be sure what the right ones are, where they come from, or how to apply them to complex situations, especially if they seem to conflict. Our students feel comfortable in expressing their familiar sophomore relativism by asking, "Who's to say what's right or wrong?" Second, even if we agreed on what one ought to do, we might still not know why an agent has any self-interested reason to do it. Business students want to learn accounting, finance, management, and so on because it will make them successful and prosperous in business. It is not clear that learning ethics will benefit them, or that they will want to be ethical if they see no benefit. It does not look like a competitive advantage, particularly for the individual.

If we cannot deal with either of these problems satisfactorily, we can hardly expect success in teaching business ethics to students who are typically skeptical about ethics.

Perhaps it is not surprising, then, to find evidence that business students are less honest than those in other disciplines.[1] It appears to be a problem that feeds on itself: if our students learn not to trust other businesspeople, they will themselves be less trustworthy. The cycle will continue, and honesty will become an ever-less-viable policy, and compliance a more expensive matter.

My claim is that Aristotle helps us deal with these difficulties. He succeeds in part because his aims are modest. He acknowledges that ethics does not offer the level of certainty that we find in mathematics, and that one should not demand that level of certainty of a field that does not have it to offer.[2] But it is not an arcane discipline. He bases his ethical views largely on common sense, supplemented by what he calls science. In his view, if we can arrange the deliverances of intelligent common sense and science into a coherent whole, we (or at any rate the best of us) can indeed make sound ethical judgments, and we can show that there is good reason to act accordingly.

Aristotle's Views

Aristotle takes ethics to be primarily about character, which we may define as one's standard pattern of thought and action with respect to one's own and others' well-being.[3] Character includes virtues and vices, and involves certain values and the right emotional makeup as well. (Aristotle does not use the term "values," but he does countenance desires for the most important human goods. He would surely hold—quite correctly—that one may value something unimportant or even something not good.)

Having a virtue involves having what Harry Frankfurt calls second-order desires: one not only is but wants to be motivated by a certain sort of consideration.[4] Values involve our higher-order desires, especially those concerning the sort of person one wants to be, which may be good or bad. To have a strong character is to have values that consistently guide one's actions. (Aristotle attends to some personal features that are not clearly moral: a sense of humor, for example.) Character determines your identity in that maintaining your character is tantamount to continuing your life.[5]

Aristotle does not reject principles; in fact they play an important role in his ethics. A courageous person, for example, will act on the principle that one should take appropriate risks to achieve some good result. But principles are secondary, in the sense that we act on principles of courage because we are courageous, and not the other way around. If you are a courageous person, your immediate thought in rescuing a friend from a pit bull is not that one ought to be courageous in a case like this, but that Smith needs help. A friend's peril is a reason for action, from your point of view.

Aristotle and other virtue ethicists do not, however, believe that we can find principles that will tell us exactly how much trouble the friend should be in before we help her, or how much of a risk we ought to take, nor any algorithm to prioritize competing principles. The principle that one should take appropriate risks to achieve some good result is vague, and cannot be made less vague without provoking arguments.

Having a virtue is not a matter of being able to produce an air-tight definition of a virtue. It is more like having certain enduring desires that can serve as reasons to act because they have to do with one's well-being or other important concerns and commitments. A person of generous character acts generously, wants to do so, and thinks it good to do so. If you are generous, you are and want to be the sort of person who is normally motivated by thoughts like this: "Jones is in need, so I'll give him what he needs." To be a person of truly generous character entails having and wanting to have a settled disposition to assist needy friends, and emotions to match—in this case, sympathy. The next-best thing, though, short of a truly generous character, is acceptance of one's obligation: "Jones is in need and I'm his friend, so I ought to give him a few dollars."

Note that one's generosity may not only justify one's action but also explain it. If you help Jones out of generosity, your generosity is causing you to help him. You are not doing it to show off or because you want to get leverage over Jones or because you are drunk.

Virtues involve attitudes and emotions in an essential way. Aristotle does not claim that you can make yourself feel grateful on a particular occasion, but you can in time become the sort of person who is grateful on appropriate occasions.[6] Good parents raise their children to be honest, hence to be strongly inclined not to lie, to feel a sense of repugnance when lying even in circumstances that justify it. In this respect he sets a demanding standard.

He believes that growing up in a good community is the primary way to become a virtuous person, in part because he believes that common opinions about ethics are on the whole correct, and in part because he believes that the needs of a good community help determine what counts as virtuous. One comes to apprehend courage first by being told as a child that some acts are courageous, and some others are cowardly. Over time one gets into the habit of acting courageously, and comes to have a pretty good sense of what courage looks like. Then through a process that Aristotle calls dialectic, which we shall discuss, one may acquire a fuller understanding of courage and its contraries, cowardice and foolhardiness, and can reliably identify instances of them.

But a virtue is more than a disposition.[7] Rationality is involved as well. Acting courageously just by imitating courageous people will not suffice. To be truly courageous one needs a clear idea of what is most important to one, and to be concerned about the kind of person one is. Not knowing one's values means that one cannot assess the importance of anything, and therefore cannot rationally consider the appropriate level of risk to accept to protect what one values. Courage and recklessness are psychologically similar but morally different, and the rationality required to act on the first rather than the second is rare. Still, a courageous person need not give an unassailable definition of courage or prove conclusively that a certain act is courageous.

Though ethics involves rationality, it is not like geometry.[8] It is more like navigation, medicine, or comedy.[9] One has to develop a feeling for navigation and medicine. There are rules, although they are not as definite as those of geometry, but there are still right and wrong answers, and the wrong ones can be catastrophic.

Aristotle's approach requires some elaboration and defense. First, we need to see why he seems to think it self-evident that being ethical serves the agent's best interests—that in fact ethics is principally about the agent's best interests.

Second, we need to understand how he uses dialectic to shore up common sense. Third, we need to see how Aristotle's virtue-based ethics deals adequately with morally complex situations.

Character and Interests

Utilitarianism, like other typical principle-based ethical theories, purports to tell us what we ought to do, but it does not even try to show that an agent is better off for being ethical. If it will be truth forever on the scaffold, wrong forever on the throne, then business ethics is a mistake, if not an oxymoron. This is a serious matter. If acting ethically makes the agent worse off, we are going to have a difficult time persuading our students to take business ethics as seriously as they take subjects that will indeed serve them well. There is some evidence that ethical organizations do well, but most studies make facile assumptions about what an ethical company looks like and offer correlations instead of causes.[10]

Utilitarian theories do not usually characterize the good life that ethics is supposed to promote, while Aristotle does: it is a matter of living according to nature—humankind's communal and rational nature—and so flourishing, to use the now popular rendering of the word *eudaimonia*. Since human beings are social and rational creatures, the good life is a matter of living according to reason in a congenial community.

Let us be clear: according to Aristotle, ethics is about the good life of the agent. Insofar as you are virtuous, unless you are unlucky in some important way, your life is good, satisfactory, happy, flourishing. It is significant that Aristotle claims that *phronesis*, which normally translates as prudence or practical wisdom, is coextensive with virtue as a whole. As "practical wisdom," *phronesis* is appropriately self-interested and is not theoretical as mathematics is.

This leaves unanswered any question about the relationship between personal happiness and what we today would say is the subject matter of ethics: the interests of others. Aristotle seems to believe, moreover, that there is some self-evidently good state toward which every substance develops, and that humans will flourish when they have achieved a state of maturity that includes rationality and sociability. A skeptic will deny that human beings tend toward some identifiable end state, and will not accept that we can know that our natural end, if such there be, includes rationality and sociability.

We cannot entirely rehabilitate Aristotle's teleology, but we can create a plausible and generally Aristotelian view on which ethics and happiness overlap. I want to make three broad points in so doing. First, we are indeed social creatures whose happiness depends to some degree on our sociability. Second, rationality of a certain kind is a necessary condition of our well-being: we are better off if we are in a state of psychic and logical harmony. Third—and this point is closely related to the second—the satisfaction of our desires is a good thing only insofar as we have desires that, from a broader and longer-term point of view, we want to have.

That humans are in some important sense social creatures seems beyond doubt. Hence the good life involves living satisfactorily in a congenial community and to be the sort of person who fits well into a good community. Your happiness depends in part on your being a productive and congenial member of the community. Desires that are at odds with this can create serious problems. You have good reason to be virtuous, and not merely to act sometimes as though you were.

Aristotle claims that your character is a matter of what you enjoy doing: good things if you are a good person, bad things if you are a bad one.[11] Good character is not just a matter of doing the right thing, but of having the right desires and emotions.[12] You should be grateful for kindnesses, angry if and only if you are seriously wronged, sympathetic toward the wretched, glad to help your fellow citizens. Emotions of the right sort support good character.

It does not follow that one is better off being virtuous; the argument shows only that people of good character enjoy being virtuous. Aristotle attributes virtue to the one who gladly does the right thing, but not all who consider ethics and happiness would agree. Kant does not require that the good person act on inclination; in fact, the "dear self" seems to be a kind of natural enemy of the good will. St. Paul, a tormented man, is eloquent on the battles of the (bad) flesh against the (good) spirit, whereas Aristotle takes the second to be the form of the first, and the flourishing of the virtuous to be psychic harmony rather than torment.

Aristotle does take notice of the situations in which we steel ourselves to do the right thing against inclination. In those cases, however, we exhibit self-control, which is ethically inferior to temperance, in which inclination does not oppose virtue. There are costs associated with virtue. Acting courageously is often unpleasant: after all, one may be risking one's life, and one is not being courageous if one holds one's own life to be worthless.[13] But whereas self-control is a matter of choosing to do the right thing in spite of wanting to do the wrong thing, courage is a matter of choosing to perform an act that essentially includes fear.[14]

Yet we may wonder whether Aristotle can give a convincing argument against those who claim to enjoy being successfully rapacious rather than just. One possible answer would be that in the long run your unscrupulousness will catch up with you, perhaps because your reputation will repel people with whom you want to negotiate or work. Indeed it might, but it also might not.

We need to look closely at Aristotle's claim. Since a good person enjoys doing the right thing and has the right desires, when you are asking yourself whether you want to be a good person, you are asking yourself what desires you want to have. To put it another way: given that you want to serve your own interests, *what do you want your interests to be?* Now that is a profound question—a question about a higher-order desire. Do our students want to be people who can enjoy only great financial success? Or do they want to be people who enjoy a life in which work plays an important but not dominant role and offers challenge, fun, association with interesting people, and compensation that lets them live comfortably? The question is not which one business students prefer. It is a higher-order question about *which one they would choose to prefer* if they could choose their preferences. It would be difficult to answer that question by reference to self-interest, since it is difficult to see what would count as a straightforwardly self-interested answer to the question, "What do you want your interests to be?"

Is there any reason at all to prefer one of those two answers? One reason for preferring the second is that you are more likely to get what you want. Most students who give it are indeed happier in the end than those who give the first.[15] Great wealth is hard to achieve, and many who achieve it turn out to enjoy it less than they expected to. A good life must be achievable and sustainable. It is not good for you to value something that you are unlikely to be able to get and keep.

It may seem impossible to decide what one is going to prefer, but there is a sort of situation in which one in effect does. If students learn how a strong organizational culture can affect one's character, they will know that the choice of an employer is a most important one. I may (depending on the organization) like being the sort of person who enjoys acting ruthlessly, or the sort who maintains a professional attitude. Choosing an employer, like choosing any sort of community, may in effect be choosing which desires to cultivate, hence to some degree choosing a character.

On what basis can a student choose to have one sort of character or another? Certain choices will cause the student to develop certain desires that are likely to be frustrated, while others will lead to a life easily attained but so narrow and impoverished as to be not worth attaining. This leaves an existential choice, one not made in a way an economist would recognize as rational, but surely not irrational.

Making a decision about one's employment may be such an existential choice. A vulnerable character can be overridden—that is, people can be made to act out of character—but over the long haul one's higher-order desires may change to adjust to one's organization.[16] On the Aristotelian view, that is a significant change in character. So choosing to take a job with Company A may cause Jones to want to be highly professional, honest, and so on, but taking a job with Company B may cause him to want to be ruthless and very rich and will feel contempt for the dullards and wimps who toil for honest pennies. But perhaps if Jones had taken the job at Company A, ten years later he would have been contemptuous of the racing rats at Salomon. The choice is between two options that are not comparable; it cannot be made rationally in the standard sense. (For one thing, we often do not know how much we shall enjoy some experience, or for how long, and it is probably even more difficult to predict the results of a significant change in higher-order desires.[17]) It is possible that Jones will eventually be happy with either choice (in which case ethics can be the tiebreaker).

It will not do to try to convince Jones that a particular kind of life will be best for him. We ought to recognize a great variety of forms of satisfying life. At the same time we ought to respect the limits on that variety implied by our rational and social nature. As business students plan their lives, we who teach business ethics should encourage them to consider their strengths and limitations, their opportunities, and what they can and cannot learn to enjoy. Let us not encourage them to assume ahead of time that whatever they happen to want is possible, or that they will enjoy it if they get it.

Rationality and Psychic Harmony

Aristotle has arguments in support of his conception of the good life, and therefore of ethics. He believes that the good life will have a certain wholeness, rather than being a series of unconnected experiences. Happiness requires desires that are rational in the sense of being consistent with one another, and actions that are consistent with one's desires.[18] Hence a happy person is in a state of psychic harmony: the faculties of the soul are working well together, as they are supposed to.

Aristotle clearly does not regard rationality as just a matter of the efficiency with which a means leads to the satisfaction of some desire, as Hume and many mainstream economists hold. Surely there is something irrational about desiring (say) health, while eating and drinking to excess, smoking, and avoiding exercise. It is also irrational not to desire health, physical or psychic, at all: these are goods, desirable for anyone. And it is at least arguably irrational to accept near-term gratification rather than postpone greater gratification—a form of weakness of the will.[19]

Consistency of desires is not sufficient for good character or for happiness, but it does seem to be necessary. There are difficulties in prizing both idleness and personal achievement, or heavy drinking and fitness, or feeling free to offend and having many friends. But can't you do well if you hide your hostility or rapacity? Aristotle says no: if you do it for strategic reasons, as when people are watching, you will be doing something that you do not enjoy.[20] You will be in a state of disharmony. In any case, you are going against your sociable nature. How many true friends are you going to have? Will you be a happy citizen of your community? A satisfied employee?

Leon Festinger was the most important pioneer in investigating cognitive dissonance. He and his followers found that people will go to great lengths to maintain a coherent set of desires and principles.[21] In particular, they will interpret their own judgments and sometimes the facts of the case to keep their words and actions consistent with the principles that they want to hold. We suffer not only because we are not as good as we claim to be, but from the inconsistency between what we claim to be and what we are. This is evidence in favor of Aristotle's view that we are uncomfortable with psychic disharmony.

We might object that Aristotle does not show that integrity of the sort that he has in mind is sufficient for good character. Some have argued that one may have this kind of integrity but be a bad person, because rationality in the sense of coherence of beliefs and desires is not enough to guarantee an ethical life, though it might be sufficient for a happy one. However, remember that Aristotle claims that, as humans are social beings, the satisfactions of family, friends, and community—necessarily reciprocal—are not optional. They are essential human goods: if you do not desire them or cannot bring yourself to act on your desire of them, your desires just will not be coherent.

Good character is essentially a matter of the healthy state of one's own soul. It is natural to wish to achieve psychic health, which is self-evidently a good thing. It is not a state that nature reliably brings about—not everything flourishes—and it is not the final state of most people. It is a state in which one is not at war with oneself, torn by inconsistent desires, constantly frustrated by life, cognitively dissonant. It is attractive to almost anyone, surely including most business students, if they consider it.

From Aristotle's point of view, to say that there are no right or wrong answers in ethics is to say that there is no difference between happiness and unhappiness, or between a fulfilling life and a miserable one. That is truly absurd, an affront to common sense. And Aristotle takes common sense very seriously.

Common Sense

Plato and many philosophers since have doubted that common sense could be the basis for ethics, or much else worth knowing. Questions like "What ought I to do?" and "What reason have I for doing what I ought to do?" were thought to be beyond the reach of common opinion—to be the sort of thing that philosophers should tackle.

Aristotle does not think this way, in part because he does not demand iron-clad certainty and because he starts with common sense—with familiar and widely shared opinions and makes it coherent. He does not put forward radically new conceptions of courage, justice, or friendship. He does not suggest that becoming a good person is a superhuman achievement, though it is not easy or even very common. The effect of the *Nichomachean Ethics* is not to undermine our ideas about ethics but to refine and rationalize them.

There is much to be said for Aristotle's fidelity to common sense. If an ethical theory generates conclusions at variance with our common and firm convictions, we have reason to question it. For example, if Kant's ethical theory implies that one ought not to lie to the Nazis even to save the lives of innocent Jews, we have reason to question his theory. On the other hand, insofar as Aristotle countenances slavery, as most of his contemporaries did, we should recall that morality is not merely a matter of consensus.

Aristotle's process of dialectic starts with common opinions, with the intention of finding principles that are consistent with most of those opinions and explain them, or improve on them insofar as they can be shown to be inadequate in some way.[22] In the best case, one's beginnings (*archai*) form a coherent whole. The *archai* with which we begin thinking about ethics are particular moral judgments or intuitions. Aristotle seems to have in mind something such as John Rawls's reflective equilibrium.[23] There are no unassailable propositions that serve as the foundation of all ethical knowledge. One compares one's principles and one's considered judgments about particular cases, and if they do not form a coherent whole, adjusts one or both to create an internally consistent set of principles that are also consistent with most of our judgments on ethical cases. In the case of what Norman Daniels has called wide reflective equilibrium,[24] we bring in pertinent science, settled beliefs about human nature, and other facts. Wide reflective equilibrium seems close to Aristotle's view that at our moral best we have a set of background beliefs, intuitions, and principles that cohere, with emotions to match. Rawls has in mind logical rather than psychological coherence, whereas Aristotle seems to be thinking of both, although he does not sharply distinguish them.

We—amateurs as well as professionals—still talk about ethics in this way. We test and sometimes reject an ethical theory because it generates strongly counterintuitive results. We will reject a standard form of act utilitarianism that would violate fairness and undermine rights, but we will also reject a certain claim about people's rights because permitting it would have catastrophic consequences, on the theory that ethical action does not normally have catastrophic consequences.

Aristotle does not claim that those who go through the process of dialectic will find principles that apply perfectly to complex situations. Ethics still is not geometry. But the principles that one does have will be clearer and more defensible, though possibly somewhat more complicated and not always easily applied, and one will have better and more trustworthy intuitions for those situations in which principles compete or are hard to apply. In particular, one's intuitions will lead one to apprehend the situation under the right principle rather than on a principle that social pressure forces on one or one that rationalizes one's preferred behavior.

Consider large stock options for executives, for example. Proceeding on the basis of intuition, consistent with some egalitarian principle, liberals are likely to claim that they are unjustifiably generous; conservatives will defend them as being what the market dictates, and as being a good way to align the interests of the executives and the stockholders. Liberals might take executive pay to be a counterexample to the notion that we ought to determine pay by reference to markets, or they might deny that the CEO's friends on the board constitute a market. Conservatives will reject the egalitarian conception of fairness that liberals embrace. How might the standoff be resolved? Conservatives could suggest that we consider the likely consequences of eliminating stock options—a typical utilitarian argument. The liberals might take the position that fairness trumps utilitarian considerations.

Part of the background for the conservative position is agency theory: we can count on executives to work effectively for the stockholders if and only if they are paid to do just that. This view presupposes a particularly pure and narrow form of self-interest that motivates executives, and its proponents do not exactly offer a sophisticated argument for it.[25] But if agency theory is what we teach our students, then they may come to believe uncritically that the presupposition is true. It is all the more important that we examine the presupposition.

Agency theorists tend to be utilitarians. I once heard Michael Jensen give a talk in which he scornfully asked, "What is justice, anyway? Where do I find it?" He seemed to have little difficulty in defining and finding utility, with no thought of whether his view of utility was adequate from a moral point of view. Thus suitably reduced, utility fits comfortably into economic theory. In a characteristically dialectical conversation we might challenge this form of utilitarianism and offer considerations based on justice and rights. We might seek a way to make considerations of utility, justice, and rights fit together and fit our intuitions as well. Reducing justice and rights to the economist's notion of utility is a facile way to do it: it will make a poor fit with other principles that we hold, with many of our views about the nature of the good life, and with our intuitions.

Many of us have heard economists say something like this: executive compensation is an economic issue, not an ethical one. We might take this to mean that it is a matter to be handled by the sort of utilitarianism that standard economic theory presupposes. But as our students should discover in discussing matters such as this, there are many different ways in which a situation may be described or framed. A law limiting stock options might be framed as preserving fairness, or as an unwarranted diminution of corporate autonomy, or as a way of undermining managerial effectiveness. We hope that our students become better at understanding and describing these multifaceted situations correctly, and therefore at making better judgments. This is a way to improve their ethical perception.

Ethical Perception Done Correctly

Aristotle claims that the person of good character perceives a situation rightly—that is, notices and takes appropriate account of its salient features. The faculty of imagination (*phantasia*) enables you to understand what a perceived object is, or to grasp the ethical quality of an act.

You are morally responsible for perceiving the act correctly—that is, for framing it right. To frame it incorrectly by failing to apprehend the ethically salient features of the situation is a mark of a bad character.[26] A person of good character can perceive that a certain act is courageous rather than foolhardy, generous rather than vainglorious, right rather than wrong, and will act accordingly. Aristotle seems to believe that emotion helps us frame properly (an irascible person will take offense inappropriately, for example), but weakness of the will is sometimes the result of wrong framing.[27] *Moral imagination* is the name we now give to the ability to frame ethically significant states and events.[28]

People may make judgments and act on the basis of how they describe a complex situation to themselves. You can frame eating a doughnut as a pleasurable experience or a fattening act, but a person concerned with health should take the second as salient. A good accountant will frame the Enron-related tricks as misrepresenting the financial position of the firm rather than as good client service. Those who teach business ethics face the task of teaching students to do better at ethical framing. A typical business course will not normally put an ethical frame around the problems and issues that it covers. It will present them as economic issues, and not ethical ones. Its language is about items such as incentives rather than obligations, and it is a powerful language. Insofar as a business ethics course helps students become more fluent in the language of right and wrong, it enriches their moral imagination and increases the probability that they will give salient descriptions of morally significant situations.

Our students' environment will influence the way they frame a situation: they will likely do it as others do it, as is the custom in their profession, as the client wishes, etc. Ethical behavior depends upon the employee's ability to recognize ethical issues, and this ability appears to be a function of corporate culture more than of individual employees' attributes.[29]

Consider the Milgram experiment, in which experimental subjects willingly administered what they believed to be painful shocks to innocent people who had given wrong answers.[30] At least some of the participants did not see themselves as causing pain to an innocent subject, but instead as following directions and helping Dr. Milgram in his important work. Your ego will be influential as well: you are likely to describe your failure to confront the boss as a piece of thoughtful diplomacy, whereas others will see it as self-serving and cowardly. Your interests will influence the framing, too: you tend to argue for the moral rightness of actions that favor you, and to describe those actions accordingly. Rationalization to evade cognitive dissonance is depressingly common. No doubt this sort of thinking afflicted the Arthur Andersen accountants working for Enron.

How can we help our students improve their framing? At the very least, we ought to show them that there are alternative ways of framing situations without giving the impression that one way is as good as another. It will be helpful to teach business students about social psychology. Those who understand organizational culture, for example, will be able to take its possible effects, on framing in particular, into account. Former students who have learned about the Milgram experiment in a business ethics course testify that they do sometimes think of it when they are in similar situations, and act accordingly, show that people can be protected against crowd-induced culpable indifference by being taught to recognize the crowd's influence and to act appropriately despite it.[31]

If managers are aware, as Aristotle was, of how easily stray desires, emotions, social pressure, and unexpected emergencies can divert us from our most rational intentions, they should try to avoid getting into those situations in which they are vulnerable. This is "self-management."[32] Finding ways of protecting the company from the kind of bad behavior that pressures and emergencies encourage is a corporate form of self-management. Graduate school is not too soon for thinking this way, and a business ethics class is a good place to consider how foreseeable but unforeseen emergencies and other pressures may sway those whose character is vulnerable—that is, most people.

How, then, does a person of good character make a decision in a complex situation? The kind of person you are will have as much to do with the decision as will your reasoning about it. Dialectic will give you somewhat sharper, though still not perfectly sharp, principles and intuitions and improve your reasoning about a given situation because you are better at noticing and evaluating aspects of it that people of less character do not handle so well. Your decisions will seem intuitive, in part because you will not be able to defend them in a way that convinces everyone. But the intuitions of a person of good character, sharpened by experience and by dialectic (perhaps in a business ethics course) are a good basis for action, although it will not necessarily protect you from bad culture or rationalization.

In part because one cannot accurately calculate with all the variables in mind, and in part to avoid rationalization, people of good character will often stick with certain nearly unexceptionable rules, such as, "We don't lie to our employees. Period." They may say, "We're just not that kind of company," or "That's something I'm just not prepared to do."

Ethics and Strategy

One way to help students learn to see business issues as moral issues and to grasp their salient features is to discuss case studies with them. In a typical strategy course the students consider cases that challenge them to apply principles to a real situation. This is the beginning of developing their intuitions about strategy. There are principles for strategists to follow, but in real life corporate strategy there is much to be said for trusting the intuitions of an intelligent person with a good track record. There will be some easy cases, but there will always be some hard cases, when the experienced and wise manager makes a decision that relies on intuition to a significant degree. Some managers are consistently better than others at framing these situations appropriately. So, for example, one might see a business as low-profit or high-cash-flow, and the strategic situation may determine which description is salient. Successful strategists often cannot say in any detail how they favor one frame over another, or how they rank pertinent considerations.

Case studies in ethics substitute to some degree for experience. In particular, they develop the students' moral imagination. Properly taught, complex cases exercise students' moral judgment about particulars, as when justice and economic efficiency conflict. In looking at a case and considering the many ways in which one can frame a situation and which ways of framing capture its salient features, students are developing moral imagination and thus practical wisdom and thus good character.

One might say that in strategy we can assess the strategist's skill by reference to the track record, but in fact the track record does not always prove very much. Phil Rosenzweig has argued that it is a mistake—one made by Thomas Peters and Robert Waterman, James Collins and Jerry Porras, and many others—to look at successful companies and try to identify the features that account for their success.[33] The standard diagnosis is that a real winner has a supportive culture, focuses on customers, cleaves to a widely understood mission, and so on. However, many such companies, having been held up as examples of what you, too, can do to succeed, perform not nearly as well after the book in question is published.

The problem with the diagnosis, says Rosenzweig, is that people in successful companies are likely to say that their culture is supportive, their focus on customers, and their mission before everyone's mind: profitability has a halo effect; everything else looks good. It is no doubt true that having a culture of mediocrity, ignoring customers, and lacking a mission will do a company little good, but the rules that the strategic gurus have identified are almost trivial as stated. The economic and competitive environments have effects that the gurus ignore.

Rosenzweig has something like a virtue theory of strategy. His shining examples, Bob Rubin and Andy Grove, know that deciding on a strategy is a matter of dealing with uncertainty. What is needed, in addition to the ability to gauge the probabilities insofar as you can, is something like courage: you take a leap into the unknown with the appropriate amount and kind of fear; and if things go wrong, you are ready to weigh the odds and do the same thing again next time. You do not worry about looking bad; you do not retreat to the safety of doing nothing or of groupthink. You have the courage to act rationally. Things may go wrong—fortune is not always on your side, and you may incur short-term obloquy, which will be unpleasant—but failure does not undermine your satisfaction in having done the best you can do, or your confidence on the next attempt. That attitude is more effective than any principle that a strategist is likely to propound.

Courage can help a strategist make deals, but there are usually new deals to be made tomorrow. What really tests character is to make decisions on which the future of the company depends.[34] The virtues of courage, wisdom, farsightedness, honesty, fidelity to the stockholders, respect for the cautionary opinions of other senior managers, and so on do not guarantee success, and sometimes the strategist does not get another chance.

Can students also gain in critical understanding of their values? Can we help students to find and stick with good values, whatever their career choices? At the very least, we can encourage them to reflect on what is most important to them and on how to protect it.

Reading fiction is a way to do this. In fact, Richard Rorty argues that literature is better for this purpose than is philosophy. Sometimes non-fiction will do equally well.[35] Michael Lewis's *Liar's Poker*, for example, can help students to reflect on their values as they consider the addictive Dash Riprock and the predatory Human Piranha, and ask themselves why selling equities in Dallas should be inappropriate for anyone with any self-respect.[36] Considering Salomon or the Milgram experiment may enable them later to stop and reflect, and to undertake moral reasoning rather than rationalization. A measure of self-knowledge, a component of good character, will lead them to protect their best values not only by choosing a congenial environment but also by avoiding if possible, and resisting if necessary, the pressures to do the wrong thing wherever they are.[37]

Conclusion

Becoming ethical is not a matter of discovering arcane principles that ground our decisions in certainty, for ethics is neither arcane nor certain. Being ethical is primarily a matter of being a person of good character, with virtues, emotions, values, and practical intelligence to match. The ethical values that experience teaches us are at least the beginning of wisdom about ethics. Ethical progress is a matter of refining and adjusting these values, learning to bring them to bear in making decisions, and protecting them from hostile environments. Our part of the project is to encourage reflection on values and to offer exercises in putting the values into practice. Then perhaps our students will go on to flourish.

Notes

1. Donald L. McCabe and Linda K. Treviño, "Cheating among Business Students: A Challenge for Business Leaders and Educators," *Journal of Management Education* 19, no. 2 (1995): 205, cited in Jeffrey Pfeffer, "Why Do Bad Management Theories Persist? A Comment on Ghoshal," *Academy of Management Learning and Education* 4 (March 2005): 99.

2. Aristotle *Nichomachean Ethics* 1.3.1094b12–14, 23–27 (Aristotle, *Ethica Nicomachea*, ed. Ingram Bywater [Oxford: Oxford University Press, Clarendon Press, 1894]; Aristotle, *Nichomachean Ethics*, trans. Terence H. Irwin [Indianapolis, Ind.: Hackett Publishing, 1985]).

3. Joel Kupperman, *Character* (New York: Oxford University Press, 1991), 17.

4. Harry G. Frankfurt, "Freedom of the Will and the Concept of a Person," in *Free Will*, ed. Gary Watson (New York: Oxford University Press, 1982), 81–95.

5. Aristotle *Nichomachean Ethics* 9.4.1066a13–29, b7–14.

6. See Ibid., 1.3.1095a2–13.

7. On this and related points I am indebted to Miguel Alzola, "Character and Environment: The Status of Virtues in Organizations," *Journal of Business Ethics* 78 (March 2008): 343–57.

8. Aristotle *Nichomachean Ethics* 1.7.1098a29–34.

9. Ibid., 3.3.1112a5–7, 4.8.1028a23–34.

10. The criteria for being an ethical company are questionable as well. More pseudoscience.

11. Aristotle *Nichomachean Ethics* 2.3.1104b5ff.

12. Ibid., 10.8.1178a9–24, etc.

13. Ibid., 3.9.1117a34–b17.

14. This interpretation, which I owe to Eugene Garver, "Aristotle on Virtue and Pleasure," in *The Greeks and the Good Life*, ed. David J. Depew (Indianapolis, Ind.: Hackett Publishing, 1980), 157–76, is controversial. Fortunately my thesis does not require getting this passage exactly right.

15. Russell W. Belk, "Materialism: Trait Aspects of Living in the Material World," *Journal of Consumer Research* 12 (December 1985): 265–80; Tim Kasser and Richard M. Ryan, "Further Examining the American Dream: Differential Correlates of Intrinsic and Extrinsic Goals," *Personality and Social Psychology Bulletin* 22 (March 1996): 280–87, cited in Jonathan Haidt, *The Happiness Hypothesis: Finding Modern Truth in Ancient Wisdom* (New York: Perseus, Basic Books, 2006).

16. Stanley Milgram, *Obedience to Authority: An Experimental View* (New York: Harper and Row, 1974); Philip Zimbardo, *The Lucifer Effect: Understanding How Good People Turn Evil* (New York: Random House, 2007); Edwin M. Hartman, *Organizational Ethics and the Good Life* (New York: Oxford University Press, 1996), 143–65.

17. Daniel T. Gilbert et al., "Immune Neglect: A Source of Durability Bias in Affective Forecasting," *Journal of Personality and Social Psychology* 75 (September 1998): 617–38.

18. Aristotle *Nichomachean Ethics* 9.4.1066b7–11.

19. To understate, the nature of rationality is a matter of controversy. Rationality has a normative aspect, and differences in definition reflect different views of how we should think. I shall not discuss objections to the standard views about consistency and transitivity.

20. Aristotle *Nichomachean Ethics* 9.4.1066b7–14.

21. See Leon Festinger, *A Theory of Cognitive Dissonance* (Stanford, Calif.: Stanford University Press, 1957).

22. See Aristotle *Nichomachean Ethics* 7.1.1145b4–8, for example.

23. John Rawls, *A Theory of Justice* (Cambridge, Mass.: Harvard University Press, 1971), 48–51.

24. Norman Daniels, "Wide Reflective Equilibrium and Theory Acceptance in Ethics," *Journal of Philosophy* 76 (May 1979): 256–82.

25. Michael Jensen and William Mechling, "Theory of the Firm: Managerial Behavior, Agency Costs, and Ownership Structure," *Journal of Financial Economics* 3 (October 1976): 305–60, cited in Sumantra Ghoshal, "Bad Management Theories Are Destroying Good Management Practices," *Academy of Management Learning and Education* 4 (March 2005): 75–91.

26. Aristotle *Nichomachean Ethics* 3.5.1114a32–b3.

27. Ibid., 7.3.1147a32–b6.

28. See Patricia H. Werhane, *Moral Imagination and Management Decision-Making* (New York: Oxford University Press, 1999).

29. Al Y. S. Chen, Roby B. Sawyers, and Paul F. Williams, "Reinforcing Ethical Decision Making through Corporate Culture," *Journal of Business Ethics* 16 (June 1997): 855–65.

30. Milgram, *Obedience to Authority*.

31. Arthur L. Beaman et al., "Increasing Helping Rates through Information Dissemination: Teaching Pays," *Personality and Social Psychology Bulletin* 4 (July 1978): 406–11; see also Lauren Slater, *Opening Skinner's Box: Great Psychological Experiments of the Twentieth Century* (New York: W. W. Norton, 2004), 109f.

32. Jon Elster, *Ulysses and the Sirens: Studies in Rationality and Irrationality*, rev. ed. (New York: Cambridge University Press, 1984); Jon Elster, *Sour Grapes: Studies in the Subversion of Rationality* (New York: Cambridge University Press, 1985).

33. Phil Rosenzweig, *The Halo Effect . . . and the Eight Other Business Delusions That Deceive Managers* (New York: Simon and Schuster, Free Press, 2007).

34. My colleague Bruce Buchanan made this point in conversation.

35. Richard M. Rorty, "Is Philosophy Relevant to Business Ethics?" *Business Ethics Quarterly* 16 (July 2006): 369–80, and elsewhere.

36. Michael Lewis, *Liar's Poker: Rising through the Wreckage on Wall Street* (New York: W. W. Norton, 1989).

37. For encouraging evidence of the possibility of doing this, see Jonathan Haidt, "The Emotional Dog and Its Rational Tail: A Social Intuitionist Approach to Moral Judgment," *Psychological Review* 108 (October 2001): 814–34, and Beaman et al., "Increasing Helping Rates."

Chapter Thirteen

ARISTOTLE AND THE MBA: THE ODD COUPLE

James O'Toole

A Harvard MBA on vacation hired a fishing guide named Joe to help him land a marlin. Joe lived in a modest house by the sea with his wife and children. Every day, he rose when the sun was warm and took a swim in the ocean with his family. Three days a week he took clients to sea in his boat. The other days he would lie in his hammock and read from breakfast until lunch with his wife.

Almost every afternoon he picked his kids up after school and took them on "an adventure." After a long dinner, *en famille,* Joe and his wife would walk to a nearby café where the locals gathered every evening.

Joe's fishing expeditions were first-rate. The MBA explained to Joe how to put together a group of venture capitalists to "build your underperforming business." Instead of inefficiently taking one client out at a time, he could have a fleet of large, high-tech fishing boats. With a little strategic advice he could branch out into related businesses, perhaps build a high-rise hotel on the beach.

Most important, Joe could go on TV and become the "marketing face" for his business, creating a "brand" that could be franchised at other sleepy fishing communities: "A guy like you could become a celebrity." The MBA then delivered the clincher: "When that happens, we have an IPO and you get rich!"

Joe asked "And what then?" The MBA answered: "Well, you retire to some nice place on the beach, do a little fishing and reading, and get to spend some time with your wife and kids."

—*Story circulating on the Internet*

OVER the last few years, MBA programs have come under increasing criticism from scholars, environmentalists, business journalists, investors, and (some) corporate leaders for:

- ignoring the "soft side" of business, particularly social, moral, and ethical concerns;
- being overtechnical and narrow, not the generalist programs they were originally intended to be;

- failing to develop true leaders with relevant skills;
- encouraging their students' tendencies toward arrogance and greed; and
- enculturating short-term thinking among executives who then cannot build sustainable enterprises.[1]

A good place to start addressing these concerns is with the first, and arguably most profound, of Western philosophers to consider what we today call organizational leadership. The moral concerns Aristotle addresses in the *Politics* and *Nichomachean Ethics* are largely absent from the curricula at most major U. S. business schools.[2] Absent, in particular, is a focus on how leaders create ethical and sustainable corporate cultures, although research shows that the values of corporate executives are the prime determinants of a corporation's culture, and that culture in turn drives organizational behavior.[3]

The world according to Aristotle corresponds remarkably with contemporary thinking about human capabilities and meritocracy, and about how business organizations should be structured to maximize effectiveness. He also was concerned with what we today call social responsibility. His ideas are consistent with modern economic concepts, particularly the linkage of rewards to contributions.[4]

Aristotle's Assumptions

Aristotle's writings are practical, but they are hard-slogging for modern readers. Hence, it is helpful to keep in mind that his moral philosophy rests on five fundamental precepts:

1. Having the capacity to reason is the essence of being human.
2. The highest forms of reasoning are abstract and moral thought, including choosing between the right and wrong ways both of living one's own life and of organizing human institutions.
3. Personal virtue comes from developing the capacity to reason. That is, we fulfill our humanness by developing our naturally given potential.
4. Everyone is capable of learning and of development. The good life comes from the process of *fulfilling,* and not from the impossible end of having *fulfilled* our capacities.
5. While developing one's natural capacities is the "highest good," it is not the "complete good." We do not develop ourselves for selfish reasons, but to better contribute to the good of the communities of which we are members.

The measure of the importance of an activity is the degree to which it requires the highest-order, most abstract, mental capabilities, and we can assume that Aristotle would have placed the leadership of modern business organizations at, or near the top, of his hierarchy of human endeavors. The highest-order, most-human activities are "politics and philosophy" because they require the greatest deployment of abstract reasoning. "Philosophy" includes what we call the sciences, arts, and learned professions. Thus, engineers, lawyers, and doctors are "philosophers," as are journalists, teachers, playwrights, and so on. Likewise, "politics" includes not only serving in elected office, but the leadership of business organizations.

The important thing to Aristotle is not a person's job, but the extent to which that person is using his or her higher-order mental capabilities. His concepts of philosophy and politics should be thought of as inclusive: a factory worker who participates in problem-solving is using those higher-level capabilities as much as the company's CEO.

Aristotelian Microeconomics

An astute economist, Aristotle anticipated Adam Smith's work on the division of labor by over two thousand years. People should be engaged in tasks where they can make the maximum social and economic contribution. It would do the people of Athens no good if those who possessed the greatest aptitude to design and build large structures, such as the Parthenon, were not doing so because they were denied the opportunity to develop their engineering capabilities. The reason why Athens was such a highly developed society in 400 BC, while most other places in the world were mired in subsistence agriculture, was because the Athenians had freed their most talented individuals from the tyranny of toil and given them the leisure to develop science, medicine, engineering, and the arts. No wonder barbarians didn't create acropolises: they treated everyone as equals.

How could justice be served if those with limited capabilities were made leaders of society, or the bosses of enterprises, while those with the greatest natural capacities were held down at the bottom carrying out orders? Aristotle concludes that what we would call meritocracy is the most just form of governance since everyone benefits from the rule of the most competent.

Paradoxically, Aristotle's point of reference is the good of the community. He believes that the natural hierarchy of humans should not serve as an excuse to reward those at the top for having been born with advantages, but that the people at the top are responsible for making it possible for those lower down to lead good lives. When they do, everyone benefits from inequalities based on real capabilities and economic contribution. Who would want to work at Microsoft if equality were its main goal, and the company's executive team had an average IQ of 100, while Bill Gates and Steve Ballmer were assigned work as security guards? Individuals capable of making greater contributions should be treated differently—but only in some respects. In particular, they should be freed from lower-level work so they can concentrate on activities making maximum use of their potential.

The question then becomes: how large a share of the bounty produced by an organization are those at the top entitled to reap? Below I examine several Aristotelian tests of fairness of the distribution of rewards, but suffice it to say here that corporate leaders such as Gates and Ballmer are rewarded justly for their contributions if they have (1) contributed value, (2) increased the overall wealth of the community, and (3) made it possible for everyone in their organization to develop their full potential. Note that the MBA curriculum generally focuses on only the first of those three criteria.

Modern Perspectives

MBA students often have told me that their goal in life is simply "to be happy," a condition they associate with beer, beaches, blondes, and Beemers. Aristotle argued, instead, that happiness is the objective result of how we live. His highest good, *eudaimonia,* has little to do with feelings of pleasure and contentment. What he means by happiness is something more like "the deep sense of satisfaction one gets when one grows as a human being." Yet he complicates matters when he elaborates on the nature of the good at the top of his hierarchy: "If happiness is activity in accordance with *virtue,* it is reasonable that it should be in accordance with the highest virtue; and this will be *the best thing in us. . . .* That activity is *contemplation.*"[5]

Contemplation is the only activity that is absorbing "good work" for all one's life. It includes what former California Governor Jerry Brown did when he meditated and what Einstein did while creating elegant equations and other forms of positively absorbing mental work: playing a piano, woodworking, solving a business problem, writing a scholarly paper.

If going to the beach isn't the best use of our time, shouldn't we spend it developing our greatest talent? Aristotle answers "yes and no." Yes, a person who is born with a high aptitude for science, mathematics, and spatial thinking obviously should study to become the best engineer she is capable of becoming, and never be satisfied with the depth of engineering knowledge she possesses. But no, she will still be unidimensional if she fails to develop her potential in the arts and social sciences. While her potential may not be as deep in those fields, she nonetheless has almost unlimited potential in terms of breadth: she can study Chinese, history, ecology, psychology, anthropology, and learn to play the piano.

There is no limit to the contemplative challenges awaiting her if she chooses to grapple with such profound questions as "Am I leading a good life?" and "Am I doing the right thing?" To Aristotle, men and women who devote as much of their lives as possible to fulfilling their potential in such ways are engaged in true leisure, which he called philosophy, and are on their way to being happy.

Instead of doing what we have always done, writing yet another academic article or playing another round of golf, Aristotle encourages us to stretch ourselves, try new things, learn new skills, and learn about new places. Each of us must pursue happiness in our own way. Growth for an artist may entail starting a business, and growth for a business executive may entail becoming an artist. Yet, Aristotle says, even such adventurous personal choices are not enough to constitute a good life. In addition, virtuous men and women pursue. . . .

The Complete Good

Aristotle argues it is not enough merely to *possess* the capacity to reason, and not even enough to *develop* it. In addition, to be virtuous, humans must *use* our reasoning capacity to meet the needs of our communities. We are "political animals," and virtuous men and women engage in the practical world of politics in addition to philosophy.

With that two-pronged requirement in mind, we may summarize Aristotle's philosophy of virtue, excellence, and happiness: there is a moral difference between just living and living well. Individuals become virtuous to the extent that they strive for excellence, choose to develop their many talents and capacities, particularly their highest-order reasoning abilities. They "complete their virtue" to the extent that they, as leaders of communities and organizations, provide conditions under which others can pursue happiness and achieve excellence.

The Role of Money

Among the panoply of instrumental goods needed to pursue happiness, the foremost and most morally complex is money. Without wealth creation, we cannot have food, clothing, shelter, and other necessities. And because we are not beasts, we want to enjoy good food, nice clothes, and a safe and secure home, not to mention an occasional trip to Paris. So work is a natural activity and, like the wealth it produces, is instrumental to a higher end: We work to live, we don't live to work.

But Aristotle asks, "Is it enough merely to live, or even to live comfortably?" No, he answers: "What we really want is *to live well*." Living well must mean doing things so blissful that we do them for their own sake, not for the sake of any extrinsic compensation. Aristotle doesn't categorize professional activities as *work*: computer nerds are not working when they are hacking, scientists are not working when they are doing research, and professors are not working when they are writing, because they would do those activities even if they weren't paid to do them. Such contemplative activities are *leisure*.

If we are not fortunate enough to have intrinsically "leisurely" professions, Aristotle says we have to find a way to free ourselves from work-work in order to make time to contemplate. Ergo, we need money to afford the leisure time required to pursue happiness. Money isn't the root of evil; it is actually a good *when* it is instrumental to the higher end of creating the opportunity for leisure.

In some ways, the Aristotelian goal is to carve out a lifestyle and work-life much like the one enjoyed by the Internet's fictional "Fisherman Joe." Because Aristotle had known people who behaved like Joe, he concluded almost everyone is free and able to choose to live the good life, even if they do not have great educations or oodles of money.

The issue isn't material goods vs. the free "best things in life." It is about how we will live, and the sign of virtue is to act consciously, choosing one's ends rationally and from the "proper disposition" of seeking excellence. The key to virtue is "to deliberate well." Virtuous people are introspective, self-critical, rational, and curious, not necessarily affluent.

So, How Much?

Today we face the same ethical question people have been asking themselves since the glory days of ancient Greece: *How much is enough for me?* Aristotle offers the barest outline of an answer: we need enough wealth not to worry where the next drachma is coming from. Further, we need enough to be comfortable and to have adequate savings, for without a sense of security we won't have the peace of mind needed to concentrate on higher pursuits. On the other hand, he explains:

> It seems to some people that good fortune is the same as happiness. But it isn't. It is actually an impediment when it is excessive and, in that case, perhaps it is no longer right to call it good fortune. For wealth has a limit in its relationship to happiness.

In sum: too little money and one is unable to develop oneself effectively; too much money and one may become lost in materialism.

The Golden Mean

In answering the question "How much is enough?" Aristotle warns us not to expect precise answers from philosophical inquiry. Ethical analysis is not scientific; it does not produce clear and quantifiable results (which may be a reason why philosophical discussions are not part of the MBA curriculum), but "has as much clearness as the subject matter admits of."

What matters more to Aristotle than the conclusions we reach is how we construct, and think through, such problems. When we answer the question "How much is enough?" he doesn't care what amount we arrive at, but whether we engage in a disciplined moral analysis.

To begin that process, we must pose our question in an appropriate context. We should start with a definition of the good life. We always must keep the highest end in view to think effectively. We should also engage in honest dialogue with friends who are also struggling with it, and try to answer the objections of those who disagree with our conclusions. The one person we typically fool in moral analysis is ourself.

Aristotle offers a disciplined process by which we can decide. First, we must distinguish between needs and wants. We need incomes that cover the costs of necessities, of raising and educating our children, of leisure activities such as travel that help us to grow, and of investments sufficient to provide income for our retirement. But we do not need everything we want. Second, we must avoid the defects of want and of excess. On the one hand, we must be realistic and not underestimate what we need. The precise amount one needs depends upon factors such as age, interests, family situation, and place of residence. Older, single people who live in rural areas do not need as much as younger couples raising kids in Manhattan. On the other hand, we must also avoid conspicuous consumption. We need clothes and art, but we don't need Brioni suits and original Picassos.

Objections, Reasonable and Otherwise

Implicit in Aristotle's reasoning is the conclusion that a great many more people can afford to start pursuing happiness *now* than are currently doing so. But should everyone spend less time toiling, and more time engaged in philosophy and politics? There are two reasonable objections to that claim.

First, some, perhaps many, people are perfectly happy pursuing more, and prefer their material goodies to the (for them nonexistent) benefits of contemplation. People who dedicate their lives to making money are already leading full lives, and Aristotle is a condescending elitist to say otherwise. But Aristotle is not trying to impose his views on anyone. He is responding to the wealthy and powerful people who asked, "Is that all there is?" In response, he suggested to all those capable of doing so to consider what it would mean for them to live a fuller, more interesting life. He asked everyone to do this because he worried that too many bright, hard-working people will miss out on the greatest joys in life because they get caught up in the pursuit of the material goods.

The struggles that matter aren't those between practical people and intellec-
tuals. Virtuous people are, again, introspective, self-critical, rational, and curious, and Aristotle thinks practical people also possess, and benefit from, those
traits. He even doubts they can prosper in their business affairs for long without
them. Virtuous, practical people ask tough questions about what is right for
themselves and for others. When they do so habitually, they come not only to
understand what is right for themselves, they also do what is right.

The second objection is more substantive and complex. This is a version of
Adam Smith's belief that individual unhappiness breeds productivity: economists would say Aristotle is naive to assume that there is a limit to the amount
of wealth people should accumulate. They ask what would happen to the economy if everyone said, "That's enough": Wouldn't growth and innovation stop,
jobs cease to be created, and the economy collapse?

In fact, Aristotle doesn't disdain wealth and doesn't condescendingly argue
that the rich should be social workers instead of entrepreneurs. He wants to
help those who are well-off *also* to live well. He sees no reason why a practically
minded businessperson can't live a full life. To that end, he argues that people
shouldn't unnecessarily foreshorten their horizons, limit their activities, narrow
their experiences, and use only a part of the potential they were born with.
The professor who churns out narrow, technical articles year after year is no
more leading the good life than is the business person who spends an entire
career only pursuing wealth.

There is nothing wrong with making more money—unless doing so eclipses
other, morally higher, concerns. In fact, the issue isn't economic at all: we
aren't going to quit being Homo Economicus. The issue is that we are *also*
social, political, and philosophical animals. So Aristotle asks us to consider
how we might spend our time in useful and rewarding ways in addition to
making money.

Here is Aristotle's answer to the second objection: habitually deliberative
people are more likely to hit on what is right for themselves, their business,
and their communities. Although they will choose to limit their wealth, entrepreneurial activity will not (and should not) cease.

Practical Wisdom

MBA students are taught technical skills, and Aristotle says it is right that
they are. A "statesman" (a leader, and this would include those in business)
needs special traits and skills, among which are intelligence and technical
knowledge. To gain such intelligence one needs first to master some discipline,
whether a science or an art. People who do so effectively are said to possess
intellectual excellence, a trait measured by their skill in calculations (such as
designing a computer chip) or in theoretical reasoning (such as making invest-

ments in futures markets). Possessing, then developing and effectively using, this kind of intelligence is necessary to succeed at work, make contributions to knowledge, create wealth, and realize one's personal potential.

But Aristotle adds that more importantly, a leader needs *practical wisdom*, which has nothing to do with science, theory, disciplinary knowledge, or knowledge of facts in any way. It is concerned "neither with eternal and unchangeable truth" but "with matters where doubt and deliberation are possible," and in particular with "how things can be other than they are." It requires "the use of one's faculty of opinion in judging matters" relating to what is right and wrong for a business, or society as a whole.

Such practical wisdom is the prerequisite of "moral excellence," the *sine qua non* of *leadership*: "That is why we say Pericles and men like him have practical wisdom. They have the capacity to see what is good for themselves and for humankind." Pericles used his practical wisdom to identify the policies that would make Athenians collectively happy and create a good society characterized by justice for all. Hence, while virtuous leaders have skill-based *intellectual* excellence, more importantly, they possess the *moral* excellence that derives from practical wisdom.

At all times, the conscious goal of a just leader is to help followers achieve what is good for them (which, on occasion, may be something different from what they think they want). In other words, leaders must have the technical skills and the practical wisdom to be effective, with effectiveness defined as the capacity to discern and provide justice. (In contrast, business schools teach "contingency," an amoral theory of leadership.)

The Social Contract

Aristotle writes that the unwritten constitutions, or social contracts, of the small-scale societies he observed were the prime determinants of the degree to which people led good lives. In the few just societies he observed, the constitution provided opportunity for people to develop their natural abilities and thus pursue happiness.

The leader is to create conditions under which followers could achieve their potential. Political leadership is therefore a task and a responsibility rather than a privilege, right, or reward. Aristotle says, "It is the mark of a man of practical wisdom to be able to deliberate well about what is good and expedient for himself . . . and about what sorts of things are conducive to the good life in general."

But how does a leader know what is conducive to the good life for others? This is a tricky business. On the one hand, Aristotle believes that Platonic paternalism is morally wrong and impractical, while, on the other, he says that it is virtuous and practical for leaders to place the good of others above their own narrow self-interest. That is a fine line to draw. Usefully, he then shows how leaders begin the process of deciding what is in the interest of others *without* dictating how they should behave. A virtuous leader starts by putting himself in the place of his followers, asking "How would I want to be treated if I were a subject of this state?" Because the welfare of the community takes priority over the interests of individual members, a virtuous leader asks a second question: "What form of social contract would allow all members of our community to develop their potential in order that they each may make their greatest contribution to the good of the whole?"

How is this to be determined? Because wisdom is never the sole province of any individual, the practical and just way to determine the conditions of a social contract is through discussion among all the participants in the system. This should not be confused with political democracy. Aristotle was no enthusiast of democracy, believing that only the virtuous few who actively pursue both the highest and the complete good are fit to participate in political decision-making. Nevertheless, his political oligarchs are not tyrants.

In his model of governance, all qualified people in a community come together to discuss rationally the issues and problems they face. While that participation is limited to virtuous individuals, all those so qualified are equal in terms of their right to participate. These equally enfranchised participants nonetheless will be *un*equal in that some will be smarter, some wiser, some more articulate, and some will have more technical knowledge in particular fields. But all participants will be equal in terms of being able to ask questions and then to evaluate the various policy ideas put forward by experts. No one person will dominate every discussion because political issues are so complex and varied that no one ever has all the information needed to make the best decisions in all cases, and no one ever has a monopoly on wisdom.

Aristotle was not naive: he understood that people have real and legitimate differences of opinion, and that they are divided by competing and conflicting interests. Still, he could not imagine a situation in which qualified people who come together to achieve justice for their community could not, after free and rational discussion, eventually arrive at a rough agreement about matters that affected them.

The Aristotelian Workplace

How does this apply to business? Extrapolating from the Ancient's writings on politics, a modern Aristotelian workplace would have four primary characteristics:

- it provides a real opportunity for all workers to learn and to develop their talent and potential;
- all employees participate in the decisions that affect their own work;

- all employees participate in the financial gains resulting from their own ideas and efforts; and
- the leaders are virtuous.

The second and third points are inextricably linked: Participation in decision-making without participation in financial gains is unjust because the fruits of employee contributions are reaped by others (executives and shareholders). Participation in a company's financial gains without participating in decision-making also is unjust because workers are powerless to influence the conditions that determine the size of their paychecks. Importantly, the first three characteristics derive from the existence of the fourth, virtuous leadership.

Modern workplaces are the moral equivalent of Aristotle's small-scale communities. As political societies grow more complex, workplaces become the arenas in which modern men and women expend most of their energies, and in which they have the most influence. Hence, business leaders have inherited the ethical roles, tasks, and responsibilities of Aristotle's virtuous political leaders.

However, few modern workplaces are Aristotelian, in at least three ways. First, the terms of our employment contracts tend to be greater determinants of our lifestyles than provisions in the social contracts that we have with our city, state, and national communities. Modern businesses have the greatest power to create conditions under which individuals can realize their potential.

Second, research on group behavior reveals that Aristotle's face-to-face model works when the number of people involved is very small and that in small groups most people will behave rationally and cooperatively, as he posited.[6] However, when the number exceeds twenty or so, as it does in most businesses, the group starts to break into factions, participants stop listening to each other, and the strongest individuals come to dominate.

Third, Aristotle believes the ability to reason to be the main qualification for participation in political decision-making, and would believe the modern organization's criteria—status, titles, salary, power, ego, and the like—to be unjust and irrelevant. Because the goal of governance is to determine "the good" and the best means to achieve it (in business terms, the right strategy, structure, policies, and products), work organizations should tap into all sources of practical wisdom. Useful ideas from middle managers, or even front-line workers, should be as welcome as those from the executive suite.

If Aristotle is right in that the good life entails developing one's potential, leaders of work organizations have a moral responsibility to provide conditions in which employees can do so. Organizations that deny them the chance to develop their potential deny them the opportunity to realize their humanity. Hence, business leaders have inherited the ethical roles, tasks, and responsibilities of Aristotle's virtuous political leaders. Virtuous business leaders serve not to make themselves rich, famous, adored, or powerful, but to provide society with the goods and services it needs in an economically efficient manner while at the same time providing the environment for the intellectual and moral development of employees. Like Aristotle's political leaders, their task is to make "the good" of the company commensurate with the good of its employees; in fact, to make the two mutually reinforcing.

Hence, the first challenges of virtuous business leadership are to create (a) processes for eliciting and evaluating ideas from across the organization, and (b) systems of governance in which all employees find themselves in groups small enough for all to have a meaningful say in decisions directly affecting their own work.

Workplace Applications

Here is an example of these principles in action. In the early seventies, a corporate executive wrote the following Aristotelian words:

> The employer's obligations to society, stockholders, and workers [are] intricately interrelated. One cannot, in effect, serve society at all if he does not serve its people. One cannot serve shareholders effectively if he does not act to make business itself an agent for human growth and fulfillment.[7]

At the time, he was cooperating with the United Auto Workers in a workplace experiment in an old, unproductive facility where auto mirrors were manufactured. Workers were given the opportunity to manage themselves, even though most of them were relatively uneducated and came from disadvantaged backgrounds. The workers produced x mirrors per day. The workers, the union, and management agreed that, whenever they produced $x + n$ mirrors, they would be free to (a) go home, (b) continue working and earn a bonus, or (c) attend a company-sponsored school where the courses offered ranged from work-related subjects to basic education to the piano. Fully a third of the workers chose to attend the company school on their found time.

Workers were allowed to find ways to organize their tasks in almost any way they wished, and allowed to redesign plant conditions to make their tasks less tedious and more interesting. The work itself became a learning experience, and the workers began making changes, experimenting with better, faster, more efficient ways to make mirrors. Ultimately, they improved their productivity to the point where they were reaching their quota around midday. Moreover, as they gained confidence and experience, they began to suggest ways to redesign other jobs in the plant, and they invented imaginative ways to share in cost savings resulting from the changes that they either initiated or supported. This was an Aristotelian workplace, designed not only to be successful economically, but, equally, to allow for worker self-fulfillment, learning, and growth.

Similar Aristotelian efforts have been implemented to make work into learning experiences and, in particular, to permit blue-collar and other front-line workers to find the kind of intellectual rewards in their jobs that professionals and managers often find in their "leisure-work." In the early eighties, Jack Stack, CEO of the rust-belt SRC Holdings, taught all of his employees, mostly blue-collar workers with no more than high school educations, the financial skills he learned when he had earned his MBA. When they were as adept as he was at reading the company's cash-flow statements and balance sheet, he gave them full authority to act on their knowledge and shared with them the gains resulting from their ideas and efforts. For the last twenty years, every SRC employee has had access to all financial and managerial information, and the net effect, in the words of the company's CFO, "is like having seven hundred internal auditors out there in every function of the company."[8] This example illustrates how leaders can create ethical, sustainable corporate cultures. Unfortunately, learning how to design such high-involvement workplaces is not in the curriculum of major business schools.

Developing Managers and Leaders

Many current CEOs claim the mantle of virtue based on their apparent commitment to the development of their top management teams. The problem is that their CEO egos, and the related misuse of their power, prevent their effectively creating other leaders. Aristotle, according to philosopher Richard Kraut, believes that great leaders observe "decent limits" to allow others to lead and develop: "No virtuous person wants to be best if this turns his equals into people who are predominantly passive recipients of his moral feats."[9]

In practice, celebrity CEOs sometimes behave as if there were only one leader, themselves, and not only garner credit for all good decisions, but amass for themselves the best opportunities to learn through leading. Worse, they dismiss executives who challenge their authority, particularly upcoming stars who shine too brightly and thus threaten their CEO status as the sole source of organizational enlightenment. Here we might recall Aristotle's assertion that political leaders, even effective ones, who amass too much power should be exiled because they limit the opportunity for others to participate in decision-making and, thus, to develop fully. Note that the advantages of shared leadership are seldom taught in top-tier business schools.

One need not be a CEO to be concerned with the issue of employee development. Whatever our level in any organization, public or private, many of us have the authority to affect positively the quality of life of those who work for us, or with us. If we choose to lead them virtuously, here are some questions that Aristotle might say we need to ask ourselves:

- To what extent do I consciously provide learning opportunities for everyone who works for me?

- To what extent do I encourage full participation by all my people in the decisions affecting their work? To what extent do I allow them to lead in order to grow?
- To what extent do I measure my own performance as a manager-leader both in terms of my effectiveness in realizing economic goals, and in terms of using my practical wisdom to create conditions under which my people can seek to fulfill their potential in the workplace?

In business schools, such Aristotelian measures are often dismissed as inappropriate, impractical, and irrelevant to the task that boards hire executives to do: create wealth. MBA students are taught that their responsibility is to shareholders, not employees, and if employee development interferes with profit-making, then trade-offs must be made. Aristotle would answer that virtuous leaders have responsibilities to *both* their owners and workers and, if there is a conflict between the two, it is their duty to create conditions in which their interests can be made the same. He would remind us that, while most leaders measure themselves solely in terms of their effectiveness at obtaining and maintaining power, virtuous ones also measure themselves by ethical standards of justice. It is appropriate that business leaders be evaluated by their effectiveness at generating wealth for shareholders, but also by their ability to provide their followers meaning and the opportunity for development in the workplace.

Just Distribution of Rewards

In light of recent corporate scandals, it is dismaying to find many executives still concerned that they might be getting less than their fair share of the wealth produced by the companies they lead. To them, the measure of what they are entitled to receive is the amount executives in comparable companies earn. As often noted, this amount has little to do with their performance or with their relative contributions to their organizations. Instead, it has everything to do with power and leverage.

Looking at the *Fortune* 500, the average CEO currently takes home over $10.8 million per year—in real terms, some twenty times more than in 1981, and some four hundred to five hundred times what their front-line workers earn. Even moderately well-paid CEOs of large corporations make about as much in a day as their workers make in a year.

While boards and investors may say that this growing disparity is acceptable, the Ancient says that being willing to take less than the share a contract permits one to take is a sign of fairness and virtue. By definition, one never takes less than one's fair share when one does so voluntarily. Thus, there would be no question of a CEO receiving less than his fair share if he were to voluntarily choose to absorb some of the costs of the increase in, say, his employees' insurance premiums, or grant some of his stock options to others in his organization who have none.

Harder to reckon is what is just and fair, but it is not impossible to do so. For example, Disney's board compensated its CEO, Michael Eisner, with $285 million between 1996 and 2004. We don't have the data required to decide how much Eisner deserved, but, thanks to Aristotle, we have a question that a virtuous member of the Disney board's compensation committee might have asked: "Is our CEO's proportionate contribution to the organization ten, or one hundred, or one thousand times greater than that of a cartoon animator at our Burbank studios or the operator of the Space Mountain ride at Disneyland?" While asking such a question is practically unheard-of in the boardrooms of giant companies, a few small- and medium-sized companies have done so, and have gone on to establish ratios as low as twenty to one between the compensations of their highest-paid executive and their average worker. While that may sound unrealistic, when the numbers are run it makes some sense: if the average worker makes twenty dollars per hour, the CEO in even a "low-paying" company can make one million dollars. It only seems out of the question when the actual ratio in *Fortune* 500 companies approaches five hundred to one.

Deliberation about the just ratio between the highest- and the lowest-paid person in an organization is a good way for corporate boards and executives to begin including ethical analysis in their compensation discussions. Alas, most large corporations use distributive compensation processes more reflective of their employees' relative power than of objective and ethical analyses of their relative contributions. And it *is* hard to do such a just and objective analysis. As Aristotle would be the first to recognize, employees must be paid market wages. However, markets do not determine the compensation of executives. In many cases, this particular market is rigged: the widespread use of compensation surveys allows executives to ratchet up their salaries continually.

At the other end of the salary scale, a company would price itself out of business if it paid its clerks as much as it pays managers, so that boards tend to skip over the issue of relative justice for lower-level workers, leaving the market to determine that. However, the market does not work in quite the same way for workers as it does for top managers and skilled professionals. Because jobs are offered to lower-level workers on a take-it-or-leave-it basis, their conditions of employment often amount to unethical "exchanges of desperation." In contrast, professionals and managers may have other employment opportunities and, as a result, some bargaining power.

Granted, that's the way of the world, and corporate executives and board members cannot be expected to repeal the laws of economics. However, they are not without power to increase opportunities for even first-line employees to raise their own standards of living. For example, boards can distribute stock and stock options more broadly, and there are a number of well-tested methods for objectively and fairly linking rewards to relative contribution: profit-sharing, gain-sharing, ESOPs, and the like, all of which are consistent with the rules of the market.

Another Exam

Aristotle does not provide a single, clear principle for the just distribution of enterprise-created wealth, nor would it be possible for anyone to formulate such a monolithic rule. Nonetheless, here are some Aristotelian guidelines in the form of questions that virtuous leaders need to ask of themselves:

- Am I taking more in my share of rewards than my contributions warrant?
- Does the distribution of goods in the organization preserve the happi-ness of the community, or does it harm morale and others' ability to achieve the good?
- Would everyone enter into employment under the current terms if they truly had other choices?
- Would we come to a different principle of allocation if all of the parties concerned were represented at the table?

Again, the only hard-and-fast principle of distributive justice is that fairness is most likely to arise out of a process of rational and moral deliberation. Pre-scriptively, all Aristotle says is that virtue and wisdom will certainly elude lead-ers who fail to engage in rigorous ethical analysis of their actions.

Coda: Why Ethics Matter

Unlike most of today's business school professors, Aristotle was comfortable with the language of ethics: he spoke clearly about right and wrong, virtue and vice, should and shouldn't. He advocated the virtues of duty, responsibility, accountability, prudence, and magnanimous action. He saluted the character traits of moral courage and excellence. He required that leaders consider the interests of their followers and contribute to the welfare of their communities.

In recent times, those on the left have shied away from such language, and those on the right have claimed that questions of morality have no place in the pragmatic world of business (instead, they say that markets should be the ulti-mate judge of our public actions). To both, one can only reply: Enron, WorldCom, Tyco, Global Crossing, and Arthur Andersen.

Aristotle understood what we in America conveniently chose to forget in the heady nineties: free economies cannot function effectively without a strong ethical foundation. Ancient Athens was no welfare state. There was no Social

Security, no public assistance, and no free schooling, but there were many poor and needy citizens. If an old person fell on hard times, and a poor but promising child needed schooling, then it was expected they would be taken care of by "friends." Such friendship was not based on dependency or utility. It was predicated on the value of respect for others, and the concomitant virtue of generosity. Or so it should be, according to Aristotle. If the state did not provide for the needy, then it stood to reason that the wealthy had to. Aristotle could not imagine a society with a market economy that did not also have an inherent commitment to social ethics and philanthropy.

Since the fall of communism and the subsequent rise of market economies in formerly Stalinist and Maoist countries, the problems of corruption, cheating, stealing, price-gouging, and tax-evasion have become common, if not chronic. There is no enculturation to ethical norms of behavior. New laws have helped, but have not been sufficient. The conclusion to be drawn is that people have to be taught the professional, personal, and social merits of virtue. That's why new business schools in formerly communist countries spend so much time dealing with ethics, a subject that had been foreign to the curriculum of communist universities.

Curiously, in the 1990s, ethics and social responsibility disappeared from the agenda of many American corporations and business schools. Too many successful executives during that era came to understand freedom to mean that they owed nothing to society. They called for drastic reductions in federal, state, and local taxes, and for cutting back government programs and regulations. What they then didn't do was to increase their support of charity and take responsibility for ethical and moral self-regulation of their economic enterprises.

Over two thousand years ago Aristotle argued that a strong ethical foundation was a requirement for an open society. In fact, history has shown that no advanced society can go outside of these two alternatives: private enterprise/ethics/philanthropy/individual responsibility, or, socialism/regulation/state welfare/social entitlements. The former leads to freedom, progress, and affluence, the later to tyranny, stagnation, and poverty.

Aristotle understood otherwise. His teacher, Plato, had opted for a controlled society in which paternalistic guardians would make all the political and moral decisions for a dependent populace, who then could devote all their time to making and spending money. Aristotle advocated a free society, but he warned that such a society would function only for as long as, and to the extent that, its citizens engaged in moral deliberation and then chose to pursue the path to virtue. The Athenians did not heed Aristotle's advice, and, as Edith Hamilton explains, the consequences were dire:

[T]hey wanted . . . a comfortable life, and they lost it all—security and comfort and freedom. . . . When the Athenians finally wanted not to give to the state, but for the state to give to them, when the freedom they wished most for was freedom from responsibility, then Athens ceased to be free. . . .[10]

We business professors ought not to let our students make the same mistake as the Athenians. If we incorporate the kinds of moral questions Aristotle raises in all our MBA classes—finance, marketing, accounting, management— we can begin to help tomorrow's executives to create ethical corporate cultures.

Notes

1. Warren G. Bennis and James O'Toole, "How Business Schools Lost Their Way," *Harvard Business Review,* May 2005; Henry Mintzberg, *Managers Not MBAs: A Hard Look at the Soft Practice of Managing and Management* (San Francisco: Berrett-Koehler, 2004).

2. Aristotle is not the final word in philosophy. He is wrong about many things— slavery, for instance—and business students would do well to read Robert Heilbroner, *The Worldly Philosophers: The Lives, Times, and Ideas of the Great Economic Thinkers* (New York: Simon and Schuster, 1999) for a marvelous introduction to a range of serous philosophical thought relating to economic matters.

3. James O'Toole and Edward E. Lawler, *The New American Workplace* (New York: Macmillan, Palgrave Macmillan, 2006).

4. Aristotle is the focus of a large number of books and articles by business school professors, including Edwin Hartman, "Can We Teach Character? An Aristotelian Answer," *Academy of Management Learning and Education* 5 (March 2006): 68–81; George Bragues, "Seek the Good Life, Not Money: The Aristotelian Approach to Business Ethics," *Journal of Business Ethics* 67 (September 2006): 341–57; and Robert Solomon, "Aristotle, Ethics, and Business Organizations," *Organization Studies* 25, no. 6 (2006): 1021–43.

5. The quotes are my own (often simplified) translations, found in James O'Toole, *Creating the Good Life: Applying Aristotle's Wisdom to Find Meaning and Happiness* (Emmaus, Pa.: Rodale, 2005), 33.

6. Edward E. Lawler, *High-Involvement Management: Participative Strategies for Improving Organizational Performance* (San Francisco: Jossey-Bass, 1986).

7. Cited in James O'Toole et al., *Work in America,* a report of a special task force to the U.S. Secretary of Health, Education, and Welfare (Cambridge, Mass.: MIT Press, 1973), 25.

8. O'Toole and Lawler, *New American Workplace,* 157.

9. Richard Kraut, *Aristotle on the Human Good* (Princeton, N.J.: Princeton University Press, 1989), 127.

10. Edith Hamilton, *The Ever-Present Past* (New York: W. W. Norton and Company, 1964), 37.

CONTRIBUTORS

Antonio Argandoña is Professor of Economics and holds the "La Caixa" Chair of Corporate Social Responsibility and Corporate Governance in the IESE Business School at the University of Navarre. He is a member of the Spanish Royal Academy of Economics and Finance (Barcelona), chairperson of the Professional Ethics Committee of the Catalonia Economics Association (Collegi d'Economistes de Catalunya), and a member of the Anti-Corruption Committee of the International Chamber of Commerce (Paris). Professor Argandoña has been the treasurer and a member of the Executive Committee of the European Business Ethics Network (EBEN). He is the author of numerous books and articles on economic and business ethics, corporate social responsibility, corporate governance, and monetary and international economics.

Anthony Daniels is an English writer and retired physician, who frequently uses the pen name "Theodore Dalrymple." He has written extensively on culture, art, politics, education, and medicine, both in Britain and overseas. Before retiring from medicine, Dr. Daniels worked as a physician and psychiatrist in Zimbabwe, South Africa, Tanzania, and more recently at a prison and a public hospital in Birmingham, in central England. He has written columns appearing in *The New Criterion, The Spectator,* and in *City Journal,* a magazine of the Manhattan Institute. Dr. Daniels is the author of such books as *Coups and Cocaine* (John Murray, 1986), *Zanzibar to Timbuktu* (John Murray, 1988), and most recently, *In Praise of Prejudice: The Necessity of Preconceived Ideas* (Encounter Books, 2007). He is the Dietrich Weismann fellow at the Manhattan Institute.

R. Edward Freeman is a philosopher and Professor of Business Administration at the Darden School of Business at the University of Virginia. He also has taught at the University of Minnesota and the Wharton School. Professor Freeman is particularly known for his work on stakeholder theory and business ethics. His latest book is *Managing for Stakeholders* (Yale University Press, 2007, with Jeffrey Harrison and Andrew Wicks). Professor Freeman is currently working on a book called *Stakeholder Theory: The State of the Art.* He received a BA from Duke University in 1973 and a PhD from Washington University in 1978.

Robert P. George is the McCormick Professor of Jurisprudence and founding director of the James Madison Program in American Ideals and Institutions at Princeton University, and the Herbert W. Vaughan Senior Fellow of the

Witherspoon Institute. He is a member of the President's Council on Bioethics and formerly served as a presidential appointee to the United States Commission on Civil Rights. Professor George was a Judicial Fellow at the Supreme Court of the United States, where he received the Justice Tom C. Clark Award. His books include *Making Men Moral: Civil Liberties and Public Morality* (Oxford University Press, 1993), *In Defense of Natural Law* (Oxford University Press, 1999), *The Clash of Orthodoxies: Law, Religion, and Morality in Crisis* (ISI Books, 2001), and *Embryo: A Defense of Human Life* (Doubleday, 2008, with Christopher Tollefsen). Professor George is a winner of the Bradley Prize for Civic and Intellectual Achievement, the Philip Merrill Award of the American Council of Trustees and Alumni, and the Stanley Kelley, Jr. Teaching Award in Politics at Princeton. A graduate of Swarthmore College and Harvard Law School, he holds a doctorate in legal philosophy from Oxford University.

Samuel Gregg writes and speaks on questions of political economy, ethics in finance, jurisprudence, and medicine. He is Director of Research at the Acton Institute, an adjunct professor at the Pontifical Lateran University, and a consultant for Oxford Analytica Ltd. He holds an MA in political philosophy from the University of Melbourne, and a DPhil in moral philosophy from the University of Oxford. He is the author of several books, including *Morality, Law, and Public Policy* (St. Thomas More Society, 2000), *Economic Thinking for the Theologically Minded* (University Press of America, 2001), *On Ordered Liberty* (Lexington Books, 2003), and *The Commercial Society* (Lexington Books, 2007). The last was awarded a 2007 Templeton Enterprise Award for being one of the best books published on the culture of enterprise.

Edwin M. Hartman is Visiting Professor of Business Ethics and the Peter and Charlotte Schoenfeld Visiting Faculty Fellow at the Stern School of Business at New York University. He was previously director of the Prudential Business Ethics Center at Rutgers Business School. Professor Hartman is the author of *Substance, Body, and Soul: Aristotelian Investigations* (Princeton University Press, 1977), *Conceptual Foundations of Organization Theory* (Ballinger Publishing, 1988), and *Organizational Ethics and the Good Life* (Oxford University Press, 1996), along with many articles.

Kevin T. Jackson is Professor of Legal and Ethical Studies at Fordham University in New York City and Visiting Professor of Politics at Princeton University. Formerly on the faculty of Georgetown University and Peking University, he has published numerous journal articles as well as books, such as *Charting Global Responsibilities: Legal Philosophy and Human Rights* (East-West Press, 1997) and *Building Reputational Capital* (Oxford University

Press, 2004). Professor Jackson frequently gives analysis of legal and moral issues for the media and has presented seminars on business integrity and leadership. His advice on mutual-fund industry-regulation reform has been published in *The New York Law Journal.*

Harold James, who holds a joint appointment as Professor of International Affairs in the Woodrow Wilson School of Princeton University, and as Marie Curie Professor at the European University Institute in Florence, studies economic and financial history and modern German history. He was educated at Cambridge University (PhD, 1982) and was a Fellow of Peterhouse for eight years before coming to Princeton University in 1986. Professor James's books include a study of the interwar depression in Germany, *The German Slump* (Oxford University Press, 1986); an analysis of the changing character of national identity in Germany, *A German Identity 1770–1990* (Routledge, 1989); and *International Monetary Cooperation Since Bretton Woods* (Oxford University Press, 1996). He was coauthor of a history of Deutsche Bank (Weidenfeld and Nicholson, 1995), which won the *Financial Times* Global Business Book Award in 1996, and he also wrote *The Deutsche Bank and the Nazi Economic War against the Jews* (Cambridge University Press, 2001). Professor James's most recent works are *The End of Globalization: Lessons from the Great Depression* (Harvard University Press, 2001); *Europe Reborn: A History 1914–2000* (Pearson Longman, 2003); *The Roman Predicament: How the Rules of International Order Create the Politics of Empire* (Princeton University Press, 2006); and *Family Capitalism: Wendels, Haniels, Falcks, and the Continental European Model* (Harvard University Press, 2006). In 2004 he was awarded the Helmut Schmidt Prize for Economic History, and in 2005 the Ludwig Erhard Prize for writing about economics.

Sean Kelsey has been Associate Professor of Philosophy at the University of California, Los Angeles, since 1998. He received his BA from Thomas Aquinas College (1992) and his PhD in philosophy from Princeton (1997) within the Program in Classical Philosophy. Professor Kelsey specializes in ancient Greek philosophy, especially Plato and Aristotle.

Thomas R. Krause, PhD, is Chairman of the Board for BST, a consulting firm specializing in comprehensive safety solutions. Since he founded BST in 1979, he has helped thousands of companies worldwide to prepare and implement successful change systems. Dr. Krause is actively involved in leadership coaching. He has spoken widely on a multitude of topics at national and international conferences and is regularly quoted by the media. Dr. Krause has authored several books and articles on safety and leadership, including *Leading with Safety* (Wiley, 2005). His next book, *Taking the Lead* *in Patient Safety: How Leaders Influence Behavior and Create Culture,* will appear in 2008. Dr. Krause received his MA in liberal arts from St. John's College in Santa Fe, New Mexico. He received his PhD from the University of California, Irvine. Dr. Krause is a licensed psychologist.

Wilfred M. McClay is the SunTrust Bank Chair of Excellence in Humanities at the University of Tennessee, Chattanooga, where he is also Professor of History. Professor McClay also has taught at Georgetown University, Tulane University, Johns Hopkins University, and the University of Dallas, is a Senior Scholar at the Woodrow Wilson International Center for Scholars in Washington, D. C., and is a Senior Fellow at the Ethics and Public Policy Center in Washington, D. C. He is the author of *The Masterless: Self and Society in Modern America* (University of North Carolina Press, 1994) and *Figures in the Carpet: Finding the Human Person in the American Past* (William B. Eerdmans Publishing, 2007). Professor McClay was educated at St. John's College (Annapolis) and Johns Hopkins University, where he received a PhD in history (1987).

David Newkirk is CEO of Executive Education at the University of Virginia's Darden School of Business. There he is responsible for the development and delivery of a range of open enrollment and custom programs for senior executives. Mr. Newkirk has spoken and written widely on issues of strategy and marketing. He holds degrees in mathematics and philosophy from Carleton College in the United States and from Oxford University, where he was a Marshall Scholar.

David Novak has held the J. Richard and Dorothy Shiff Chair of Jewish Studies as Professor of the Study of Religion and Professor of Philosophy at the University of Toronto since 1997. He is a member of the University of Toronto's University College, Centre for Ethics, and Joint Centre for Bioethics. Previously, Professor Novak taught at the University of Virginia. He is the author of fourteen books, most recently *The Sanctity of Human Life* (Georgetown University Press, 2007). Professor Novak received his AB from the University of Chicago in 1961, his MHL (Master of Hebrew Literature) in 1964, and his rabbinical diploma in 1966 from the Jewish Theological Seminary of America. He received his PhD in philosophy from Georgetown University in 1971.

James O'Toole is the Daniels Distinguished Professor of Business Ethics at the University of Denver's Daniels College of Business. He received his doctorate in social anthropology from Oxford University, where he was a Rhodes Scholar. Professor O'Toole is the author of fifteen books, including

Creating the Good Life: Applying Aristotle's Wisdom to Find Meaning and Happiness (Rodale, 2005), on which his essay in this volume is based.

Roger Scruton was until 1990 Professor of Aesthetics at Birkbeck College, London, and subsequently Professor of Philosophy and University Professor at Boston University, Massachusetts. He is now Research Professor at the Institute for the Psychological Sciences in Arlington, Virginia. Professor Scruton has published over thirty books, including works of philosophy, literature, and fiction, and his writings have been translated into most major languages. His most recent books are a study of Wagner's *Tristan und Isolde*, titled *Death-Devoted Heart* (Oxford University Press, 2004), *Gentle Regrets* (an intellectual autobiography) (Continuum, 2005), and *Culture Counts: Faith and Feeling in a World Besieged* (Encounter Books, 2007).

James R. Stoner, Jr., is Professor of Political Science at Louisiana State University, where he has taught since 1988, and where he now chairs the Department of Political Science. He is the author of *Common Law and Liberal Theory: Coke, Hobbes, and the Origins of American Constitutionalism* (University Press of Kansas, 1992), and *Common-Law Liberty: Rethinking American Constitutionalism* (University Press of Kansas, 2003), as well as a number of articles and essays. Professor Stoner received his AB from Middlebury College in Vermont and his MA and PhD degrees from Harvard. In academic year 2002–2003 he was a Visiting Fellow of the James Madison Program in American Ideals and Institutions at Princeton University, and he served from 2002 to 2006 on the National Council on the Humanities.

Robin Fretwell Wilson is Professor of Law at Washington and Lee University School of Law, where she teaches in the areas of family law, insurance, children and violence, and healthcare law. She is the editor of two recent books, *Reconceiving the Family: Critical Reflections on the American Law Institute's Principles of the Law of Family Dissolution* (Cambridge University Press, 2006) and the *Handbook of Children, Culture, and Violence* (Sage Publications, 2006, with Nancy Dowd and Dorothy Singer). Professor Wilson's work on child maltreatment and child welfare has appeared in the *Cornell Law Review*, the *Emory Law Journal*, and the *San Diego Law Review* as well as numerous peer-reviewed journals.

INDEX

A Note on the Social Trends Institute

Any citizen looking at the world today can see a number of changes that are taking place in modern society. Some of these include global terrorism, the enlargement of the European Union on one hand and nationalist splits on the other, increasing concern for the environment or the transformation processes in India or China.

However, after some reflection, this same citizen can also perceive certain social trends that are shaping a new world and affecting the role of its main institutions (Corporations, Education, Governments, the Family, and Religious Institutions). These trends, which include globalization, demographics and immigration, biotechnology, new lifestyles, and changes in family patterns, will have a significant impact on the future.

In order to understand these social trends and analyze their impact, STI conducts interdisciplinary, international research. This "bridging research" connects governments, civil society, families, individual citizens, information and communication technologies, and corporations, among others.

The individuals and institutions that support STI share a common Judeo-Christian vision of society and the individual, a deep respect for freedom of thought, and a willingness to contribute to social progress, understanding between peoples, and the common human good.

A Note on the Witherspoon Institute

The majority of the essays in this volume were presented to an audience of scholars of business and the liberal arts as well as business practitioners at a conference at Princeton University organized by the Witherspoon Institute in May 2007.

The Witherspoon Institute works to enhance public understanding of the political, moral, and philosophical principles of free and democratic societies. It also promotes the application of these principles to contemporary problems.

The Institute is named for John Witherspoon, a leading member of the Continental Congress, a signer of the Declaration of Independence, the sixth president of Princeton University, and a mentor to James Madison. As important as these and his other notable accomplishments are, however, it is Witherspoon's commitment to liberal education and his recognition of the dignity of human freedom, whether it be personal, political, or religious, that inspire the Institute's name.

In furtherance of its educational mission, the Witherspoon Institute supports a variety of scholarly activities. It sponsors research and teaching by means of a fellowship program; it organizes conferences, lectures, and colloquia; and it encourages and assists scholarly collaboration among individuals sharing the Institute's interest in the foundations of a free society. The Witherspoon Institute also serves as a resource for the media and other organizations seeking comment on matters of concern to the Institute and its associated scholars.

For more information about the work of the Witherspoon Institute, please visit www.winst.org.